Effective Learning and Teaching in Engineering

Written to meet the needs of teachers, lecturers and tutors at all stages in their careers, this is the authoritative handbook for anyone wanting to understand the key issues, best practices and new developments in the world of engineering education and training.

The book is divided into sections which analyse what students should be learning, how they learn and how the teaching and learning process and your own practice can be improved.

With contributions from experts around the world and a wealth of innovative case study material, this book is an essential purchase for anyone teaching engineering today.

Caroline Baillie is Dupont Chair in Engineering Education Research and Development at the Faculty of Applied Science, Queens University, Ontario, Canada. **Ivan Moore** was formerly Director of the Department for Learning Development at the University of Portsmouth, UK.

Effective Learning and Teaching in Higher Education Series
Edited by Sally Brown

> ### The Higher Education Academy 'Effective Learning and Teaching in Higher Education' series
>
> The Higher Education Academy is the UK national organization committed to the support of teaching and learning in higher education.
>
> It seeks to increase the professional standing of all HE staff by facilitating professional development and awarding professional accreditation in teaching and learning.
>
> The Higher Education Academy is also committed to improving the student experience, providing a wide range of support and services to aid the whole spectrum of higher education activity, including networks of subject centres and centres of excellence in teaching and learning through the promotion of evidence-based practice.
>
> The 'Effective Learning and Teaching in Higher Education' series is written in accordance with the aims of the Higher Education Academy, and these titles will be essential reading for subject specialists wanting to improve their practice, and also for those studying for professional accreditation.

Effective Learning and Teaching in Law
Edited by Roger Burridge, Karen Hinett, Abdul Paliwala and Tracey Varnava

Effective Learning and Teaching in Business and Management
Edited by Bruce Macfarlane and Roger Ottewill

Effective Learning and Teaching in Mathematics and its Applications
Edited by Joseph Kyle and Peter Kahn

Effective Learning and Teaching in Medical, Dental and Veterinary Education
Edited by John Sweet, Sharon Huttly and Ian Taylor

Effective Learning and Teaching in Social Work and Social Policy
Edited by Hilary Burgess and Imogen Taylor (*forthcoming*)

Effective Learning and Teaching in Engineering
Edited by Caroline Baillie and Ivan Moore

Effective Learning and Teaching in Computing
Edited by Alastair Irons and Sylvia Alexander

Effective Learning and Teaching in Engineering

Edited by
Caroline Baillie and Ivan Moore

RoutledgeFalmer
Taylor & Francis Group

LONDON AND NEW YORK

First published 2004
by RoutledgeFalmer
2 Park Square, Milton Park, Abingdon, Oxon OX14 4RN

Simultaneously published in the USA and Canada
by RoutledgeFalmer
270 Madison Avenue, New York, NY 10016

RoutledgeFalmer is an imprint of the Taylor & Francis Group

Typeset in Bembo by
Florence Production Ltd, Stoodleigh, Devon
Printed and bound in Great Britain by
TJ International Ltd, Padstow, Cornwall

British Library Cataloguing in Publication Data
A catalogue record for this book is available from
the British Library

Library of Congress Cataloging in Publication Data
A catalog record for this book has been requested

ISBN 0–415–33488–8 (hbk)
ISBN 0–415–33489–6 (pbk)

Contents

Illustrations

Figures

Tables

Contributors

Phil Barker Heriot-Watt University, Edinburgh

David Baume Higher Education Consultant

Pam Bishop Birmingham University

Shirley Booth Department of Education, Lund University, Lund, Sweden

John A. Bowden RMIT University, Melbourne, Australia

Jennifer Case University of Cape Town, South Africa

John Cowan Heriot-Watt University, Edinburgh

Claire Davis School of Engineering, University of Brighton

Mark Endean Department of Materials Engineering, The Open University

Christine Hirst Loughborough University

John B. Hudson Rensselaer Polytechnic Institute, USA

James McCowan Queen's University, Kingston, Ontario, Canada

Alan Maddocks Loughborough University

Fred Maillardet University of Brighton

Linda S. Schadler Rensselaer Polytechnic Institute, USA

Elizabeth Wilcock School of Engineering, University of Brighton

John Wilcox Bradford College

Sarah Williamson Loughborough University

Introduction: reflecting on effective learning and teaching in engineering education

Caroline Baillie

Engineering education can be seen as an emerging discipline but more usefully as a merging of other disciplines. In order to understand how we can help our students prepare for a changing future, we need to consider what that future might bring, the important implications of engineering on society and how future engineers will influence this. We will then need to turn this outcome into a set of learning experiences that actually cause the student to develop as a human being and, in many cases, shift their awareness of their place in the world. This handbook is intended to act as an energy source for lecturers who need to revitalize and draw strength when faced with resisting students and other faculty. It can also be seen as a collection of work representing a developing community of practitioners who have a common goal. In reflecting on this goal – why we are interested in spending our waking hours thinking and worrying about our students, Shirley Booth guides us through the 'pedagogy of awareness' and helps us to see the relation between teaching and learning. John Cowan completes the cycle by looking 'Beyond reflection'. Learning, Shirley tells us, is about coming to see things in important new ways. John suggests that we need to be able to ask questions in order to do that. He evokes the need for identifying critical incidents in order to formulate ideas for improvement as a teacher. Shirley reinforces the need to discern critical aspects, to find out what is critical and what can be varied around this aspect. It is certainly our hope that we have prompted a few questions, uncovered a few critical aspects and that you will have learned something about yourself and your teaching while reading the book and reflecting on the process of your students' learning.

What we intend to do is to find a pathway through the multitude of obstacles facing us as we travel along the education development pathway. We suggest that the first thing to consider is what we would like the students to learn. This is obviously not a list of content as we often find in course descriptions, but a careful consideration of what we would like students to be 'capable' of or 'able' to do. In Part 2 of the book, Fred Maillardet explores the 'ability to' statements of the Engineering Professors' Council which have been introduced to develop a 'way of thinking' for the professional engineer rather than a shopping list of requirements as has often been the case. This model has its failings as pointed out by John Bowden. John claims that his 'capability' theory addresses the problem of separation between knowledge and skills by the notion of 'knowledge capability' – that learning knowledge is a means to developing capabilities and not an end in itself. In his chapter he develops the theme of variation also discussed in Shirley's chapter, explaining that a capability focus 'encourages reflection about variation with context so that principles and contextual elements are differentiated, thus enhancing the capacity to apply the principles to new contexts in the future'. We, again, see the need for reflection in order to discern the relevant or critical aspects about our teaching or for students in their learning. We must learn to value our own way of seeing about engineering education while 'pondering its efficacy' in order to help students do likewise.

It is, of course, part of the message of this book that curriculum development is a cycle in which we iterate between all the relevant aspects of what, how and why – but we will address them here in turn. Evidently, if we have sufficiently 'pondered our efficacy' in the consideration of what we want students to learn we will already have answered most of the questions relating to how we will help them learn those things. And in considering how to teach the students we will inevitably realize that some things are very difficult to 'teach'.

Many of these issues have been addressed by our authors in Part 3. Claire Davis and Elizabeth Wilcox demonstrate the importance of preparation and planning in their use of case studies in teaching. It is an interesting thought that many new Faculty will spend long hours writing course notes which are sometimes no more than a regurgitation of a text book. They could, instead, be spending that time thinking about how they could help students really learn, and planning this in detail. Claire and Elizabeth point out the need to develop appropriate problems or cases which address certain key theoretical concepts. How often do we sit back and think about what these are? It's a little too easy to lose the key concepts in a multitude of 'facts' which are, often, no more than a set of constructs used to understand the concepts but which we teach as if they hold equal importance (Baillie, 2003). Planning is also dealt with in detail by Mark Endean and David Baume for their distance learning material. Because we don't have the ease of lectures to fall back on, the development of distance learning material seems much more complete than in face-to-face settings. What is also very apparent is the order in which the curriculum is designed. The aims are decided and then the learning outcomes, followed by the assessment of those outcomes. For distance learning it becomes clear that a key element of the design is to make sure that the students have learned what you want them to learn. Only after that do you design the learning activities. Finally, you consider what staff activities and resources are needed. It would be useful to reflect on the lessons that distance learning can give to face-to-face teaching and learning.

Another key part of the planning process is to consider what the students already know, the range of knowledge and abilities of the class and how to work this into lesson plans. In his chapter on work-based learning, John Wilcox discusses the official mechanism of giving credit to students for their prior learning and experiences. This is a much more mature way of dealing with students who have a huge knowledge from industry but, perhaps, little theoretical knowledge. It also focuses the degree programme on individual needs. Although it is hard to see this working with larger groups of students in mainstream degree programmes, some mechanism like this would be extremely useful in order to enable the teacher to frame their classes based on what the students already know, rather than assuming this knowledge and that it is the same for all.

Where there are obvious gaps in the knowledge this has, of course, been attempted, e.g. in areas of maths. Christine Hirst and colleagues describe the increasing problem with maths deficiencies in engineering students and how it has become common in many universities to introduce a 'diagnostic' test followed by streaming of students. If we reflect back to Shirley's work we remember that she warned us about the numerous dead-ends that students would find themselves in and that we should discover 'their hitherto taken-as-given understanding' and centre their learning around 'critically important knowledge', or 'threshold concepts'. If we were to first decide what these threshold concepts might be, we would better create diagnostic tests and develop programmes for students which truly did reflect their various needs.

The next stage in the planning process is to consider the most appropriate mechanism for helping students grapple with the concepts, capabilities and case studies. Phil Barker presents us with the notion of conversations with computers, ways in which different styles of conversation can be enhanced. He suggests that even assessment 'provides a form of communication between the student and the tutor' but stresses the need to match learning objectives against the form of assessment used in order to address the level of learning which is desired from students. It might be worth considering at this point the words of Ursula Franklin (1990) who considers 'communication technologies' to be 'non communication technologies'. She believes that technical arrangements reduce or eliminate reciprocity – 'some manner of interactive give and take, a genuine communication among interactive parties'. She suggests that 'reciprocity is not feedback', that 'reciprocity is ruled out by design' and describes a Ben Wicks cartoon which illustrates her point. The cartoon shows a repairman in a living room removing a television set with a smashed screen. Next to the set stands a man on crutches, one foot heavily bandaged, to whom the repairman says, 'Next time Trudeau speaks, just turn the set off'. In the light of Ursula's words we should consider if we, as educators, are seriously considering the effects of the technology on our 'conversations' with students. As Shirley reminds us 'approaches to learning are not characteristic of individual students but are rather the result of the student's interaction with the task in the learning context in which it is experienced'.

Hence, our choice of 'teaching' approach, or our way of helping the students learn, needs not only to match the learning objectives and assessment methods, to help students develop a deep approach to learning, but needs to do so in ways which will not have serious side effects. Often we do not really know the effects of our teaching on our students. We need to evaluate the educational experience (in Shirley's holistic meaning – the whole educational experience) of students – and this needs to happen even before we begin to teach. It should not just be added on at the end, to check that we did something right and adjust if not for the following year. That is, of course, necessary but if we wait until the end to reflect, we will miss out on all sorts of important aspects that happened weeks before.

Jennifer Case describes a sobering tale of things not quite working out as planned. And this is worth planning for. She describes a case where a lecturer introduced an innovation into her teaching, replacing lectures with more interaction and use of groupwork, the use of a workbook, and journal tasks. For many this course did, indeed, serve to promote deep approaches to learning and conceptual understanding. However, for many others it did not. For those students there were distinct reasons why they did not respond well to the new approach. Students who relied too heavily on a procedural approach and those who considered lectures to be the only way to develop understanding would find these approaches impenetrable. Jennifer demonstrates the need to watch for time pressure and also to 'teach for the development of the whole person' and that 'tinkering' with our programmes may not be effective as desired because we have not 'pondered the efficacy' of the whole learning experience for the students.

An example of such a 'paradigm shift' in mode of teaching is brought to us by Linda Schadler who describes the 'studio mode' of teaching. Rensselaer realized the limitations to traditional teaching, those of timing labs to lectures and poor attendance at lectures, and created a studio concept which would combine lecture and active learning. It addressed the need for a new learning environment with studio rooms, the need to help students train in team building in order to work in groups and, as Claire demonstrated with her case study-based learning, the need to develop new experiments and problem solving material. It is clear that such whole-scale approaches will be even better if faculty are trained in the new approaches to teaching, as many are simply not used to the very different style of interaction with students that is required.

Throughout the chapters on 'how' we go about our teaching, we also in many cases see reference to a completely new assessment scheme. Certainly most of the authors note the influence of assessment on student motivation and approach to learning and the need to match the assessment to the learning objectives. It is important to consider, however, that learning which may not necessarily be summatively assessed but which helps students to learn. In the UK all higher education institutions are required to have policies on 'Personal Development Planning', (PDP) in place by 2005–6. PDP is described by Alan Maddocks as a 'means by which students could monitor, build and reflect upon their personal development'. By engaging in the development of the PDP (with adequate staff support, integration into the learning programme and appropriate induction) students are expected to improve their capacity 'to understand what they have learned, how that learning was acquired, take responsibility for their own future learning through the processes of planning and reflection'.

A recurring theme of many of the chapters discussed so far has been in highlighting the need for an integrated approach to education. In Linda's chapter we see the integration of lecture with lab, theory with practice and learning space with learning need. A further example of this is demonstrated by James McCowan in his description of the integrated learning concept at Queens University Faculty of Applied Science. James focuses on the need to manage the transition from conventional to integrated learning and describes the approach taken to introducing change gradually. He demonstrates that integrated learning is seen by different people in different ways and that this builds the potential for integration. If each group could discern the critical aspect in focus for them, the integration and success of such a venture would be even deeper.

The journey which we go through in order to plan our students' learning will, in itself, be a learning experience for us. We may find after all that what we wanted the students to learn no longer seems appropriate and that we cut out whole components of the programme to replace them with others. We may have completely changed our own view of teaching and learning. And so we come full circle to end on reflection beyond reflection. We are now in a position of taking John Cowan's advice, sitting back and pondering and allowing for serendipity to take place.

References

Baillie, C. (2003) 'Negotiating scientific knowledge', in W. Lepenies *Entangled Histories and Negotiated Universals*, Frankfurt: Campus Verlag, pp. 32–57.

Franklin, U. (1990) *The Real World of Technology*, Ontario: Anansi Press, p. 48.

Part 1

Why do students learn
what they learn?

1

Engineering education and the pedagogy of awareness

Shirley Booth

Introduction

In this chapter I will put forward what I believe to be a fruitful pedagogical[1] view of learning, and its implications for certain aspects of teaching. It is not a view of education as a whole – it does not, for example, touch on the design of curriculum as far as content goes, or offer prescriptive advice to teachers on pursuing their practice. What I try to do is to problematize teachers teaching by bringing the spotlight onto learners learning, within the prevailing professional, institutional and national guidelines that circumscribe engineering education.

The view of learning has a number of levels. At a micro-level it concerns the structure of human awareness and how certain pedagogical situations support a productive restructuring of awareness to lend greater understanding; at the individual level it concerns variation in the knowledge relations that people have with the phenomena in the world around them; and at the pedagogical level of classrooms, laboratories and workplaces it concerns the variation in ways of experiencing phenomena that can arise through pedagogical measures. Learning can be characterized as changing one's way of experiencing some phenomenon, and teaching is then creating situations where such change is fostered.

The view of learning has its roots in empirical phenomenographic studies[2] where the object of study is variation in ways of experiencing phenomena that are met in pedagogical settings and the result of which is an analytical description of that variation in terms of a set of qualitatively distinct categories.

From this empirical work has emerged a theory, the theory of variation, which extends the research into learning to a consideration of creating conditions for learning.

Background

Engineering education can trace its origins to two distinctly different roots. The first is the tradesman apprentice education, where boys with indentures to the local trades studied to advance their theoretical and practical knowledge of the tools of their trades. Thus began Chalmers University of Technology, in Sweden, with mechanical marine engineering as its early specialisation in support of the merchants of the port of Gothenburg, and Georgia Institute of Technology in the US with mechanical engineering in support of, among other things, the textile industry. The other sort of root is the university or college that took the natural sciences as a starting point and specialized in applications to engineering; Imperial College in London and MIT in the US are examples of this origin. All four institutions are, today, research-led and education-intensive universities of engineering, offering programmes of study across all the traditional engineering disciplines as well as in the cross-disciplinary fields of study that are increasingly important: not only chemical engineering, but also biochemical technology; not only marine engineering but marine technology and logistics. Increasingly there is a move to incorporate humanities subjects into the programmes and students are expected to learn to communicate with others, to become problem-solvers, to become aware of ethical aspects of their professional work, and to prepare for a life of entrepreneurship.

What was once getting an engineering degree through a complex programme of technical and mathematics courses is now moving towards a complex process of becoming a professional engineer through exposure to a wide range of technical and mathematical challenges, spanning a variety of disciplines and reaching out to the professions and society at large. More than ever, engineering educators have to consider the learning processes they are expecting from their students and take considered steps to match them with appropriate pedagogical environments and instructional tasks.

In this chapter I am proposing a view of learning that can support teachers who engage with the educational challenge, as the scholars they are in their own research discipline. This is not a behavioural view with a focus on training students to act in certain ways when they meet certain sets of circumstances. For engineering, as for other professions, the future sets of circumstances are as yet unknown and it is in order to function in this unknown future that students invest four or five years of their youth (Bowden and Marton, 1998). Nor is it a purely cognitive view where the mind is seen as a computer which might process incoming information now or save it until later when there is spare capacity, and where efficient algorithms in the mind are responsible for giving correct responses based on the structured data held there and the perceived context. Both behavioural and cognitivist views of learning have their places in the discipline and practices of psychology, but what engineering education needs is a view of learning with roots in the discipline and practices of the pedagogy of higher education: the field of knowledge and research which specifically focuses on people who are intentionally moving towards personal goals with support from the efforts of institutions and teachers, and the knowledge and practices that are articulated there.

A relational view of learning and teaching

The view of learning I am espousing is that learning, in its most profound form, is a question of coming to 'understand' things in distinctly new ways, where 'understand' can be replaced by 'see', or by 'conceptualize', or by 'experience'. There are other ways of viewing learning, even in a strictly educational sense. Learning can also mean acquiring more facts or skills, much like those already known; learning to program in a new procedural programming language such as Ada, for instance, when already competent in Pascal, or learning to handle a new and refined version of a piece of equipment. But it is this learning as understanding (or its synonyms) that I am focusing on. Learning is seen neither as the behavioural response to a stimulus nor as the cognitive manipulation of algorithms and data structures in the mind; learning is seen as a qualitative change in the relation between the learner and that which is learned, which can be expressed as a move from one way of seeing the phenomenon to another or, equivalently, as the phenomenon appearing to the learner in a qualitatively new way compared with earlier appearances. The relation is bipolar – the learner sees the phenomenon in a particular way and the phenomenon appears in a particular way to the learner.

Let me elaborate on this idea, now sticking mostly with the verb 'to understand'. In any subject there is *important* content – phenomena, concepts, theories, principles, skills – and there are particularly productive ways of understanding these, which form the backbone of the subject. Without a clear and multi-faceted understanding of the computer science concept of recursion, for example – what it signifies qualitatively, how to write programs using it, how such programs are implemented, what functions it serves in different environments, how it relates to analytical induction, and so on[3] – the student will face numerous dead-ends in computer science studies. This is what can be thought of as a *threshold concept* (Meyer and Land, 2003), one which is pivotal for successful learning at later stages of a subject, and which calls for particular attention from the teacher who is sensitive to the demands of learning her or his subject.

It is an anecdotal truism that people understand things in different ways, whether it is the debate on genetically modified food or on how to develop a computer program that needs a recursive solution. What is well established by educational researchers is that the variation in ways in which people understand an issue or a concept can be analysed and described in a small number of qualitatively distinct ways (Marton and Booth, 1997). And this analytical description enables the teacher to gauge where the students are in relation to the phenomenon being studied and thereby formulate goals, offer feedback and assess learning in line with shifting their understanding to desired goals.

To stay with the recursion example (with apologies to those who are not turned on by programming), among students in the process of studying the techniques of functional programming (Booth, 1992) three distinct ways of understanding it have been found: as a template that is provided in a programming environment to enable programs to be written according to certain rules; as a way of bringing about programs that can repeat particular functions thereby filling the important role of iteration; and as a mathematically grounded construct that makes use of self-reference with a base case as stop condition. They can be seen as increasingly inclusive and increasingly complex; the third is the way an experienced programmer (and the teacher) is capable of understanding recursion and which is generalizable through its mathematical underpinnings to other programming environments – even though, in most practical cases, the second is sufficient to make a good job of writing a program. The first is naive in that it does not prepare the student for a future of unknown challenges but, rather, traps her or him in textbook problems with straightforward solutions.[4]

I hope that the example of ways of understanding recursion can illustrate that there are not only qualitatively different ways of understanding, but that there are distinctions between these ways that are critical for development from less productive to more productive ways of understanding. Thus, between the first (template) and the second (repetition) there is the distinction of bringing the problem to be solved and its interpretation into focus (rather than the program that is to be written according to rules), and between the second and third (self-repetition) there is the distinction between a programming heuristic (specific for this environment) and a mathematically related (and thereby generalizable) concept.

To generalize this somewhat, we see, first, that the ways of understanding become wider, embracing more concepts associated with recursion and computer science and engineering in general. Further, we see that each one tells of a more elaborate whole: only the act of writing a program in the first, then the originating problem is brought into view, and then the mathematics that underpins such functional programming (and which is its great strength) is incorporated into the whole.[5] The variation in ways of understanding recursion is a variation in ways of conceptualizing the whole, and the parts within that whole, and the relations between those parts.

We can say that the categories reflect qualitatively different ways of being aware of the nature of recursion. Here, 'awareness' signifies what, out of all the many signals reaching the student in the act of considering recursion, becomes focal and what is related to that focus. As you sit and read this chapter you might be focusing on a number of aspects of it – hopefully seeking its meaning, though that might be focusing on the example of students' ways of understanding recursion, or of what is being said about the principles under-lying this view of learning, and most likely a switching back and forth between the example and the principles.[6] The context in which you are reading is significant. If you are unfortunate enough to be reading it for a written exam-ination tomorrow you might well be reading it in a different way, and focusing on different aspects, than if you are reading it for general interest as a profes-sional engineering educator. The student working with a typical half-solved, textbook problem involving recursion might well experience recursion in a different way than if the problem related more to personal experience and therefore required a degree of interpretation.

The point I am making is that, in this pedagogically grounded view, learning is about coming to understand something of importance in a way that is qualitatively more in line with desired goals, and that this is a matter of expanding awareness to embrace greater wholes, more parts within the wholes, and stronger relations between parts – and, in particular, that critical aspects can be brought into focus. Note that in what I have written I have consist-ently avoided relating one way of understanding to an individual student. An individual might be capable of ways of understanding that exceed that demonstrated in a particular context, which is related to the nature of aware-ness and its contextual dependence. Learning also requires matching the way of understanding to its appropriate context.

Teaching threshold concepts

Now that we have established the outline of the view of students' learning, teaching can come into the argument. A fundamental role of teaching is to bring critical aspects of subject matter into focus, in particular in designing tasks, whether lectures, or problems, or labs, or projects – and giving feed-back on them, in tutorials or lab assistance or in assessment. So, two new tasks are given to the (already overburdened) teacher – finding out, analysing, describing the qualitatively different ways in which subject matter can be understood and designing tasks that support shift from one way of under-standing to another that is more elaborated, complex and inclusive.

In fact, the first task comes more or less naturally to the experienced teacher. They know what students need to know and the ways in which it should be understood in order to move on in their subject, though they might have difficulty in articulating it unless challenged and encouraged to do so.

Ask yourself: what do my first-year students often find difficult to understand? What distinguishes the ways of understanding of those students who demonstrate a lack of understanding from those who clearly do understand? What might be critical for the sort of understanding that I want for my students, in order, maybe, to be able to continue their development in other subjects, or relate it to future professional issues? What obstacles to understanding might they find hard to overcome?

Having analysed these critical aspects they can become focal for the effort of teaching at the micro-level of concept and learning task. If an alien from another planetary system landed on Earth and showed themselves to have a physical sense of colour but no concept of colour, how would you teach them to distinguish red from the other colours? One way, the obvious way maybe, is to show them red objects and tell them that they are red. This would lead to a connection between objects of that colour and the concept of red. But would they be able to distinguish red from the other colours? Not unless the difference had been grasped, and that would mean the teaching effort would have to bring red objects into the alien's awareness at the same time as objects of other colours and the distinction brought to focal awareness. Now suppose that the objects to hand are children's building bricks in a variety of colours, including red. Which would be more effective – to show red only in terms of bricks of one shape and size in relation to blue and green and pink bricks of different shapes and sizes? Wouldn't that be to risk that particular shape and size being associated with redness, thereby losing generality? No, surely, to show different shapes and different sizes while maintaining redness as a common feature is the way to bring about a general awareness of red as a colour. To continue with flowers of different colour and form would add to the effect. It is *variation* and *invariance* that are the key points here. The concept of red is brought into focal awareness by exposure to a deliberate *variation* of size, shape and type of object in relation to objects of other colours, while the property of redness is maintained *invariant*.

So can it be with the design of learning tasks, or sequences of tasks. Having identified a critical aspect of a phenomenon that is known to be important for learning, teaching can be designed such that the aspect is maintained while other aspects of the phenomenon are varied. Returning to the recursion example, in order to support a shift from the first to the second category of understanding, exercises can be set, or examples worked on in class, where problems that have to be interpreted in terms of repetition of one kind or another is maintained and thus brought into focus while the syntactic form of the solution falls into the background. And to shift from the second category to the third category, a number of programs need to be considered where the self-referential nature of the function and termination on reaching a base case come into focal awareness through varying the syntactic and semantic (template and forms of repetition) features of the program.

We can think of these examples in terms of *dimensions of variation* – whether colour as in the concrete example or aspects of writing recursive programs in the more abstract example. A dimension of variation is a feature of a particular class of phenomenon (colour, aspect of a programming construct) that can either be taken as given or can be contemplated as being other than the given. And it is necessary (though certainly not sufficient) for learning that teaching should raise the 'taken as given' to focal awareness and to impose a variation that opens up alternative ways of understanding.

It is not only in the design of tasks for learning that this lesson on variation can be valuable. In discussing phenomena or telling of phenomena there is room for supporting learning to a greater or lesser degree by the forms of exposition that are used in presentation or discussion. Let us move now to physics: a feature of virtually every physics phenomenon is that it is expressed in a mathematical form and much of physics is taught through dealing with, or manipulating, the mathematical forms. For engineers, physics is generally brought in to support an application which is technical rather than mathematical. In a recent paper by Ingerman and Booth (2003), the ways in which physics students and research physicists expound on physics was studied and implications for teaching and learning were drawn from the results.

Four different ways of expounding on physics were analysed from the data gathered in asking advanced students to tell of a solution to a well-known problem in quantum physics and researchers asked to tell of their research. They were named as Expounding (a) in bits, (b) in a single perspective, (c) in multiple perspectives and (d) through contextualization. The first was observed only in students and comprises hopping from one idea to another with no coherent line of argument – hardly to be recommended for teaching. The others were seen in both groups of participants, though (c) and (d) were more pronounced in the researchers. Typical for (b) is describing one's research through long passages of narration on a single feature such as the mathematical formulation or the technical equipment, without relating it to the physics problem at the heart of the work. Typical of (c), in contrast, is shifting back and forth between two aspects of the research, maybe the physics for a qualitative sense and the mathematics for the formal sense, so that for the listener there is a stream of references between the two lines of argument. And in (d) the exposition places the research phenomena in different contexts so that it is illuminated from different directions.

This gives an indication of the way that explanations and expositions can be presented that offer more or less opportunity for students to see their hitherto taken-as-given understanding opened to potential variation. Both (c) and (d) offer this potential[7] as long as the shifts in perspectives and in contexts are centred on critically important knowledge, threshold concepts, rather than arbitrarily.

Finding out what is learned

So far I have been considering what teachers can do in order to support a meaningful structuring of their students' awareness of the subject matter they are studying, bringing critical features of important knowledge into focus. And the device for this is grounded in exposing the variation in the dimensions in which those features are otherwise taken as given. But so far I have begged the question of how this can be adapted to the subjects of study and the whole programmes of professional development that engineering educators are engaged in.

In the case of recursion, which I do not intend to labour further, I offered an analytical description of the variation in ways of understanding (or experiencing) the concept, pointed to critical differences between the three categories that comprise the description, and suggested ways in which those critical features could be subject to variation in teaching. The engineering educator needs first of all to identify the important knowledge, what has the threshold quality described earlier. In elementary calculus this could be *integration* which can be understood in many ways, and some are more fruitful for subsequently handling differential equations than others are. In environmental science it could be *energy*, which is a troublesome concept at the best of times but which takes on special significance in the closed systems of the environment (Carlsson, 1999). In many fields of engineering the notion of a *model* is problematic and students can confuse the model with the phenomenon that is being modelled, with consequences that vary from area to area. Such key concepts and principles as these are worthy of extra teaching effort in order to support students' understanding across the field they are studying.

There are many ways in which practising teachers can collect evidence of the variation in ways students understand such key phenomena. Diagnostic tests can be devised around them and the scripts that are collected can be analysed; examination questions that intend to test understanding can be studied for puzzling deviations; questions that come up directly after a lecture can be collected and analysed, such as the method of 'muddy cards' devised at MIT (Hall *et al.*, 2002); tutorials can be organized so that students have time to discuss concepts and report on differences in understanding they discover in the group (Svensson and Högfors, 1988). And alliances can be made with educational researchers who can conduct more systematic studies of interest for their own purposes. But the most important factor in any of this is the critical perspective the teacher can bring to the data thus collected: a critical perspective grounded in a thorough and profound knowledge of the field and an open mind on variation in the experience of learning.

Fostering meaningful approaches to learning

All of the view of learning being espoused has its origins in an empirical research approach to studying student learning collectively known as phenomenography (Marton, 1981; Marton and Booth, 1997) and the emergent variation theory of learning (Marton and Booth, 1997; Bowden and Marton, 1998; Pang and Marton, 2003). And the initial empirical research was a study of how students go about their tasks of learning, and with what results (Marton *et al.*, 1997). The overriding outcome of that research is now rather well known. It points to two distinctly different approaches to learning tasks: a *surface approach* in which focus is on the task as given, on the sign, on doing what the task seems to call for in the educational situation; and a *deep approach* with focus on the meaning embedded in the task, that which is signified, on relating the task to prior knowledge and experience. These approaches are not characteristics of individual students but are, rather, the result of the student's interaction with the task in the learning context in which it is experienced. Thus, a student might well (and without choosing) take a deep approach in a task that is of intrinsic interest, where it is felt that the teacher will give significant feedback, and where the context invites engagement with the subject matter. And the same student might take a surface approach in a context that is uncertain, where the task seems arbitrary or busywork, where the study programme is crowded and time is short.

Every task or situation has a perceived relevance which is structured partly around perceived demands and constraints but, more importantly, in this argument, around perceived relations between prior knowledge and aims for future knowledge. Questions naturally emerge in the meeting between student and learning task, and those questions might circle around 'What do they expect from me here?' or around 'What does this mean, what is involved here?' In both cases the student is extracting meaning from the task, but in the former there is no engagement with subject matter or quest for understanding in focus. The teacher who creates a sense of curiosity in what might be the outcome of understanding is on the way to creating a deep approach to the tasks to come.

That is well enough, but those early studies (for example Säljö, 1975) – and many since, as well as the theoretical developments (Marton and Booth, 1996) – have shown decisively that a deep approach is connected with a grasping of critical features of subject matter, while a surface approach, being a temporary response to the immediate situation, gives knowledge that is easily misunderstood and quickly forgotten. It has to be pointed out that the deep and surface approaches are generic terms and individual types of task (reading, solving problems, doing labs, undertaking projects in industry) all have their own peculiar forms which can be observed and analysed *in situ*. Writing computer programs, for instance, has been seen to have four distinct approaches, two of which can be construed as equivalent to deep and two to surface (Booth, 1992).

The nature of the task and the context it is embedded in are paramount for understanding the field of knowledge it is intended to offer the students. A study carried out by a teacher in materials science can illustrate this (Lundström and Booth, 2002). In a course on reinforced polymer materials he felt that his students were failing to bring the various forms of reinforcement, the underlying theories, the methods of manufacture and the properties of the materials into a coherent whole where choices could be made on suitable ways of making objects with particular properties. Constrained by course requirements and parallel courses he could not introduce the projects that he would have liked to, so he took another approach where the students had to relate the subject matter of the course to a particular and individual application object that could be made from the materials being studied – such as a cycle helmet, a truck cab, a flagpole, a rocket nosecone – and report critically on its relevance. These reports were collected by email and after one such course a scheme of criteria for grading and giving meaningful feedback was devised for a repeat course. A careful analysis (helped by a grant from the university) showed three qualitatively different ways of writing the email reports (Figure 1.1).

On the one hand, the *application object* was treated in three qualitatively different ways across the large collection of written reports:

- it might be taken as given, without consideration of its conceivable potential functions and forms;
- it might be treated from various perspectives of function and form; and
- it might be placed in different contexts, thus illuminating the potential for different functions and forms.

On the other hand, the *subject matter* was also treated in three qualitatively different ways:

- it might be copied into the report from the textbook or lecture notes;
- it might be condensed into a general description; or
- it might be interpreted in the light of the object and the function and form under consideration.

Thus, with the help of phenomenographic insights, we can describe the equivalent of deep and surface approaches in this particular task. A surface approach, focus on the sign, is shown in a report where subject matter has been copied or condensed and related to the application object which is taken for granted. A deep approach, focusing on the signified, interprets the subject matter in relation to the application object, which is either considered from

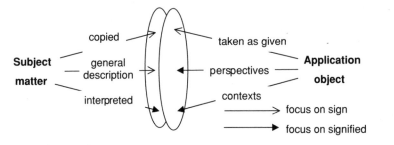

Figure 1.1 Ways of relating subject matter of a course in reinforced polymeric materials to a specific application object

various perspectives or considered in various contexts. In the first case we can say that the student's awareness has been unmoved by the task while in the second there is potential for variation to have brought critical aspects of subject matter into focus.

With this schema for understanding how students were going about their learning task, feedback could be given not only on the content of the report as such but also on the ways in which approaches could be improved in order to foster understanding.

Constituting the whole

A passing reference to the relevance structure of a learning task was made above, but no education is constituted of isolated learning tasks! Learning tasks constitute – in most traditional programmes of study – courses that run in parallel groups of two, three or four. Even in traditional programmes these courses are given by teachers from different disciplines, with their assumptions and conceptual frameworks, and the students are expected to focus into the course to learn that particular subject, and out towards other courses to inte-grate the subjects into a coherent whole. In the programmes that were mentioned at the start of this chapter, where new cross-disciplinary fields are being articulated, and a greater interest in humanities and human aspects of engineering are being fostered, this discipline-based programme structure makes demands for teachers to understand one another's starting points. And one starting point that is common for all, and largely neglected, is the students' own experience of what constitutes the whole.

A study into how students experience the whole of an engineering physics programme (Booth and Ingerman, 2002) can serve to illustrate the concerns that teachers could be addressing in this large-scale perspective on a pedagogy for supporting students' awareness of their own professional development. The study came about because of a sudden and drastic drop-out in the second year of a four and a half year programme, conjectured to be a result of packing more humanities and problem solving into the already packed first-year curriculum. That conjecture remains a conjecture, but what emanated from the study has a more general significance.

Students with varying degrees of success were interviewed and asked, among other things, to tell how the 16 or 17 courses they had taken so far related to one another. On analysis, six qualitatively different ways of relating them came to light. One group of three tell of the courses as (a) encapsulating isolated fragments of knowledge, (b) ordering these fragments, and (c) fitting fragments together. 'The fragment' is the dominant nature of the course, and finding the teachers' intentions in presenting these fragments, or putting them in a particular order, or fitting them together in some predetermined way, is how they are conceptualized as a whole. In contrast, a second group of three make more sense of these fragments and their internal relations, and speak of them being (d) meshed and rearrangeable, integrated by understanding, or (e) coming together into a single object of knowledge, and finally, (f) becoming a knowledge object that is related to oneself and to the world of physics.

So, here we have a schema of qualitatively different ways of making sense of the whole of the engineering physics programme, and only the most advanced feature of that sense-making brings physics, as such, into the picture. For the most part we hear of second-guessing the teachers' intentions and trying to fit parts of an incoherent puzzle together. We see these six categories as inclusive – all students almost certainly scratch their heads over how some particular course is relevant to the rest or to their future careers (and maybe it puzzles teachers too), but only some students demonstrated the capability to look away from their immediate puzzlement over the programme and focus, first, on seeking points of contact in their understanding of the various fragments, and then on bringing them into relation to a growing understanding of what constitutes engineering physics.

There is another thread to this argument, and that is the ethical stance of the students with respect to their teachers and their learning. In the first three categories of ways of experiencing the first year (a, b and c), authority is seen as residing firmly with the teachers and it is their responsibility that students should learn, whereas in the second group (e, f and g) responsibility for learning has shifted towards the student – first in relation to the degree programme and finally with physics as the point of reference. Even here there is an inclusivity in the later categories – authority is hardly likely to be removed from teachers altogether, except by students who, for some reason, become alienated by the programme, but not all the students interviewed expressed a sense of autonomy.

Seeing this as a shift in awareness of themselves in the context of their studies and the opening world of engineering physics as a profession, one can say that dimensions of variation have opened – from a taken-as-given assumption that teachers would see that everything was right, to a realization that the way is open for them to question their assumptions and take control of their sense-making, to looking forward and including the future in engineering physics in that sense-making process.

Implications can be drawn for teaching on two levels. First, teachers need to problematize the whole that their own fragment fits into, and see to it that there are conceptual hooks for students to latch on to. It might be a question of mathematics teachers taking the phenomena of particular engineering disciplines or subjects as the starting point for their theoretical developments and as a source of examples and problems. Or, it could be teachers in the macroscopic aspects of a field relating their models and experiments to the microscopic aspects, whether backwards as references to subjects already studied or forwards in the form of questions that, one day, can be addressed more fully. But it does demand a collegiality among teachers across the disciplinary boundaries, with their teaching in focus, and with a pedagogical theoretical framework to illustrate and question their diverse experiences.

Second, teachers need to encourage autonomy among their students from the outset. There is a common assumption that students need to master a fundamental body of work before they can begin to tackle original problems and projects, but a number of innovations, such as problem-based and project-oriented approaches to teaching, question that assumption. Learning is seen to be more happily supported by engagement in solving genuine problems that give rise to genuine questions. That these questions have no answers in the immediate subject of study does not detract from the long-term benefits of having an interest in discovery. Such autonomy needs to be encompassed in course goals and descriptions, in curriculum material and in examinations, in order to be convincingly articulated for students to see and understand.

Conclusion

I have tried here to condense into a few pages some of the ideas on learning and teaching that have emerged from the research specialization of phenomenography, with both empirical studies and theoretical developments as support. These ideas might be alien to some engineering teachers, but I ask them to examine their own teaching experience with the ideas in mind and see if there are, indeed, points of contact. I suspect there are. And teachers for whom this strikes a chord, I ask you to investigate and articulate your experience and relate it in a similar framework to contribute to the body of scholarly knowledge that your colleagues can have use of.

Notes

1 'Pedagogy' is being used in this chapter to signify particular sorts of meetings between students, teachers and knowledge, where there is an intention to learn. Here, it is meant to be less encompassing than 'education' which can include institutions, political and professional regulations, and the needs and demands of society, as well as pedagogy.

2 The book *Learning and Awareness* written by Ference Marton and myself (Marton and Booth, 1997) can be referred to for elaboration of much of the theoretical outline which underpins this chapter.

3 For more on this refer to Booth (1992).

4 The qualitatively different ways in which people might understand genetically modified food is left to the reader to analyse and describe (preferably in terms that go beyond for and against).

5 The study being referred to was in the context of a course that deliberately avoided discussion of implementation; in another context this would certainly come into the whole of another category and with it would come concepts such as environment and stack.

6 And which characterizes what will later be introduced as a deep approach to learning through reading a text.

7 Which is not to say that (b) should be avoided, giving as it does the opportunity for coherent argument on one aspect or another of the phenomenon in focus.

References

Booth, S. (1992) *Learning to Program: a phenomenographic perspective*, Gothenburg: Acta Universitatis Guthobergensis.

Booth, S. and Ingerman, Å. (2002) 'Making sense of physics in the first year of study', *Learning and Instruction* 12 (5): 493–507.

Bowden, J. and Marton, F. (1998) *The University of Learning*, London: Kogan Page.

Carlsson, B. (1999) 'Ecological understanding; a space of variation', Doctoral thesis, Luleå University of Technology, p. 39.

Hall, S. R., Waitz, I., Brodeur, D. R., Söderholm, D. H. and Nasr, R. (2002) 'Adoption of active learning in a lecture-based engineering class', Paper presented at the ASEE/IEEE Frontiers in Education Conference, Boston, MA, 6–9 November.

Ingerman, Å. and Booth, S. (2003) 'Expounding on physics. A phenomenographic study of physicists talking of their physics', *International Journal of Science Education* 25 (12): 1489–1508.

Lundström, S. and Booth, S. (2002) 'Journals based on applications: an attempt to improve students' learning about composite materials', *European Journal of Engineering Education* 27 (2): 195–208.

Marton, F. (1981) 'Phenomenography – describing conceptions of the world around us', *Instructional Science* 10: 177–200.

Marton, F. and Booth, S. (1996) 'The learner's experience of learning', in D. Olson and N. Torrance (eds) *Handbook of Education and Human Development: new models of learning, teaching and schooling*, Oxford: Blackwell.

Marton, F. and Booth, S. (1997) *Learning and Awareness*, Mahwah, NJ: LEA.

Marton, F., Hounsell, D. and Entwistle, N. (1997) *The Experience of Learning*, 2nd edition, Edinburgh: Scottish Academic Press.

Meyer, E. and Land, R. (2003) *Threshold Concepts and Troublesome Knowledge: linkages to ways of thinking and practising within the disciplines*, ETL Project Occasional Report 4 (referenced from http://www.ed.ac.uk/etl/publications.html on 27 October 2003).

Pang, M. F. and Marton, F. (2003) 'Beyond "lesson study": comparing two ways of facilitating the grasp of some economic concepts', *Instructional Science* 31 (3): 175–194.

Säljö, R. (1975) *Qualitative Differences in Learning as a Function of the Learner's Conception of the Task*, Göteborg: Acta Universitatis Gothobergensis.

Svensson, L. and Högfors, C. (1988) 'Conceptions as the content of teaching: improving education in mechanics', in P. Ramsden (ed.) *Improving Learning. New Perspectives*, London: Kogan Page.

Part 2

What do we want students to learn?

2

What outcome is engineering education trying to achieve?

Fred Maillardet

Introduction

The year 1997 was significant for UK Engineering Higher Education. The report of the National Committee of Enquiry into Higher Education (the Dearing Report) was published, the Quality Assurance Agency (QAA) was established, and the Engineering Council's Policy Document Standards and Routes to Registration 3rd Edition (SARTOR 3) was published.

While the Dearing Report drew attention to the need to articulate more clearly exactly what was being offered by the education provider, and the QAA established the mechanism by which this articulation could be formulated and monitored, SARTOR 3 set out the criteria for the appropriate educational base for registration as an engineer. This featured the use of minimum engineering course input standards defined in terms of A-level point scores, a response in part to the criticisms of some employers that the Higher Education (HE) system was not producing sufficient engineering graduates with the skills and attributes they required.

A definition of engineering

The late George King often referred to engineering as 'a three legged stool' relying on mathematics, science and techné as the three legs. By techné he meant the whole range of creative abilities which distinguished the engineer from the scientist; to conceive, design, make, actually bring to fruition. One grave danger inherent in the current tendency to categorize education as 'academic' or 'vocational' is that it overlooks the key role of the engineer to operate and be at ease in both areas, often acting as an arbiter between the views held by those operating solely in one or other area . It is thus important to restate that engineering is more than understanding science; it is essentially a vocational subject which relies upon a sound understanding of scientific principles together with an appropriate facility in mathematics, the vital communication and modelling language.

Input standards and quality

The SARTOR 3 approach led all-too-quickly to the use of input standards as a convenient and readily quantifiable proxy for quality of a course. Market forces, it was claimed, would ensure that the 'best' courses would be able to attract the 'most able' students who, in turn, would produce the 'best quali-fied' graduates. This is not the place to explore the paucity of understanding of the current UK education system exhibited by this approach, and the games which started to be played by some Admission Tutors, but suffice it to say that, to engineers at least, the use of one *input* criteria to indicate *output* quality from any process is deeply flawed. It is particularly inappropriate in engineering where many of the topics to be mastered and skills to be devel-oped are simply not widely available at A-level; most engineers would agree that A-levels are the place to assemble and develop the core scientific and mathematical building blocks.

Other factors

In addition to the excessive focus on input standards, a number of other factors were leading many to question the need to articulate output standards more clearly. Among these were:

- Concern among employers of falling standards, although many in HE argued that it was a lengthening of the 'tail' of qualifications rather than an overall reduction in standards which was of prime concern.
- Uncertainty among employers of what attributes could be anticipated in graduates.
- Recognition of the lack of a common format or language for the articu-lation of output standards.
- Growing concern within HE over assessment practices and, particularly, the increasing load being imposed on both students and staff by excessive volumes of assessment, partly as a result of the spread of modular structures.

- Growing unease over the increasing fragmentation of the engineering profession as evidenced by the growing range of interpretation of Engineering Council policies by the main professional bodies.

The EPC output standards project

At its 1997 Annual Assembly, the Engineering Professors' Council (EPC) discussed both input and output standards at length, and expressed its concern about the over-emphasis on input standards, stressing that the profession should be measuring output standards. Indeed, EPC support for SARTOR 3 was on the explicit understanding that appropriate output standards would be in place by the time that the new criteria had worked their way through to the graduate level, say five years. The EPC resolved to address this need and established an Output Standards Working Group later in the year. This working group contained representatives of all the major branches of engineering (chemical, civil, electrical, electronic, manufacturing and mechanical) and consulted widely both within HE and beyond.

The importance of gaining the support of the key stakeholders was recognized so that an Advisory Group was formed including representatives of the Engineering Council (EC), the Engineering Employers Federation (EEF), the Engineering and Marine Trades Association (EMTA), the Department for Education and Employment (DfEE), the Department of Trade and Industry (DTI) and the QAA. This advisory group met regularly over the next three years and fed back valuable reactions to the Working Group as the output standards model evolved.

The outcomes

EPC conducted a survey of its members, asking them to rank the qualities, skills and capabilities which they valued most highly in prospective engineers. The earlier work of the Council for National Academic Awards (CNAA), the Accreditation Board for Engineering and Technology (ABET) and the Higher Education Quality Council (HEQC) was also studied and a composite list of the essential attributes and capabilities needed to define a reasonable expectation of the graduate engineer developed. It was a key objective that the result should apply to all engineering disciplines, so that it needed to be generic. Given the vocational nature of engineering, it was also concluded that the expectations of engineering graduates were best conveyed in competence terms of what they could do rather than what they knew; that is 'ability to' statements.

These considerations led, eventually, to the decision to base the requirements on the engineering design process which appears fundamental to all engineering, together with the associated key skills.

The list of 'ability to' statements was thus expressed in terms of seven primary elements:

1   ability to exercise key skills in the completion of engineering-related tasks;
2   ability to transform existing systems into conceptual models;
3   ability to transform conceptual models into determinable models;
4   ability to use determinable models to obtain system specifications in terms of parametric values;
5   ability to select optimum specifications and create physical models;
6   ability to apply the results from physical models to create real target systems;
7   ability to critically review real target systems and personal performance.

The last six of these were decomposed into 25 component elements to describe in detail the steps normally required to complete the primary activities; that is, how an engineer actually solves real engineering problems. These secondary elements are listed in full in the Appendix.

The determination to keep the statements as generic as possible led to challenges over wording as each of the engineering disciplines interpreted the underlying process in terms with which they were familiar. The EPC Working Group had avoided words like 'familiarity' and 'understanding' which they considered to be too vague and open to an excessively wide range of inter-pretation. Instead, they used more precise but less traditional language in terms of what students should be able to do, together with generic terms like 'determinable models'.

The EPC Working Group anticipated the 'ability to' statements being applied to individual students rather than expectations resulting from course claims. A student would be expected to demonstrate all of the abilities at the specified threshold benchmark standard in order to graduate with the award of an engineering degree. Differentiation between degrees (e.g. those designed for Chartered Engineers and Incorporated Engineers, or B.Eng. and M.Eng.) could be achieved by using different benchmark specifications. The specifications of additional benchmarks set above the threshold would enable higher levels of attainment to be recognized for purposes of honours classification.

A pilot study of the application of the framework was carried out among nine UK engineering departments spanning the major disciplines and the results were encouraging, demonstrating that it was possible to express exem-plar benchmarks for each of the different disciplines using the generic framework. Employer focus groups were also consulted and, although they found the language 'difficult', they did accept that it provided an efficient and effective means of communicating between informed practitioners. This achievement could be seen as a watershed not just in terms of creating a common framework for all the disciplines, but in terms of describing engineering as a process or way of thinking. The practice as opposed to the study of real engineering was being addressed.

The stakeholders' views

The EPC issued an Interim Report in 2000 as an occasional paper: The EPC Engineering Graduate Output Standard. This was generally well received. EPC recognized, however, that the approach needed to be reviewed by all the key stakeholders if it was to be widely accepted. Five Working Groups were thus established, their findings being reported formally to the EPC Congress in 2002.

Employers

The employer WG recognized that, with the transition from an 'elite' to a 'mass' HE system, norm-referencing of students' abilities was no longer adequate. They welcomed the use of clear 'ability to' statements, and saw the standard as a means of developing clear co-operation between employers and academia. They confirmed the earlier employer view that they found the language difficult, but recognized the need for precision. They proposed a simplified presentation for non-technical colleagues. The EEF, in particular, were keen to sustain the development of this initiative, and sponsored some of the assessment studies.

Assessment issues

This WG recognized that without appropriate assessment, output standards were meaningless. It also recognized that assessment is a 'driver for learning' for many students and, as such, is a critical aspect of overall course design. However, the excessive assessment load being placed on both students and staff needed to be addressed; a radical overhaul of assessment practices was called for, particularly to avoid multiple assessment of the same (or similar) abilities. A series of workshops was mounted in conjunction with the Learning and Teaching Support Network (LTSN) for Engineering during 2002 and 2003, helping course leaders to articulate the output standards anticipated from their own current or planned courses, and including discussion of assessment issues. A number of papers were also published focusing on assessment, for example Peter Knight's 2001 paper on the implications of adopting output standards.

Professional bodies

This WG served a particularly valuable role in providing a forum for discussion between the major engineering institutions, who were all in the process of considering how to articulate more clearly what was required in accredited engineering courses. A number of the institutions began developing frameworks using the EPC output standards model.

Incorporated Engineer

SARTOR 3 reinforced the need to consider carefully the relationship between the Chartered Engineer (C.Eng.) and the Incorporated Engineer (I.Eng.). This WG provided a timely opportunity for the major institutions to explore this challenging area together. The conclusion of the WG was that there was no reason why the output standard framework could not be applied to I.Eng. degrees as well as C.Eng. degrees; indeed, the approach helped to identify more clearly where differences needed to exist between I.Eng. and C.Eng. courses as greater emphasis could be placed on different primary and secondary 'ability to' statements according to the type of course being mounted.

Compatibility with QAA benchmark statement

The QAA published their benchmark statement for engineering a little before the EPC report. This WG had the critical task of comparing the two statements; if they were fundamentally at odds, engineering HE would face a dilemma regarding which to use. A sophisticated cross-matching of outcomes (in both directions) led to the conclusion that the approaches were different but entirely compatible, the main difference being the EPC use of the engineering design process as the framework spine.

The overall conclusion to be drawn from the working groups' reviews was that the requirements of all the key stakeholders had been generally satisfied without ignoring their different perspectives and, thus, needs.

Conclusions: what has been achieved

The EPC drive to articulate output standards has produced a framework of 'ability to' statements for engineering which enables course designers to develop programmes of study which have a 'whole course' approach to assessment rather than a fragmented module-based regime. The latter invariably results in multiple assessment of some requirements with the possible complete omission of others. It also enables course designers to articulate the distinction between different types of engineer, e.g. Chartered Engineer and Incorporated Engineer. The project has met the employers' need to be able to anticipate the abilities of graduates, thus enabling recruitment processes to be designed more effectively and company graduate training schemes to be developed from a firmer foundation. Professional bodies can now express accreditation requirements more clearly, using a common language to focus on the output standards, and can discriminate more objectively between the graduates from different universities.

However, some of the most lasting benefits could well be the less tangible achievements. The EPC initiated the articulation of output standards debate which has now been taken up by others, including the QAA and EC. The improved communication and working relationships between all parties involved should lead to improved co-operation with attendant benefits in the future. This is not only true of the 'external' bodies, but also has significant implications as regards the sub-disciplines within engineering; fragmentation of the profession has been increasing over recent years and a common framework or language in which to express output standards should help to draw together the various interest groups.

Perhaps the most profound achievement in the long term is the articulation of engineering as *a way of thinking*, a creative way of approaching all engineering challenges which is shared across all sub-disciplines. This recognition could yield unanticipated benefits in terms of recruitment of able school children who are turned off currently by what they see as 'boring' science. The essential *creativity* at the core of real engineering must shine through all that the profession presents to the world at large.

Appendix

The generic 'ability to' statements

1 Ability to exercise Key Skills in the completion of engineering-related tasks at a level implied by the benchmarks associated with the following statements.

   The Key Skills for engineering are Communication, IT, Application of Number, Working with Others, Problem Solving, Improving Own Learning and Performance.

2 Ability to transform existing systems into conceptual models.

   This means the ability to:
   (a) Elicit and clarify client's true needs.
   (b) Identify, classify and describe engineering systems.
   (c) Define real target systems in terms of objective functions, performance specifications and other constraints (i.e. define the problem).
   (d) Take account of risk assessment, and social and environmental impacts, in the setting of constraints (including legal, and health and safety issues).

(e) Select, review and experiment with existing engineering systems in order to obtain a database of knowledge and understanding that will contribute to the creation of specific real target systems.
(f) Resolve difficulties created by imperfect and incomplete information.
(g) Derive conceptual models of real target systems, identifying the key parameters.

3   Ability to transform conceptual models into determinable models.

This means the ability to:

(a) Construct determinable models over a range of complexity to suit a range of conceptual models.
(b) Use mathematics and computing skills to create determinable models by deriving appropriate constitutive equations and specifying appropriate boundary conditions.
(c) Use industry standard software tools and platforms to set up determinable models.
(d) Recognize the value of determinable models of different complexity and the limitations of their application.

4   Ability to use determinable models to obtain system specifications in terms of parametric values.

This means the ability to:

(a) Use mathematics and computing skills to manipulate and solve determinable models; and use data sheets in an appropriate way to supplement solutions.
(b) Use industry standard software platforms and tools to solve determinable models.
(c) Carry out a parametric sensitivity analysis.
(d) Critically assess results and, if inadequate or invalid, improve knowledge database by further reference to existing systems, and/or performance of determinable models.

5   Ability to select optimum specifications and create physical models.

This means the ability to:

(a) Use objective functions and constraints to identify optimum specifications.
(b) Plan physical modelling studies, based on determinable modelling, in order to produce critical information.
(c) Test and collate results, feeding these back into determinable models.

6   Ability to apply the results from physical models to create real target systems.

This means the ability to:

(a) Write sufficiently detailed specifications of real target systems, including risk assessments and impact statements.
(b) Select production methods and write method statements.
(c) Implement production and deliver products fit for purpose, in a timely and efficient manner.
(d) Operate within relevant legislative frameworks.

7   Ability to critically review real target systems and personal performance.

This means the ability to:

(a) Test and evaluate real systems in service against specification and client needs.
(b) Recognize and make critical judgements about related environmental, social, ethical and professional issues.
(c) Identify professional, technical and personal development needs and undertake appropriate training and independent research.

Recommended further reading

ABET (2000) *Criteria for Accrediting Engineering Programmes*, Accreditation Board for Engineering and Technology.

CNAA (1983) *Goals of Engineering Education*, Council for National Academic Awards.

Engineering Council (1997) *Standards and Routes to Registration*, SARTOR 3rd edition, EC.

EPC (2000) *The EPC Engineering Graduate Output Standard*, Interim Report of the EPC Output Standards Project, Occasional Paper Number 10.

EPC (2002a) *An Employer Group Interpretation*, Report of the Employer's Working Group, Engineering Professors' Council.

EPC (2002b) *Assessment of Complex Outcomes*, Report of the Assessment Working Group, EPC.

EPC (2002c) *Output Standards and Professional Body Accreditation*, Report of the Professional Bodies Working Group, EPC.

EPC (2002d) *Exemplar Benchmarks for I.Eng.*, Report of the I.Eng. Working Group, EPC.

HEQC (1997) *Graduate Standards Programme: Final Report*, Higher Education Quality Council.

Knight, P. (2001) 'Implications for the assessment of engineering degree students of the adoption of engineering output standards', SEFI Annual Conference.

NICHE (1997) *Higher Education in the Learning Society*, Report of the National Committee of Inquiry into HE, HMSO.

QAA (2000) *Subject Benchmark Statement for Engineering*, Quality Assurance Agency.

QAA/EPC (2002) *The Compatibility between the QAA Subject Benchmark Statement for Engineering and the EPC Engineering Graduate Output Standard*, Joint Working Group Report.

3

Capabilities-driven curriculum design

John A. Bowden

Introduction

The design of any curriculum should emerge from the answers to a few, apparently straightforward questions:

1 What should the learner be capable of doing at the end?
2 What kinds of learning experiences and in what combination would best assist the learner to achieve those outcomes?
3 How can the learning environment be best arranged to provide access to those optimal learning experiences?
4 How can the differing needs of individual students be catered for?
5 What specifically is the role of teachers in supporting such learning by students?
6 What kinds of assessment of student learning will motivate learning of the kind desired and authentically measure the levels of achievement of the intended learning outcomes?

Of course, the questions are straightforward only in their form. Their arrangement reflects a particular view of learning and the meaning behind each question is dependent on the pedagogical theory through which it is interpreted. However, three overall themes that can be drawn immediately from the questions are that:

(a) the questions and their implications are all inter-linked;
(b) they are posited on the assumption that it is the student who develops capabilities to act and that the educational institution provides an environment that can either help or hinder that development; and

(c) planning of the activities of teachers takes place after the learning-centred questions have been answered.

In this chapter, I will concentrate on question (1) above but the answer to that question has implications for all of the others. I argue for the proposition that the learning goals in a university curriculum should be expressed in terms of the capabilities of learners on graduation. It should be noted that the capabilities-driven curriculum theory discussed in this chapter was developed in the late 1990s in Australia (Bowden *et al.* (2000) a website authored by Bowden *et al.*, accessed in 2000) independently from the comparable movement in the UK. For that reason, while there are similarities between the two, there are differences that I will mention later, especially in relation to the Engineering Graduate Output Standard (Engineering Professors Council, 2000). The latter (called the EGOS from here on) was developed specifically for engineering and deals with abilities of various kinds. My capabilities theory is a general one and deals with the capability to act, especially in real-life professional settings. Later in this chapter, I will be elaborating my four-level model of capability outcome. The EGOS subsumes notions of levels of outcome into specific descriptions of the kinds of abilities to be demonstrated. To this point the major difference between my capabilities theory and the EGOS is primarily one of general theory versus specific standards. Readers would find comparison of the two of interest and will soon see that there is an additional and significant difference that I will explain later in this chapter, i.e. the degree to which what the EGOS refers to as key skills are integrated with knowledge-based learning. I posit the notion of knowledge capability that represents that integration. The EGOS represents key skills merely as needing to be developed to 'an appropriate level'. That implies a separation that is at odds with the idea of an integrated knowledge capability. This issue will be discussed further later in the chapter.

The capabilities theory derives from the pedagogical theory in a book I wrote with Ference Marton titled *The University of Learning: beyond quality and competence* (Bowden and Marton, 1998). There, we argued that university students are always learning through interaction with current knowledge so as to become capable, some years in the future, of dealing with situations in professional, personal or social contexts that can't be specified in advance. In essence, we claim that university students are engaged in learning for an unknown future and that we have to design the curriculum with that in mind. Hence, the notion of capabilities as learning goals emerges as a central idea – capabilities to act in previously unseen situations.

This idea also appears to be central to discussions of the future of the engineering profession in a more recent book by Rosalind Williams (2002) who argues that the profession formerly known as engineering is having an identity crisis. 'The mission of engineering changes when its dominant problems no longer involve the conquest of nature but the creation and management of a self-made habitat' (see Williams, 2003). She argues further that to adapt to the new habitat, engineers have to re-tool, starting with their understanding of engineering education. The model, as represented in the 1950s by faculty at MIT, was of a tree with the basic sciences as the deep roots, the applied sciences as the shallow roots, the engineering sciences as the branches and the engineering system at the top. Williams argues that this has been supplanted by much more complex interactions as engineers participate in technoscience – depicted by Galison (1997: 46) as a 'trading zone, an intermediate domain where procedures could be coordinated locally even where broader meanings clashed'. The vitality of trading zones lies in breaking down boundaries, keeping things mixed up, developing a lot of interfaces, going with the flow. Williams (2003) goes on to depict engineering education as needing to provide an environment where students get used to justifying and explaining their approach to solving problems and also to dealing with people who have other ways of defining and solving problems. 'Only a hybrid educational environment will prepare engineering students for handling technoscientific life in a hybrid world.' Williams would find that the capabilities-driven curriculum model argued for and explained in this chapter provides just such an environment.

Capabilities-focused versus content-focused curriculum design

The two different frameworks for curriculum design that I would like to contrast are the capability focus and the traditional content focus. They are illustrated in Figure 3.1.

As an undergraduate in the 1960s, the curriculum I experienced was definitely content-focused. Each topic was dealt with separately and independently, let alone each course. Readers will recognize this pattern. Typically, in a content-focused curriculum, information about content A is provided, along with examples of content A-type problems. Students then go to a problem sheet or to the back of the textbook to practise solving type A problems. Later, content B information is provided, content B examples and then practise with type B problems, and so on with content C, D and beyond. In the examination you could expect to find type A and type B problems, (and C and D and so on) in much the same form as those at the back of the textbook. I remember scientific concepts in subjects like mechanics being addressed, with Newton's laws and rotational mechanics being dealt with separately, each with their own algorithms. The same concepts were addressed in applied mathematics using differential equations. Never were the physics and mathematics treatments compared and never were linear motion and rotational motion linked; rather, they were presented totally independently in curriculum terms.

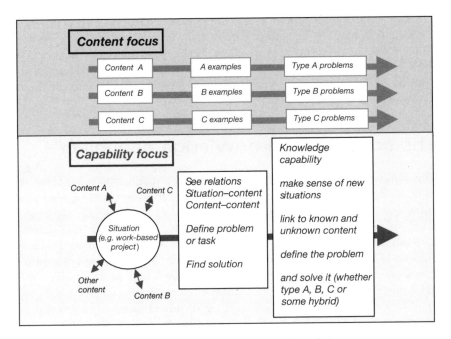

Figure 3.1 Capability-focused v. content-focused curriculum design

A remedy for this curriculum design problem is to adopt a capability focus. Students should be encouraged to speculate about real situations in which aspects of content A, B and C and, perhaps, some further unknown aspect are present or absent in different ways, depending on the situation dealt with. Students should be encouraged further to discuss these aspects and situations, to argue about them, to reflect on them and to write about them. This links to Williams' propositions (2003) described earlier. In the traditional curriculum that I experienced in the 1960s, there was little scope for such qualitative discussion and writing about ideas and concepts; there was too much emphasis on quantitative problem solving through rote-learned algorithms in isolated contexts. Research in recent decades in several different countries demonstrates that the same problem has continued to exist over the past four decades (for example, see Bowden *et al.*, 1992; Dall'Alba *et al.*, 1993; Rump, 2002 (a website authored by Rump, accessed in 2002); and Walsh *et al.*, 1993). Students learn to solve quantitative problems by using the relevant rote-learned algorithm without necessarily understanding underlying concepts and without developing the capability to draw on their learned experience to deal with new, previously unseen and, necessarily, more complex situations.

If given an opportunity and encouragement to engage in reflection and discussion, students might well conclude that the solution in a particular case may be found in applying a particular algorithm. And, of course, they need to know about and be able to handle the relevant equations. However, with a capability focus, the equations acquire their rightful status – as tools for problem solving once you've worked out that they are relevant. They are not truth in themselves. And they are not useful as tools if they are learned in isolation so that graduates are unable to work out when and how to use them to deal with real-life problems.

The concept of 'knowledge capability'

This ability to handle previously unseen, real-life situations, to make sense of them, to figure out what the relevant aspects are, to relate them to what you know and to find out what you don't know but need to use (e.g. the equations), to define the problem and only then solve it, is what I have termed knowledge capability. You still need to be able to do the quantitative solution but only after you've figured out what is needed. Mere knowledge acquisition is one thing; the capacity to use it in this way is both more complex and more powerful. I would argue that knowledge capability should be the goal of all university learning and that such a goal should be clearly expressed in programme and course handbooks or catalogues.

I would define knowledge capability more fully as the ability:

- to work out what are the key aspects to be dealt with in each new situation;
- to relate those aspects to the knowledge already acquired and/or to knowledge the graduate knows how to access;
- to determine what the underlying task or problem in that situation might be;
- to design a process or solution to deal with the situation; and then
- to have the ability to follow through and complete the task or solve the problem, either alone or with others.

In contrasting a content focus and a capability focus, I have been talking so far only in terms of the traditional content of the technoscientific disciplines. However, university education is about more than that. Over a period of 25 years I have regularly asked academics in a wide variety of disciplines, in a range of types of university and in various countries (such as Australia, England, Hong Kong and Sweden) to describe the qualities they are seeking in graduates from their programmes. I have compiled a list summarizing their responses (see Bowden and Marton, 1998: 96), which are, perhaps, surprisingly consistent across all of the variables mentioned:

- knowledge of core facts;
- general knowledge;

- understanding of knowledge structure in related fields;
- understand theory–practice relation;
- appreciate real-world variation;
- ability to solve problems;
- ability to define problems;
- lateral thinking;
- communication skill;
- insight;
- perspective;
- self-motivation;
- capacity for self-learning;
- ethics.

These deal with discipline content in various ways and also deal with other qualities commonly referred to by universities as generic skills, transferable skills or some term like these. Later, I am going to present an argument that these so-called generic skills can't be separated from the discipline content, but at this point I want to show some data about how important these other aspects of learning are rated by employers and academics.

In a study by Harvey (1993), both academics and those who recruit their graduates rated communication, problem-solving and analytical skills as the top three criteria. Employers added teamwork and flexibility next while, perhaps not surprisingly, academics added independent judgement and enquiry-based skills. Knowledge per se was rated much lower by both groups and, while core knowledge in particular was considered somewhat important, there was little interest among employers in differentiating between graduates according to their specific knowledge. Capability theory argues that learning knowledge is a means to developing capabilities and not an end in itself. That is consistent with Harvey's findings. Recruiters of graduates are interested in recruiting the right person, the person with the appropriate capabilities. Now the propositions put by Williams (2003) and Galison (1997) which I elaborated earlier are consistent with this capabilities argument and I will demonstrate later that the curriculum issue is resolved not by simply adding some new 'generic bits' to the syllabus but only by an integration of know-ledge with so-called generic capabilities.

Capability theory

For any theory to have pedagogical value, it has to explain varying levels of learning outcome, it has to apply to a range of types of outcome and it needs to discriminate between performances in one situation compared with another. It is on just these three dimensions that my capability theory is based: (1) types of capability; (2) levels of outcome; and (3) kinds of situation.

As far as type of capability dimension is concerned, I see it more as a series of overlapping continua than as discrete values associated with a particular discrete capability. However, some people still think in terms of communication capability or capability to operate in a team situation as separate from each other and from knowledge content. I believe this is not a helpful framework but in some respects it is easier to illustrate the theory by using a commonly experienced type like communication that everyone knows something about. I will do that for convenience here but, through the explanation of such an example, you will see that it turns out to be inextricably integrated with the knowledge content.

Levels of capability outcome in various situations

Let us look at the 'levels of outcome' dimension. I have defined four levels. It doesn't make sense to say simply that a graduate is capable of communication. The questions 'in what way?' or 'to what extent?' or 'for what purpose? or 'with whom?' are several among many that need to be answered.

Scoping level: defining the capability range. When dealing with communication, are we talking about written, oral or electronic communication? Is the purpose of the communication to:

- pass on information;
- help a group of people understand something in a new way;
- convince someone that your argument is valid; or
- try to understand someone else's argument (the listening side of communication)?

It might be about any or all of these and it might be about other aspects of communication. From a learning perspective, the curriculum has to be designed with these questions in mind and the student needs to scope out for him or herself just what is to be focused on in developing communication capability.

Enabling level: developing specific skills related to the capability. With the capability scoped at level one, there is no necessary demonstrable ability developed. At level two, there may be some enabling skills related to the capability that can be developed but which are not the capability itself. Here, presentation skills (oral, written or electronic), debating skills, logical argument and personal manner play a part, among others, but would need to be adapted at higher levels to the various purposes defined in the scoping level and to the characteristics of the person or persons to whom the communication is directed.

Training level: elaborating meaning of the capability in a particular field. The training level has been identified because different disciplines and different fields focus on some specific aspects related to the field. For example, a characteristic of communication in the field of law could be the importance of precision in language and the absence of ambiguity. Why? For the very purpose of communicating something to someone in ways that can withstand critical analysis of a legal kind.

On the other hand, a characteristic of communication in the field of nursing may be the importance of using language that displays empathy with the patient's situation. Indeed, in contrast with legal communication, ambiguity may be more acceptable in many nursing contexts than lack of empathy. And the attitude of empathy and support may be the very 'something' being communicated rather than the actual things spoken about.

Relating level: developing understanding of the relation between meaning and context. The relating level goes beyond the training level and is necessary because the narrower focus of the training level is inadequate both within the professional role and in other aspects of life. The relating level is about adapting behaviour to deal with the particular context.

Consider the lawyer who has just returned to her office after a successful case in court where she communicated legally in a precise, unambiguous and ultimately successful way. She has an appointment with an elderly couple in danger of losing their home and who want legal help to avoid the disaster. Upon listening to them for a few minutes during which time they talk about such things as what their daughter advised them and how hard they have worked all their lives, she imperiously tells them to get to the point. She lists the legal issues that have to be addressed and asks them not to introduce any more irrelevancies.

If the clients were the opposing barristers, that form of communication might be appropriate. But in the circumstances, a more complete professional in law would change the way of communicating according to the context and would use simpler, more supportive forms of communication in stressful situations for clients. The lawyer could well do to display some empathy with her clients' predicament and circumstances.

In a similar way, nursing professionals communicating with a patient being discharged from hospital about the medication to be taken at home need to be quite precise and clear about the detail, even perhaps using both written and oral communication to reinforce the message, irrespective of whether they communicate empathy. A more complete professional in nursing would also understand that modes of communication need to vary with context and would focus less on empathy and more on precision when necessary.

Finally, the folly of a lawyer communicating at a party in a legalistic style (or as we've all experienced at least once, an academic 'lecturing' friends on such an occasion) points to the importance of the relating level beyond the

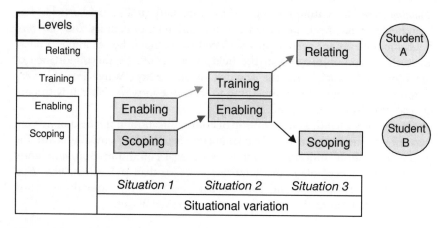

Figure 3.2 Capability outcomes – situational variation

profession. Achieving a communication capability outcome at the relating level involves contextual sensitivity of behaviour in terms of the purpose, the people involved and the circumstances of the communication process.

Of course, different students may reach different levels of outcome from one situation to another. And, as illustrated in Figure 3.2, the pathway may or may not be continual progression.

All three dimensions (types of capability, levels of capability and kinds of situation) are important from the perspective of curriculum design, learning experience and assessment. All must be provided for.

Water quality engineer – an example of integration

I want, again, to reinforce the argument that the so-called generic skills are inextricably integrated with the knowledge being learned. Consider a project aimed at cleaning up a river system that has salination problems due to a century of irrigation farming that has continuously diverted water through farmland and then returned it to the river. This is a real situation in my home state.

Imagine that two water quality engineers are engaged in the project and need to interact with a variety of people as a solution is being sought. Those people would certainly include other scientists and engineers but also local farmers and, perhaps, elected officials in the district or local bureaucrats. Most water quality engineers would be readily able to communicate with other technologists in such circumstances. You would hope so anyway. But not all would necessarily be capable of communication with the farmers in a way that helped them understand what solutions were needed and that the short-term negative impacts on them are necessary to enable a long-term solution. One engineer might be able to communicate with farmers effectively but another might not. Yet, both engineers might be very skilled at speaking at scientific meetings.

The difference is not just a question of communication skill as a separate entity; it is related to understanding of the subject matter. To refer to the need to have communication skills to the appropriate level, which the EGOS (Engineering Professors Council, 2000) seems to do, is to miss the point. If you can explain key issues of water quality engineering in a way that the farmer can understand and if another graduate is less effective in such circumstances, then you have a more comprehensive knowledge of your subject. Your knowledge is more complex and better linked to other knowledge structures. So-called generic skills and the learning of content are integrated in the notion of knowledge capability that I have defined earlier. This is one issue on which my capabilities theory differs from the UK output standard for engineering graduates.

How do we implement capabilities-driven curricula?

The overall focus is on graduates' ability to use what they know to do professional things, rather than merely accumulating knowledge. To design such a curriculum, you need to determine the programme goals first (the intended capability outcomes), then course goals, then necessary learning experiences and, only then, the teaching plans.

Authentic assessment is essential but not just at the course level. Since the capability outcomes are at programme level, there needs to be assessment across courses, i.e. at the programme level too. Inevitably, for programme capability goals to be achieved, students need to have learning experiences in which they get a chance to integrate across various disciplines – hence, integration and cooperation across courses is necessary.

There is a need for students to have not just a varied experience but also to experience the variation. The content focus I mentioned earlier provided a varied experience, e.g. Content A is different from Content B, Content C, etc. But there is no encouragement for students to reflect on that variation. Hence, they don't (certainly I didn't) actually experience the variation and, thus, they don't make the connections. The capability focus encourages reflection about variation with context so that principles and contextual elements are differentiated, thus enhancing the capacity to apply the principles to new contexts in the future. This is likely to be essential in Williams' (2003) and Galison's (1997) views of the future engineer.

Let me give a brief example from another field as an illustration. At RMIT, accountancy has been taught for decades and graduates have gone into the workplace and successfully used accounting practices quite routinely. During the past decade or two, there has been a large increase in the number of over-seas students taking studies in Australia, many from Singapore and Malaysia. After such graduates returned to Singapore for instance, they often found that the accounting practices they had learned didn't seem to work. Similarly for students from other countries. Subsequent investigations also showed similar problems for Australian-born graduates going to work in other countries. Some of them adapted but many didn't.

It was soon apparent that the problem was that accountancy was being taught with the Australian legal system being taken as given. Now, students instead are given accounting problems and asked to address them in relation to the Australian legal system and, as well, in relation to the legal systems of other countries and to reflect on the differences. Now, students are not learning accounting practices per se; instead, they are learning how accounting principles are applied in different legal systems. Such a graduate could go to any country, would examine the relevant aspects of the local legal system, and then adapt the accounting principles to build an appropriate practice. Such graduates would have accounting capability and be able to use that capability to deal with new, i.e. previously unseen, situations.

Another important issue is respect for students' ways of seeing. I put this forward not as an issue of democracy, ethics or politeness but rather as a peda-gogical issue. The students' goal should be to learn to discern relevant aspects of the situation, figure out what the problem is and how it relates to things they know or need to find out and then find a solution – developing capa-bilities to the relating level. To do that they must learn to value their own ways of seeing but continue to question their efficacy. Teachers who scorn students' responses as 'wrong' inhibit their pondering why they saw the phenomenon that way and what aspects might be relevant to a more powerful way of seeing. Lack of respect for students' ways of seeing is a barrier to learning.

Finally, I think it is a logical conclusion that with capability goals, it is the students' responsibility to learn. We can't do that for them. What we can and must do is to design the learning environment so that they are developing their capabilities and to support them as they do so. Explicit programme and course descriptions, clear capability goals in terms of know-ledge capabilities that explicitly integrate generic or key skills, coherence across the curriculum, supportive teachers and authentic assessment are a few of the essential aspects.

References

Bowden, J. and Marton, F. (1998) *The University of Learning: beyond quality and competence*, London: Kogan Page (paperback edition January 2004, RoutledgeFalmer imprint).

Bowden, J. A., Dall'Alba, G., Laurillard, D., Martin, E., Marton, F. *et al.* (1992) 'Displacement, velocity and frames of reference: phenomenographic studies of students' understanding and some implications for teaching', *Amererican Journal of Physics* 60: 262–269.

Bowden, J. A., Hart, G., King, B., Trigwell, K. and Watts, O. (2000) 'Generic capabilities of ATN university graduates: final report to DETYA', available online at www.clt.uts.edu.au/ATN.grad.cap.project.index.html (accessed 18 October 2000).

Dall'Alba, G., Walsh, E., Bowden, J. A., Martin, E., Masters, G. *et al.* (1993) 'Textbook treatments and students' understanding of acceleration', *Journal of Research in Science Teaching* 30: 621–635.

Engineering Professors' Council (2000) 'The EPC Graduate Output Standard: interim report of the EPC output standard project', Occasional Paper No. 10, Coventry, England.

Galison, P. (1997) *Image and Logic: a material culture of microphysics*, Chicago: University of Chicago Press.

Harvey, L. (1993) 'Employer satisfaction: interim report', presented to the Quality in Higher Education 24-hour Seminar, University of Warwick, December.

Rump, C. (2002) 'Assessment in engineering education' (Slide 6), presentation at Chalmers Grundutbildningskonferens, Lingården, Sweden, August. Available online at http://www.ckk.chalmers.se/cselt/cselt2002/proceedings/rump/camillarump.ppt (accessed 29 April 2002).

Walsh, E., Dall'Alba, G., Bowden, J. A., Martin, E., Marton, F., Masters, G., Ramsden, P. and Stephanou, A. (1993) 'Physics students' understanding of relative speed: a phenomenographic study', *Journal of Research in Science Teaching* 30: 1133–1148.

Williams, R. (2002) *Retooling: a historian confronts technological change*, Boston: MIT Press.

Williams, R. (2003) 'Education for the profession formerly known as engineering', *The Chronicle of Higher Education* 49 (20): B12.

Part 3

How can we help students learn?

4

Case studies
in engineering

Claire Davis and Elizabeth Wilcock

What are case studies?

Case studies are an increasingly popular form of teaching and have an important role in developing skills and knowledge. It is well documented that students can learn more effectively when actively involved in the learning process (Bonwell and Eison, 1991; Sivan *et al.*, 2000) and case studies are one way in which this can be promoted (Grant, 1997; Kuntz and Hesslar, 1998; Richards *et al.*, 1995). There are a number of ways of describing what a case study is, for example, Fry *et al.* (1999) describe case studies as complex examples which give an insight into the context of a problem as well as illustrating the main point. A case study can also be considered as a student-centred activity that presents an account of a situation or involves the study of a topic that raises issues or problems for analysis. One of the major advantages of using case studies is that they present material to students in a contextual manner, thus bridging the gap between theory and practice.

It is at this point, that it is important to make a distinction between this type of learning and problem-based learning. While problem-based learning encourages students to identify their own learning objectives, the case study approach has stricter parameters so that specific scientific principles and syllabus content is included. It may be expected that the students define some of their own learning *activities* but the learning *objectives* are usually clearly stated at the start of the case study. The structure and format of case studies can be likened to project-based learning as described by Savin-Baden (2003). Savin-Baden highlights the differences between problem-based learning and project-based learning and these are summarized in Table 4.1. In practice, there is a great deal of overlap between the two teaching modes. Many of the discussion

Table 4.1 Differences and similarities between project-based learning (similar in structure to case study learning) and problem-based learning

Project-based learning (case studies)	Problem-based learning
Predominantly task oriented with activity often set by tutor	Problem usually provided by staff but what and how they learn is defined by students
Tutor supervises	Tutor facilitates
Students are required to produce a solution or strategy to solve the problem	Solving the problem may be part of the process but the focus is on problem management, not on a clear and bounded solution
May include supporting lectures which equip students to undertake activity, otherwise students expected to draw upon knowledge from previous lectures	Lectures not usually used on the basis that students are expected to define the required knowledge needed to solve the problem

points presented here are relevant to both case studies and problem-based learning topics.

The format of a case study can include a large variety of different teaching structures, ranging from short individual case studies to longer group-based activities; these will be described later in this chapter.

Why use case studies?

Traditional teaching methods have focused on the lecture-based approach in which students are passive recipients of knowledge. However, in recent years there has been a noticeable shift towards more student-centred activities as increasingly more studies indicate that students learn most effectively when involved in active learning. Students need to be encouraged to participate in independent study and not just sit back and receive subject content and, hence, knowledge. Educational research has shown case studies to be useful pedagogical tools. Grant (1997) outlines the benefits of using case studies as an interactive learning strategy, shifting the emphasis from teacher-centred to more student-centred activities. Raju and Sanker (1999) demonstrate the importance of using case studies in engineering education to expose students to real-world issues that they may be faced with in an engineering profession. Chinowsky and Robinson (1997) describe the development of civil engineering case studies within an interdisciplinary course, where civil engineering students were encouraged to interact with students from other disciplines.

Case studies have also been linked with increased student motivation and interest in a subject (Mustoe and Croft, 1999).

Case studies typically present students with topics to be analysed and discussed. Many case studies require students to undertake a variety of activities such as independent research, attending lectures/seminars, working collectively in a group and/or presenting their work in the form of reports, posters, oral presentations, etc. It is known that styles and modes of learning differ from student to student, i.e. students have different 'preferred methods for perceiving and processing information' (Kolb, 1984). For example, not all students' working style is suited to that of collaborative learning, just as not all students work best individually. A learning environment that utilizes a variety of teaching methods and activities is more likely to draw upon a full range of learning styles. Furthermore, such an approach may help students to develop their ability to use diverse learning styles and encourage adaptability (Grasha, 1996). Case studies provide a good opportunity to accommodate a variety of learning styles so that students are able to develop their technical and key skills and so that no student should be unfairly disadvantaged compared to another.

Typical case study formats

Case studies can take numerous different styles in terms of length, content, assessment, etc. However, there are several key factors that should be included, or at least considered, in all case studies; these are discussed below.

Pre-case study sessions

Case studies are likely to involve activities such as independent research, group work, presentation requirements (e.g. poster, oral, reports, etc.). It is important to recognize that students may not already possess these key skills at a level required to participate fully in the case study. It may be necessary to organize one or more sessions before running the case study to give the students confidence in these skills, for example a group training session (Wilcock and Davis, 2003) or training on how to give effective presentations. Gibbs (1995) suggests that students should have a trial run when taking part in, or carrying out, new activities before the first time marks are awarded. In addition, it should be indicated to the students that the case studies are about developing these key skills as well as the academic knowledge of the case study topic.

Introduction

Case studies are used to encourage active learning where the student is expected to identify learning activities, carry out independent research and possibly work in a group. For many students this will be a very different learning style than they have encountered before, for example at school where traditional classroom lessons may have been common. It is essential that the students be given very clear instructions of what is expected of them during student-centred activity (Gibbs, 1995). This can take the form of specific aims and objectives (including those related to key skills development as well as specific case study topic knowledge), a support website (containing the aims and objectives and further guidance/information relating to the specific case study), a booklet (containing generic information about case study learning and other learning modes the students are expected to partake in) or a combination of these support tools.

Supporting lecture(s)/background information

Case studies can be used to teach basic concepts and lecturers can emphasize important points and procedures in a way that students can enjoy learning them (Henderson *et al.*, 1983). However, if a case study is being used to develop the students' understanding of a new topic containing complex or numerous concepts then a supporting lecture(s) may be required to ensure that all the students understand the key areas that will be included. Some lecturers may prefer to give the students the essential information via a set of notes, references to relevant literature or on a support website.

Independent research

Most case studies will require students to conduct independent research. Students may need assistance in determining which sources of information are most appropriate to consider, particularly early on in their university course where they may not have had the training in critical analysis of references before. Students may also need guidance on how to use the Internet to gather information, for example on how to determine validity of the information source (Goett and Foote, 2000). Goett and Foote state that it is important that students should understand the difference between citing a source and plagiarizing it, how copyright law applies to the resources they wish to use, and that web pages will differ in their accuracy, currency, completeness and authority. These issues could be addressed either through briefings, web pages or notes.

Facilitating group activities

Where students are expected to work in a group, care is needed to ensure that all members of the group contribute. Students should be encouraged to separate the work required into sub-tasks that can be allocated to different group members. It may be appropriate for the lecturer to carry out this task division for the students if it is their first experience of carrying out this type of activity.

For longer case studies, i.e. those carried out over several weeks, the lecturer may wish to consider having formal meetings with the student groups to ensure progress is being made (Wilcock et al., 2002). An alternative approach would be for the groups to have to keep a record of meetings they hold which would then be submitted as part of the assessment procedure. The development of group working skills in the context of case study teaching will be discussed in more detail later.

Selecting the case study topic

Obviously, the main considerations when selecting the topic for the case study are to ensure that it allows the key theoretical concepts from the course curriculum to be covered and that it is an area that has sufficient resources for the students to use. The second of these considerations will often be determined by the way in which the case study is being developed, i.e. whether the case study follows a lecturer's research interests, is delivered by an industrialist, etc. Issues that have arisen following feedback from students are that they tend to be more motivated by case study topics that they can relate to. For example, where an engineering failure is being considered, an event that is more recent and of higher profile is favoured. This is echoed by Mustoe and Croft (1999) who emphasize the importance of implementing case studies based on modern and recent technologies and applications. Another consideration is the amount of information available on a topic, for example for high-profile topics there can be an enormous amount of detail available (e.g. on the Internet) which can be daunting for some students. For these circumstances guidance to the students about core resources to be considered is important. Methods for developing case studies are discussed in the next section.

Assessment

Case studies can be used to develop key skills, as well as subject-specific knowledge, and assessment may need to take into account both aspects. The type of assessment used will depend upon the learning objectives, the length and level (e.g. first year of undergraduate course compared to the final year) of the case study. For example, when students first encounter case study learning it may be appropriate to include assessment of the learning process as well as the specific subject content. In this case, assessment of the group working process (e.g. attendance at group meetings, recording the agenda, minutes and action lists from meetings, distribution of activities, etc.) could be used. The forms of assessment that might be used in case study teaching are considered in more depth later.

Examples of case study formats

Single-session case study

A single-session case study may be used to illustrate a key theoretical concept(s) that is being covered in a more traditional lecture format, in the context of a real-world example. The main consideration here is to maintain a clear link between the concepts being conveyed and the example being used. State the learning objectives at the beginning of the session and explain that students will be addressing the main areas within the context of the case study. The following is an example of a single-session case study used to explore material properties and processing (raw materials, manufacture, marketing data, heat treatments, compositions, structures, etc.) set in the context of chocolate production. The session is three hours long and involves group work, presentation skills and time management.

Students are assigned to groups of four to six for the session. Each group is presented with a pack of information about chocolate and a set of questions to answer. There is too much information for everyone to read everything, hence the students need to set priorities and allocate tasks to ensure that all the research is completed in time. The groups are also required to give a five-minute presentation to the class on a given topic, different for each group (e.g. control of taste through composition, structure and processing/sustainable strategies for packaging chocolate, etc.). Therefore, the students have to share their findings from the reading and relate the information to their knowledge from other lecture courses (e.g. what is shell casting, tempering, etc.). A final component to the case study is taste testing of a range of different chocolate samples to illustrate the role of composition (sugar, milk, cocoa levels, particle size, etc.) on taste and texture. In order to ensure that the students appreciate why they are studying chocolate (not a material that commonly features in a materials engineering course syllabus) an introductory mini-lecture is used. During this introductory period the lecturer identifies where specific content in other lecture courses the students are taking (e.g. casting, heat treatment, crystal structure, etc.) is relevant to chocolate technology. In addition, they clearly explain the expected outcomes of the case study and provide the students with suggested methods for tackling the tasks set. This is important as this case study is used with first-year undergraduate students.

Multiple-session group case study

A multiple-session case study may be used to develop the students' key skills and knowledge of a topic while also covering theoretical concepts. Multiple-session case studies can run over several weeks and provide a good opportunity to incorporate a variety of activities and assessment strategies. Outlining the importance of project management to students is essential in such case studies as well as giving a briefing on the important factors of group working. The following is an example of a multiple-session group case study in which students investigate and perform experiments on the metallic components of a bicycle. The case study runs over five weeks and involves an introductory lecture, three practical sessions, two group sessions and a session for presentations. The main aims of the case study are to illustrate why given materials are used for a particular application and to give students the opportunity to produce and analyse experimental data in conjunction with carrying out independent research on the topic.

After the introductory lecture, in which the lecturer provides background information on the topic and then identifies the case study tasks, students are randomly allocated into groups of four to five. In the following five weeks, students undertake independent research and are expected to carry out practical work using optimal microscopy, scanning electron microscopy and hardness testing. Due to timetable and laboratory size restrictions, it is not possible for all students to attend every experimental session. To tackle this problem, each experimental session is limited to two members from each group and different pairs are required for each session. This ensures that all students attend at least one practical session. Each group then has access to a complete set of experimental data, but this depends on good group management and communication. Thus, an initial limitation is used as a means of developing group working skills. Postgraduate students help run the experimental sessions to minimize increased contact hours for the lecturer. If using postgraduate support, care should be taken that the support is of a similar level for each group. This can be achieved by using the same individual for each group or, if different instructors/helpers are to be used, by providing a briefing session for them at the beginning of the case study.

In the two weeks that follow the practical sessions, each group meets with the lecturer and postgraduate assistants for ten minutes to give a five-minute presentation and provide a one-page summary of activity and future plans. If a group member does not attend a group session, they lose marks. The aims of the group sessions are as follows:

- to ensure that progress is being made;
- to enable appointments to be made with the postgraduate students to answer specific technical questions;
- to provide an opportunity for the group to meet and detail activities for the following week;
- to ensure the egalitarian operation of groups.

The case study ends with students handing in a group report and giving a group presentation reviewing their findings. As a means of assessing the individual, students are also required to submit an individual executive summary which is a one-page outline similar to an extended abstract.

Methods for developing case studies

There are a number of ways to develop new case studies; some are more successful than others. The following list covers the main methods and discusses their advantages and disadvantages.

Developing a case study based on the research interests of staff

This can be a good method for case study development, as locating resources for the case study is easier and the lecturer's in-depth knowledge and interest in the topic will add to the students' case study experience. Examples of this approach are given below:

Example 1: Case studies on polymer foams used in sport and the health service

These case studies were developed from the lecturer's research interests in polymeric foams following many years working in this field. The case study topics are: flexible foams that cushion falls (e.g. sport crash mats, etc.), closed-cell polystyrene and polypropylene foams for packaging and foam cushions for wheelchairs. The case studies are run over multiple sessions with supporting lectures and content provided on a dedicated website developed by Dr Nigel Mills from the University of Birmingham (www.foamstudies.bham.ac.uk). Each topic on the website contains background information, videos, design programmes, laboratory experiments, links to other websites and interactive tests. Videos from high-speed photography, or from finite element analysis computation, are used to illustrate the effects of loading on complex foam geometries. The students understanding of foam mechanics and structure (density, polymer, open or closed cells) are tested and simple virtual experiments can be performed to validate the materials design process. The case studies provide added value to the students' learning experience as they involve areas of current research developed by a world expert in that subject.

Example 2: Industrial failure-analysis case studies

Professor Neil James from the University of Plymouth has developed an interactive web-based package illustrating some of the techniques widely used in industrial failure analysis, e.g. metallography, fractography and simple fracture mechanics. The examples within the package are real-life industrial failures that were chosen and presented in a way to guide the learner through the analytical steps and thought processes used in solving such problems. The case study topics were selected to illustrate unusual, interesting or potentially misleading aspects of failure investigation, often in the context of the impact of engineering decisions on litigation, insurance claims, assessment of responsibility and design/manufacturing modifications. Topics include failure of wire rope on a crane under uncertain loading conditions, failure of an aluminium aircraft tow-bar during use, failure of the main undercarriage leg mountings on a crop duster aircraft during landing and proving hail damage to polycarbonate roofing sheets. The website provides the opportunity for stand-alone case studies where the students are directed to specific examples that allow them to explore theoretical concepts that have been covered in lectures. Alternatively, the case studies can be used to introduce the concepts in context of the likely scenarios that practising engineers may encounter (see http://www.tech.plym.ac.uk/sme/FailureCases/FAILURE.htm).

Developing a case study to replace more traditional teaching on the same topic

When developing a new degree course there is considerable scope for introducing new content and new approaches to teaching. However, most degree programmes are well established with existing courses taught in a traditional style (lectures and laboratory classes). In such courses, case studies can be introduced to replace traditional teaching methods for the same subject content. While the lecture format is useful for teaching large blocks of information and theory, research suggests that students must do more than just listen and receive knowledge (Chickering and Gamson, 1987). By using case studies, or other student-centred activities, students can engage in active learning and study skills can be developed. In terms of Bloom's taxonomy, which ranks orders of learning in a pyramid with knowledge at the bottom rising through comprehension, application, analysis, synthesis and evaluation at the top, case studies and activity learning techniques allow students to move up the pyramid and take part in analytic, synthetic and evaluative work (Conway, 2001).

When teaching an existing syllabus using case studies instead of lectures it is important to evaluate whether the students receive the same breadth and depth of learning. Often case studies can result in good depth of learning related to the case study topic; however, the breadth may be reduced due to students not being able to relate the general concepts to other examples. There can also be problems with ensuring that the replacement case study equates to the same amount of student effort as the previous teaching activities, which is discussed in more detail later in this chapter.

Requesting students to develop case studies based on personal interests

Involving students in the writing of case studies can be a valuable experience and can benefit students in terms of the development of communication skills and problem-solving skills. For example, Smith (1992) suggests that students can write their own case studies and gave an account of two courses in which students were required to study and discuss a number of published cases, and then write up a case study based on a real industrial project. In each case, students worked with a project engineer ('clinical professor') to learn about a project and how it had been accomplished. Smith suggests that in using cases there are opportunities for both the user and the writer to profit and that the potential profit for the writer is, in fact, substantially greater. An evaluation of the courses using this approach indicated that the students and the instructors viewed them as educationally beneficial. Project engineers from industry involved in the courses also agreed that the experience was valuable and gave students a greater insight into real product development.

Example 3: Development of a portfolio of case studies by students

Dr Irene Turner from the University of Bath is producing a portfolio of case studies to support recruitment and teaching of the undergraduate courses in Materials Science and Engineering and initially approached the current undergraduate students for ideas and content. Unlike the example presented above (Smith, 1992), this did not form part of a student course but, instead, operated on a voluntary basis, with a competition where undergraduates and postgraduates were invited to submit proposals and a prize of £250 was offered. Unfortunately, this was unsuccessful, as students did not take part in the competition. This was felt to be because the students did not have enough confidence in their abilities to develop a case study and/or felt they did not have the spare time to work on the topic, particularly as many students take part-time jobs to help finance their studies. A more focused approach of asking graduates (who have moved into industry) to develop case studies based on their experiences/projects has been more successful.

Inviting/involving external lecturers, e.g. from industry, to contribute to a case study

Involving external sources can add new dimensions to the learning activity. For example, in a case study looking at the materials used in tennis equipment, a tennis coach was invited to brief the students on topics such as how rackets have evolved over time and how the equipment can contribute to tennis injuries (e.g. vibrations transmitted from the racquet to the arm).

The inclusion of approaches that allow students to see the relevance of the topic under consideration are well received by the students, in this case they reported that the experience added further insights into the topic. One student commented: 'links to industry, e.g. manufacturers or specialists, gives a greater perception of how our course can be used in industry, and also builds links with potential employers'.

Another approach is to use real-life examples from industry such as described by Raju and Sanker (1999). Raju and Sanker developed a case study based on an actual problem that happened at a steam power plant and which involved considerable financial and ethical decisions. In designing the case study, they worked closely with the engineer and manager involved in solving the problem to produce the written text. The engineer and manager from the plant also attended the classes where the case studies were discussed and were requested to make changes to ensure authenticity and accuracy. The feedback received for the case study was extremely favourable and students urged the authors to create more such case studies. This was also reflected in comments from the plant engineers and managers who felt that they lacked such exposure to real-life problems while they were studying. Despite Raju and Sanker stressing that developing such a case study required substantial investment of time by faculty members, they felt that, in light of the positive benefits of the learning activity, industry should encourage engineering professors to develop more real-life and cross-disciplinary case studies. There are some external organizations that do facilitate such developments, for example, in the UK the Royal Academy of Engineering support visiting professors (senior industrialists) at universities to develop industrially relevant teaching, often in the form of case studies.

Example 4: The introduction of industrial-based case studies in the third-year undergraduate programme

In this example, the lecturer involved (Dr James Busfield at Queen Mary University of London) designed seven industrial case studies each delivered by a representative from industry. The main motivation behind this was to raise awareness of materials design and the role of a materials engineer in industry, and to expose students to role models in industry. In each case, the industrialist chose the case study topic, provided written support materials for the students, presented the case studies to the students, assessed how the students dealt with the case study and provided feedback on completion. The case studies run over five weeks where students work together in teams to present a review of their conclusions and a group report. Students can usually contact the industrialist via email throughout the case study. Case study topics have included turbine blades, fighter plane tail keel design and anti-ballistic design in tanks. Student responses to the case studies have been very positive: 'Course gives an insight into my potential future role in UK industry'.

How to use case studies to develop skills

The case study-based approach is a useful method to develop transferable skills. Key skills that can be embedded into case studies include the following.

Group working

The ability to work well in a group is a valuable skill and one that can be developed during a student's time at university. Group learning can be used to promote active learning (Bonwell and Eison, 1991), aid the development of communication, leadership, organization and problem-solving skills (Butcher *et al.*, 1995) and has clear vocational relevance. Although most students recognize and acknowledge the benefits of group working, many are concerned with conflicts and uneven workload within groups (Davis and Wilcock, 2003). Feedback on group work has shown that this can present a particular problem for some students, comments include:

> It's not fair when other members of the group do not provide any input or aid the group effort yet still get marks.

> I don't like working as part of a team because there are always lazy people who don't do any work and if you don't want that to effect your own mark you end up doing everything. I work well in a team and am quite a good organiser, but tend to do too much of the work.

Many students entering their first year of university will have had little or no experience of group working and this may heighten the problems that can arise in a group situation. Hence, an initial session on group-working skills before running case studies has been found to be beneficial. This session could include a discussion of group dynamics, group roles, group meetings and a short group exercise. Student feedback from a group-working skill session linked to a case study included: 'I found the session really useful and it was interesting to look at strategies used in group working' and 'I got to know the group better and we eventually worked better as a team'. Another approach to dealing with this problem is to schedule short formal group sessions with the lecturer during the case study to ensure that all members of the group are contributing and that there are no conflicts within the group (Wilcock *et al.*, 2002). Feedback from students when this approach was adopted included: 'They [the group sessions] enabled the group to set specific targets and identify the roles of each individual', and 'A good way of motivating people to actually do some work and not to leave it to the last minute!'. While this approach is beneficial in ensuring a more uniform contribution of the students within the group it requires additional contact time with the lecturer, which is undesirable as efficiency in teaching is important, and does not allow the students to fully develop the key skills associated with group working. A compromise approach may be needed where group-working skills are formally addressed with the students early in their university career and lecturer-group sessions are used for long case studies (extending over several weeks).

Some lecturers have found that carefully selecting group membership to ensure smooth group operation can overcome the potential problems experienced by students in group work case studies. There are various ways in which group membership can be determined. Allowing students to select their own groups can go some way to alleviate problems with group dynamics, however, this can often result in the grouping of high-ability students and low-ability students which may not be useful if you want peers to support each other (Brown, 1996). Random selection is often seen as the fairer mode of forming groups and is certainly more representative of industrial and professional work (Gibbs, 1995). However, groups may encounter difficulties and conflicts, particularly if they have little experience in working with others. Another alternative is to form groups based on learning styles or abilities. This can be useful if you want to build on students' prior experiences or skills, but can be difficult to organize as it relies on you and the students having a good knowledge of the way in which individuals work and interact with each other (Brown, 1996).

Individual study skills, information gathering and analysis

Case studies are a good vehicle for encouraging students to carry out independent research, i.e. outside of the lecture/tutorial environment, and this can be useful for promoting active learning and self-regulated learning. In addition, case studies require resource investigation, encouraging students to utilize a number of different sources, i.e. Internet, library, laboratory results and contacting experts in industry. It is important to explain to students that critical analysis of resources is required to avoid a surface approach to the case study. It is important that detailed instructions are given to the students as to what is expected in terms of their independent research (e.g. minimum number of journal papers to be reviewed, examples of depth of analysis required, etc.), particularly at the early stages of their undergraduate career.

Time management

Case studies can be run in a number of different formats from a short, single teaching session to extended multi-week topics. Students need to consider how best to carry out the work so that it is completed to the set deadline. Horton (2001) emphasizes the importance of developing project-management skills in students and related skills such as the ability to work in teams, communication and co-ordination, stating that they are essential factors for professional success for today's engineering graduates. A clear explanation of project requirements, the time-scales involved, and interim meetings with academic staff will help ensure progress is made during the case study rather than all the work being left to the last week.

Communication skills

Case studies often form part of a course work requirement where the students have to present their work in a variety of formats: these include, oral presentations, articles, posters and reports. The ability to communicate effectively is strongly emphasized by employers (Horton, 2001) and it is important that such skills should be addressed during university study. By incorporating a variety of modes of communication (i.e. reports, essays, articles, presentations, posters) students will be well prepared for the range of skills required in the workplace. Co-ordination is required between all the lecturers on a course to ensure that any particular communication technique is not used excessively: for example, students only producing posters rather than giving oral presentations. Examples of good and bad practice should be available for students and feedback on performance should be provided. Asking students to self-assess and peer-assess presentations (posters and oral) in a formative manner can provide added insight.

Practical skills

Case studies can be designed to involve practical work on the application/ components that are being studied. It may be possible to use existing laboratory exercises in a course within the case study, perhaps by changing the way the laboratory exercise is presented. For example, instead of doing a laboratory exercise on microstructures of metals, the same experimental work could be carried out as part of a case study examining the materials used in bicycle frames and wheels. Hands-on activities can add extra dimensions to case studies and can give students a real 'feel' for the area they are studying. For example, practical work was incorporated into a suite of previously research-based cases and feedback on this was very positive: 'It [the practical work] was an additional source of interest and an extra dimension to case study work'.

Peer tutoring

As case studies can be used as a vehicle for students to identify learning activities and to carry out self-directed study it is possible to include students from different courses and levels in the same class (Wilcock and Davis, 2003). The presence of students with different background experiences and knowledge allows the use of informal peer tutoring. Formal peer tutoring where final year undergraduate students and/or recent graduates now undertaking postgraduate study are used to facilitate aspects of the case study can also be used. In general, peer tutoring is increasingly being used as a learning strategy in higher education, with many studies (e.g. Sobral, 2002; Solomon and Crowe, 2001) promoting it as being a valuable experience for both the tutees and tutors involved. For example, in a study of peer tutoring in a medical school, Sobral cites three points made by Whitman on the subject of peer tutoring:

- the cognitive processing used to study material for tutoring differs from that used for studying for a test;
- peer learners benefit from their peers' ability to teach at appropriate levels; and
- both the tutor and tutee appear to benefit from the co-operative relationship that peer tutoring engenders.

Feedback from the students involved in a case study, which included elements of peer tutoring, indicated that most of the group found the experience beneficial. Peer tutoring was made possible through mixed grouping (first-, second- and fourth-year students) where fourth-year students acted as peer tutors for specific sections of the case study. In this instance, peer tutoring was relatively informal and only contributed to short sessions within the case study, thus peer tutor training was not incorporated (although this may be necessary for more substantial peer tutor work). Students were, however, thoroughly briefed on what was expected of them in terms of peer assistance. Comments from the some first-year students included: 'Some of them were fourth-year students and had a broader background of information which has helped us with the case study', and 'They helped me understand the more technical elements of the case study'. However, some students stated that the mixed grouping did not add to their case study learning, for example, one student commented: 'Didn't gain much knowledge as we didn't really do any work together'. When the fourth-year students were asked about the experience, it was clear that the majority also found the interaction useful. Two students stated: 'We have done a lot on materials and it helped to be able to explain things' and 'Working with the technology students helped me to listen to their views and help them with areas that I know more about due to being in my fourth year'. Again, not all students felt that they were able to share knowledge, with some students stating that communication between their groups was limited. While it would be preferable for all students to gain from peer tutoring it should be expected that not all students will interact in a group setting.

Another method of implementing peer tutoring in case studies is to include postgraduate assistance and for this it is often useful to provide training for those involved. For example, at the University of Birmingham, the Staff

Development Unit runs courses for postgraduates that focus on 'Assessing Students' Work' and 'Small Group Teaching'. Often, postgraduates will have taken part in case studies as undergraduates so will have extra insight into the student experience of learning through case studies, which is of benefit. Targeted peer tutoring, where the peer tutor assists with certain activities within the case study (for example, embedded experimental activities), can be very effective in enhancing student learning.

Assessment methods

Case studies typically build upon both course content (i.e. knowledge) and key skills; hence, careful consideration is required on how to assess these different areas. The two main modes of assessment are formative (assessment for the purpose of improving learning and student performance) and summative (evaluation of students' performance against a set of predetermined standards). Summative assessment can be used to measure the students' understanding of course content, but a more formative approach may be appropriate for evaluating the key skills development. Formative assessment should provide useful feedback to encourage students to reflect upon their learning experience and, therefore, benefit should be seen in their approach to future case study activities. Booklet 7 of the LTSN Generic Centre Assessment Booklet Series provides informative and detailed discussions of these modes of assessment.

If group work is being used in a case study, group assessment is another area that needs to be considered. Group-based case studies often require students to produce one or more outputs between them (generally a report and/or presentation/poster). Learning to collaborate is a useful skill and to produce a group output is an important part of this. In order to meet the requirements of a university course, individual marks also have to be awarded to contribute to the final student classification; hence, for any group work a means of assessing the individual should be considered. Peer assessment is now a common approach used in higher education and there is much support for involving students in the assessment process, however, there are also associated pitfalls and problems. Swanson et al. (1991) questioned the validity of peer assessment, suggesting that the process is not truly reliable. Feedback from students has presented mixed views on this type of assessment (Wilcock et al., 2002). While the majority of students recognize its benefits, many feel that there are problems with its use. There are alternative methods for assessing the individual, for example, assessing students on an individually written executive summary (a one-page outline similar to an extended abstract). An overview of the different approaches to assessing an individual's contribution to the group can be found in Booklets 9 and 12 of the LTSN Generic Centre Assessment Booklet Series, these include:

- individual contracts;
- divided group mark;
- viva;
- project exam.

Evaluation

Case studies are introduced into courses to increase the level of student active learning and, hence, interest and motivation. It is, therefore, desirable to evaluate whether these objectives have been attained. It may be appropriate to have a scheduled session to evaluate the students' learning experience, particularly after the first time a case study is run. Evaluating students' learning can be problematic; time and consideration is needed to ensure effective and reliable results. However, it is important to be reflective in teaching and evaluation can provide some very useful and valid information. Some suggestions for evaluation are as follows:

- *Questionnaire (closed questions)*: These ask for a specific answer – yes/no, a circle round an option, items to be ranked, etc.; there are many standard university versions of this type of questionnaire. This approach can be cost-effective for processing the data and interpreting the results. However, they limit the responses from the students to predetermined answers. This may not give the depth of feedback needed for case study learning where the level of student participation, the experience of group working, identification of problems, etc., is of interest.

- *Questionnaire (open-ended questions)*: These allow students to fully explain their views and will often evoke more personal and informative answers. Care is needed to allow the students sufficient time to consider the questions and to provide full answers, for example, by providing time at the end of the case study sessions, using a separate session specifically for evaluation, or by asking students to complete in their own time. However, if allowing students to return questionnaires in their own time, be aware that the level of questionnaire return may be quite low. The disadvantage of this approach is it can take time to analyse and interpret the results and no summary numerical rating can be provided to compare to other teaching. This form of evaluation is useful following the initial use of case studies where modifications may be required.

- *Interviews and discussion*: Tutorials and staff/student liaison committees offer a good opportunity to discuss the learning experience with students. If assessing a specific case study, it is often better to use a member of staff who is not directly involved in the case study so that students do not worry that negative feedback may affect their assessment.

- *Independent evaluator.* In a teaching resource on evaluation, O'Neil and Pennington (1992) stress the importance of creating an environment that promotes open, honest and constructive feedback and one suggestion for this is the use of a 'critical friend' or 'honest broker' (an independent or outside evaluator). Having an evaluator who is not a lecturer (and not responsible for marking their work) may allow students to be more direct and honest in their comments about case studies.

Once feedback has been obtained it is good practice to tell the students how their feedback has been used to improve the quality of the teaching. This is particularly the case when the feedback obtained from the students has been more detailed (e.g. via interviews and discussion) as this will ensure the students provide good quality feedback in the future and feel involved in the learning process.

Common pitfalls

As with the introduction of most new teaching styles into a course there are several areas that can cause problems when adopting case study learning. These are outlined below.

Added workload, i.e. not replacing sufficient other teaching

In some cases, where traditional lecture-based teaching has been replaced with case studies it has been found that students actually spend more time working towards the case study than they would have been in the original mode of learning. This is often the case with project work and students will sometimes spend up to three times longer on this type of learning than they would on conventional taught modules (Gibbs, 1995). While it is encouraging to see such dedication to the topic, it is important not to overload students with case study work, which could distract them from their other studies. One way to help students manage their time and work effectively is to specify the amount of time, i.e. student effort hours that should be spent on the project. In addition, providing the students with guidelines of what is expected of them can be beneficial, for example, the number of references they are expected to read, the typical depth of analysis required, etc.

Group working

As discussed earlier, the topic of group working needs careful consideration. Students often experience conflicts or difficulties when co-ordinating work and it is wrong to assume that students entering university already know how to work effectively in a team. Formal group-work training can help to address some of the problems that students experience and will give them a better understanding of group dynamics. Group membership, group size and group assessment are also important factors and can sometimes effect students' attitudes towards a group-based project. It is always best to be clear in why you have chosen to run your project in a certain way, i.e. if you have chosen to randomly select groups in order to simulate a working environment, explain this to the students. If it is a particularly long group project, it may also be necessary to run interim group meetings with the students to ensure that they are on the right track and are working effectively.

Explanation of case-study requirements

Feedback has shown that students would like more details on what is expected from them in the case studies, e.g. level of independent research and, more specifically, sufficient information on how to write reports, give presentations and design, and present posters. This is particularly important at the start of the course as, for many students, this may be a very different form of learning to that they were used to at school. For example, one student commented after a case study which involved a poster presentation: 'A better brief for the poster would have limited the text content, and a clear aim for what needs to be included would have been helpful'. A guide for students, either text based or on the Internet, could be issued to the students before their studies, an example can be found at www.cases.bham.ac.uk.

Depth of learning

When examining students' use of resources, it has been found that many of the research-based case studies led students to derive all their information from the Internet. While this is a valuable resource it can often result in only surface learning where the students copy or paraphrase content available on the Internet. One way of addressing this problem is to provide references to textbooks, journal papers, etc. that the students are expected to consult and to specify to students that they are expected to critically analyse their work. Including a practical component to the case study (e.g. specific experiments) is also a useful way of achieving more in-depth study. Ensuring that there is progression of learning skills development (e.g. analysis to synthesis) when using a series of case studies is important, rather than repetition of the same skills.

Case-study mark allocation

As stated previously, students will often spend a disproportionate amount of time on project-related work in comparison to traditional taught courses and there needs to be careful consideration of how many credits/marks should be allocated to the case study. It is important that students feel that they receive enough credit for the effort expected. One of the main reasons for introducing case studies is to increase students' motivation and enjoyment of the topic, but if they feel that they are not being rewarded for the work it may lead them to be disillusioned with the learning process. A useful way of determining appropriate assessment weighting is to examine the proportion of student effort hours it involves (Gibbs, 1995).

References

Bonwell, C. C. and Eison, J. A. (1991) 'Active learning: creating excitement in the classroom', *ASHE-ERIC Higher Education Report No. 1*. The George Washington University, School of Education and Human Development, Washington, DC.

Brown, S. (1996) 'The art of teaching small groups 1', *New Academic* 5 (3): 3–5.

Brown, S. (ed.) (1998) 'Peer assessment in practice', SEDA Paper 102, ISBN 0–94681599–2.

Butcher, A. C., Stefani, L. A. and Tario, V. N. (1995) 'Analysis of peer-, self- and staff-assessment in group project work', *Assessment in Higher Education*, 2 (2): 165–185.

Chickering, A. W. and Gamson, Z. F. (1987) 'Seven principles for good practice', *American Association for Higher Education Bulletin*, 39 (7): 3–7.

Chinowsky, P. F. and Robinson, J. (1997) 'Enhancing civil engineering education through case studies', *Journal of Engineering Education* 86 (1): 45–49.

Christensen, C. R. (1981) *Teaching and the Case Method: text, cases and readings*, Boston, MA: Harvard Business School.

Conway, P. (2001) 'Using cases and activity learning with undergraduate economic classes', *The House Journal of the European Case Clearing House* 26: 18–19.

Davis, C. and Wilcock, E. (2003) 'Thematic booklets – case studies', to be published by the UK Centre for Materials Education, Liverpool, ISBN 09546433–0–5.

Fry, H., Ketteridge, S. and Marshall, S. (1999) *A Handbook for Teaching and Learning in Higher Education*, Glasgow: Kogan Page.

Gibbs, G. (1995) *Assessing Student Centred Courses*, Oxford: The Oxford Centre for Staff Development.

Goett, J. A. and Foote, K. E. (2000) 'Cultivating student research and study skills in web-based learning environments', *Journal of Geography in Higher Education* 24 (1): 92–99.

Grant, R. (1997) 'A claim for the case method in the teaching of geography', *Journal of Geography in Higher Education* 21 (2): 171–185.

Grasha, A. (1996) *Teaching with Style: a practical guide to enhancing learning by understanding learning and teaching styles*, New York: Alliance Publishers.

Henderson, J. M., Bellman, L. E. and Furman, B. J. (1983) 'A case for teaching engineering with cases', *Engineering Education*, January: 288–292.

Horton, G. (2001) 'The need for professional skills training in engineering programs', in *First Baltic Sea Workshop on Education in Mechatronics*, Fachhochschule, Kiel, September.

Kolb, D. A. (1984) *Experiential Learning: experience as the source of learning and development*, Englewood Cliffs, NJ: Prentice Hall.

Kreber, C. (2001) 'Learning experientially through case studies: a conceptual analysis', *Teaching in Higher Education* 6 (2): 217–228.

Kuntz, S. and Hesslar, A. (1998) 'Bridging the gap between theory and practice: fostering active learning through the case method', Paper presented at the Annual Meeting of the Association of American Colleges and Universities (AAC&U), p. 23.

LTSN Generic Centre – Assessment Series 2001. Booklet 7 'A briefing on key concepts', by Peter Knight; Booklet 9 'A briefing on self, peer and group assessment', by Phil Race; and Booklet 12 'A briefing on assessment of large groups', by Chris Rust.

Mustoe, L. R. and Croft, A. C. (1999) 'Motivating engineering students by using modern case studies', *European Journal of Engineering Education* 15 (6): 469–476.

O'Neil, M. and Pennington, G. (1992) 'Evaluating teaching and courses from an active learning perspective', Effective Learning and Teaching Module 12, Parts 1 and 2, CVCP Universities' Staff Development and Training Unit, Sheffield.

Raju, P. K. and Sanker, C. S. (1999) 'Teaching real-world issues through case studies', *Journal of Engineering Education* 88 (4): 501–508.

Richards, L. G., Gorman, M., Scherer, W. T. and Landel, R. D. (1995) 'Promoting active learning with cases and instructional modules', *Journal of Engineering Education* 84 (4): 375–381.

Savin-Baden, M. (2003) *Facilitating Problem-based Learning: the other side of silence*, Buckingham: SRHE/Open University Press.

Sivan, A., Wong Leung, R., Woon, C. and Kember, D. (2000) 'An implementation of active learning and its effect on the quality of student learning', *Innovations in Education and Training International* 37 (4): 381–389.

Smith, C. O. (1992) 'Student written engineering cases', *International Journal of Engineering Education* 8 (6): 442–445.

Sobral, D. T. (2002) 'Cross-year peer tutoring experience in a medical school: conditions and outcomes for student tutors', *Medical Education* 36: 1064–1070.

Solomon, P. and Crowe, J. (2001) 'Perceptions of student peer tutors in a problem-based learning programme', *Medical Teacher* 23 (2): 181–186.

Swanson, D., Case, S. and van der Vleuten, C. P. M. (1991) 'Strategies for student assessment', in D. J. Boud and G. Felletti (eds) *The Challenge of Problem-Based Learning*, London: Kogan Publishers, pp. 260–274.

Wilcock, E. and Davis, C. (2003) 'Group working and peer tutoring in case studies', submitted to *Journal of British Engineering Education Society (BEES)*.

Wilcock, E., Jenkins, M. and Davis, C. (2002) 'A study of good practice in group learning in sports materials science using case studies', presented at the 2nd Annual UK & USA Conference on the Scholarship of Teaching and Learning (SoTL), TUC Centre, Holborn, London (accepted, to appear in *BEES* 2004).

5

Effective engineering education at a distance: a guide for the curious

Mark Endean and David Baume

Introduction

We hope that this chapter will help you to decide whether some form of open and distance education is appropriate for your particular current or intended students, course, or educational setting. If you decide that it is, we further hope that the chapter will help you to plan how you will prepare and run your course. In writing the chapter we have made the assumption that you have a specific need and have provided opportunities for you to develop your ideas towards some form of provision for your students. If you are just reading for general interest, though, we have given you a thread to follow and some ideas to work with. More on that shortly. But first, some fundamental questions.

What do we mean by engineering?

We accept the account given by the Engineering Professors' Conference (EPC) of the fundamental processes of engineering, of the sequence of steps involved in 'doing engineering', of the high-level capabilities of an engineer. This account is described and discussed in Chapter 2. The EPC summary of this account is given below (EPC, 2000):

1.2.1 Ability to exercise Key Skills in the completion of engineering-related tasks at a level implied by the benchmarks associated with the following statements.

1.2.2 Ability to transform existing systems into conceptual models.

1.2.3 Ability to transform conceptual models into determinable models.

1.2.4 Ability to use determinable models to obtain system specifications in terms of parametric values.

1.2.5 Ability to select optimum specifications and create physical models.

1.2.6 Ability to apply the results from physical models to create real target systems.

1.2.7 Ability to critically review real target systems and personal performance.

These are high-level academic and professional capabilities, the development of which will clearly need access to considerable and specialist library, information and computing sources and resources, expert advice and support. We shall explore in this chapter whether and how these capabilities can be learned and developed through open and distance education, as long as the necessary resources are accessible by some means or another.

In this chapter we also offer a sub-set of this account of engineering capabilities, going into more detail for some of the capabilities, to inform the worked example of teaching one particular engineering topic which runs through much of this chapter.

What do we mean by open and distance education?

Before we describe the natures of and differences between open learning and distance learning, we emphasize what open and distance learning have in common. Open learning and distance learning are usefully seen as zones, not points, along a spectrum. At one end is pure distance learning, with no face-to-face teaching at all. At the other end is pure face-to-face teaching with no expectation of any student learning activity outside class. Open learning occupies much of the space between (Figure 5.1).

The UK Open and Distance Learning Quality Council says:

Open and distance learning include any provision in which a significant element of the management of the provision is at the discretion of the learner, supported and facilitated by the provider.

This ranges from traditional correspondence courses, online provision and interactive CD ROMs, to open learning centres and face-to-face provision where a significant element of flexibility, self-study, and learning support, is integral to the provision.

(ODL QC, 2003)

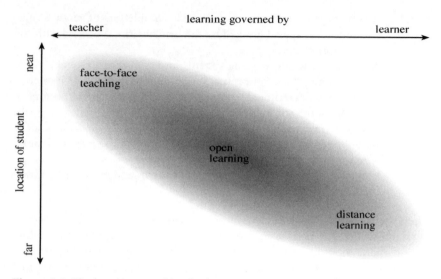

Figure 5.1 The learning v. teaching landscape

The distinction between open learning and distance learning is, thus, neither sharp nor absolute. Many of the issues and methods are common, and the great majority of this chapter will be useful to you whether you are planning open or distance education. The use of telephone and online (both asynchronous and synchronous) communications can further enrich learning, but make these distinctions even more difficult. Fortunately, we don't think the distinctions are very important.

Open learners study, at least to some extent, in their own time and at their own pace. What they study, and also how they study – what learning activities they undertake – will be in some, often substantial, measure determined by the course. Open learning is thus *not* the same as free or independent learning. Open learners may well spend time being taught face-to-face in classrooms, laboratories and workshops. It can be very productive to consider all engineering students (and, indeed, students of any other discipline) as, in part, studying by open learning. If we consider as open learning any parts of their notional learning hours that are not made up of face-to-face teaching, this prompts us to make suggestions and provide resources to support their open learning. This approach will reduce the chance of students regarding the time during which they are not actually being taught as 'free time'!

Activity 1
Write down (a) some specific productive things you could ask your students to do between taught sessions on your course and (b) any resources you would need to make this happen.

Our response
If you have done this exercise, you have planned some open learning! It may well be that you have been doing this for years.

In making your suggestions for (a) student activities, you may for example have specified questions for students to answer, tasks for them to undertake, investigations for them to make. In terms of the resources to support this (b) you may have described project and task briefings, a range of engineering resources, and also 'content', whether specially written, printed or Internet-accessible.

Distance learners are physically and/or temporally remote from each other and from their 'teachers', for most of the time at least. So the proportion of your students' learning that you have to plan and provide resources for, rather than deliver face-to-face, is much higher. One challenge with distance learning can be overcoming learners' feelings of isolation, of not being part of a group or community. Another can be that you have to take additional steps to identify the progress your learners are making, and also to identify their view of the course and the teaching. The normal cues – short conversations with students, work handed in for marking, their active engagement or not in the classroom, workshop or laboratory – are not available, and you have to take additional steps to identify student progress and feedback. Each learner has their own needs.

Activity 2
List a few ways in which can you think of connecting *distance* learners to their 'learning community'.

Our response
You may have considered the use of synchronous and/or asynchronous online working; postal, telephone or fax contact; video-conferencing; and occasional face-to-face meetings, depending on the particular learners and programme you are considering.

Activity 3
Which of the methods described immediately above could be used for *open* learners without compromising their 'open-ness'?

Our response
We thought, all of them.

So, in summary, open learners need not be distant and distance learning need not be open.

Open and distance learning (ODL) is the term coined to cover the full range. To reinforce what we said above: the ODL spectrum stretches from a mainly face-to-face programme with small amounts of guided private study to a programme in which students rarely, if ever, enter the institution.

Activity 4

Where on the scales of openness and distance do you want or expect your learners to be? To put it another way, what proportion of your students' time will and will not be spent in face-to-face learning?

To put it another way still, work out which of their learning activities, and hence what proportion of their time (a) must and must not, (b) could and could not, and (c) should and should not be spent in face-to-face learning.

Our response

Your answer to this will have been determined by your own particular circumstances and plans.

Can engineering be learned through open and distance education?

Asking this question online of one well-known North American university elicits the following response: 'As a distance education university, XXX University is unable to offer courses in the area of engineering'.

We, in contrast, think that engineering can be learned at a distance. It is, we believe, much more productive to ask *which aspects* of engineering can be learned in this way.

Activity 5

Turn to the EPC account given earlier and spend a few minutes identifying which of these capabilities:

(a) clearly can . . .
(b) clearly cannot . . .
(c) might but with varying degrees of difficulty . . .

be learned through the particular form of open and distance education that you are currently considering.

Our response

We do not of course know what your particular plans are, or what conclusions you reached. You may have felt that much of the theoretical and conceptual learning, and much of 1.2.1–1.2.4 and 1.2.7, could be learned by open and distance learning. Building and testing physical models will be more problematic in some engineering disciplines, although you may feel that the use of simulations can address some of these problems.

The style and structure of this chapter

You have already experienced something of our approach to writing about open and distance learning. As you may well suspect, you have also experienced some of our approach to open and distance education itself. Let us now make our approach explicit.

This chapter seeks to engage you in an open learning 'conversation'. There already has been, and will continue to be, liberal use of questions and activities, with which you are warmly invited to engage. Shortly there will be two strands to the activities. The first strand is a worked example, continued through the chapter. The second strand offers encouragement for those with a particular ODL need to use their own examples and develop their own materials as they work through the practical content of the chapter.

You could use the chapter in several ways. You could read it for interest. You could engage with the worked example on the bending of a beam, seeking to anticipate how we respond to each task or question. You could use the chapter as an illustrated piece of ODL material in its own right. And you could use the chapter to help you to develop an extended outline for an ODL module, which you can in time convert into finished ODL material. And, of course, you could use various combinations of these approaches.

But whatever use you choose for the chapter, we suggest taking the particular systematic approach to designing your course set out in the following sections. In the first of these we give a 'broad brush' summary of the business of designing a course. We follow this with an opportunity to go through the stages for yourself in more detail.

Before you decide to develop the course . . .

. . . you need satisfactory answers to two questions. If you have a particular course in mind, make your own notes.

Question 1
What particular subject expertise do you have?

Question 2
What persuades you that there is an unmet demand for an open learning course in your areas of expertise?

Planning an open and distance learning course can be a large, complex, expensive task. It can cost a million pounds or more to produce a single 60-point course, fully supported by print and multimedia materials.

But the core ideas and practices are very simple. Following the sequence below, you can produce a good basic open learning course in a few dozen hours. Before you start on the course proper, you need at least to sketch answers to these questions and to take these steps.

Market

Question 3
Who is the intended audience for the course?

Our response
We have in mind first-year general engineering undergraduates but the package would also be of use to trainee designers.

Question 4
What do they want to learn, to become able to do? (How do you know or how will you find out?)

Our response
We look to the EPC statements here; in particular 1.2.4 in the context of designing structures to meet specified requirements. We start from the premise that this is what our learners have signed up to do!

Question 5
How can you reach them to tell them about the course?

Question 6
What will they want to know about the course in order to decide to take it?

Income

Question 7
What price will the market bear?

Question 8
How many places will you sell at that price?

(*Either* answer these questions *or* devise a plan for answering them!)

Expenditure

There are two main headings of expenditure: production and operation. Production involves academic and administrative staff time to design the course process and to write the study support materials. Operation includes academic staff giving feedback to, and otherwise tutoring (see p. 87), the students, and monitoring and evaluating the course process to inform changes to materials and process. Administrative staff will be involved in materials production and distribution and in student record keeping.

Question 9
What are the main headings for expenditure for (a) producing and (b) operating the course you are considering?

Question 10
Quantify any of these costs you can, and identify knowledge gaps on costing and how you will fill these gaps.

Distance learning is inherently neither more nor less expensive than face-to-face teaching. But the costs are differently distributed, with more initial investment required.

A systematic course design process

To learn, all students, however and whatever they are learning, need a sense of direction, of goals. They need answers to questions such as 'Where will this course take me?' and 'What will I be able to do at the end of it?'. Clear and attractive statements of the aims and the intended learning outcomes of the course are necessary. This means that not only do you have to decide the aims and learning outcomes for your course but you also have to communicate them to the learner.

We start by stating our aims and learning outcomes. Depending on which strand you are following you can then respond to our questions using our worked example or your own chosen subject area. You can, of course, start with our example and then come back to develop your own plans at a later date.

So, first, we suggest, determine the aims of your course or programme. Overall, what is the course or programme intended to achieve?

It is important to recognize the purpose of aims. They are there to 'set out your stall' rather than to describe in minute detail the forthcoming content of the learning package. So they should be succinct. But, more importantly, they should be set at an appropriate level. A study programme has aims; each of the modules within the programme has aims; and so on. At each level, there should be no more than three or four aims which between them summarize the package, however large or small the package is.

Activity 6
Outline the aims of your proposed ODL course.

Our example
The aims of this learning package are to:

● explore the distribution of shear forces and bending moments in beams loaded at a point and uniformly along their lengths;
● introduce the principles of beam theory including the neutral axis and second moment of area; and
● examine the effect of shape and material properties on the behaviour of freely supported beams.

Second, determine the intended learning outcomes of the course or programme. These should describe what the students should be able to do on successful completion of the programme. The EPC list provides a very good starting point. You will want to extend or refine these for your particular programme, or take a subset of them for a particular course within a programme.

Below is an outcome statement for our exemplar. Note the obligatory introductory sentence.

Outcome statement
Having completed this package you should be able to:

1   describe how shear force and bending moment diagrams are derived;
2   explain the distributions of shear force and bending moment in simple beams;
3   describe and explain the effect of shape on the behaviour of beams in bending;
4   describe and explain the effect of materials properties on the behaviour of beams in bending;
5   relate the shape of simple structures to their likely behaviour under load.

You will probably have noticed that our outcome statements do not look much like the EPC statements. This is a matter of level, again. As with aims, so with learning outcomes; they should be present at each level, from programme, where they are broad and will describe the high level engineering process, to individual 'learning object' level, where you need statements about what learners can do in fine detail. We present the learning outcomes above as one small part of what a structural engineer should be able to do in order to satisfy EPC statements 1.2.2 and 1.2.3.

Third, we suggest, determine how you would assess students' attainment of your intended outcomes. This may seem odd – surely you should go on to determine content and learning and teaching methods before you look at assessment? Why consider assessment at this early stage?

Well, there are two important reasons for considering assessment now. First, you need to be sure that you know that you can assess the learning outcomes that you have specified. If you can't assess them, then you should probably change the learning outcomes so that you can assess them. Unassessable learning outcomes are misleading – they are like an engineering specification whose attainment cannot be measured. Second, the final assessment tasks will guide you as you design the rest of the programme or course, the learning activities and the learning resources and the course process, to make sure they are all consistent with each other, or in 'constructive alignment' with each other in the helpful phrase of John Biggs (1999).

Activity 7
Indicate how you will assess whether students have attained the intended learning outcomes of your course.

Our example

1   Describe how shear force and bending moment diagrams are derived. (Exactly what it says!)
2   Provide a number of examples of SF and BM distributions resulting from specified loading cases and ask for explanations. Provide loading cases and ask for resulting SF and BM diagrams *with explanations*.
3   Use the standard solutions for I to account for the relative stiffnesses of different cross-section beams.
4   Use the Engineer's Bending Equation to do simple materials substitution exercises on a given beam and loading case (including self-load) and explain the significance of the outcomes for the structural designer. Could also be linked to merit index exercises.
5   Provide examples of compound structures (e.g. a roof truss) and ask for the distribution of forces in the structure for a given loading case.

You will have noticed that these assessment tasks relate very closely to the intended learning outcomes. This is as it should be.

Fourth, in order to learn, students also need – in addition to a sense of direction, of goals – appropriate things to do. So, given clear and assessable goals, you need to decide what student learning activities will help students become able to attain the course outcomes. Again, this may seem unexpected – you may be wondering when you are going to plan the teaching? It is tempting (and very common) to plan a course as a sequence of content to be taught.

Better, much better, to plan it as a sequence of activities which students will undertake; not just practical experiments but thought experiments, information gathering, even note taking and graph drawing, all transform passive learners into active ones.

Why do we advocate this? A particular view of learning and teaching underpins this systematic approach to course design and, in particular, the current suggestion that you plan what students will do in order that they learn. This view says that learning is an active process; that learning results from appropriate student activity; and that the role of teaching is to prompt, support, stimulate, provoke and challenge students to undertake the kinds of activities that will lead to them achieving the desired learning outcomes. Hence, we suggest that you plan what students will do in order to learn. This works for any kind of teaching, but the single most important feature of good open learning is good questions and activities for students to answer and undertake. Good activities:

- engage the student's interest;
- link to the student's own aspirations, to what they want to get out of the course;
- let them practise abilities and use knowledge relevant to the course outcomes;
- help the student confirm that they have understood what they are learning;
- build on what has gone before;
- prepare them for what is to come.

Planning such questions and learning activities may sound difficult. It is. The good news is that good teachers are already good at doing these things. Further good news – you can pilot questions during the development of the course, to see if they work and how they can be improved.

Activity 8
Write down an appropriate activity that will help students to attain one of your learning outcomes (take outcome 3 from our example on p. 81).

Our response
The 'old chestnut' here is to take a ruler and attempt to bend it first across its thickness and then across its width. There is a vast range of alternatives. In order to 'explain' the effect, learners have to relate the behaviour of the ruler in both cases to the second moment of area of a rectangular beam. This could be done by inspection of the relevant equations *and writing down the conclusions*. A simple explanation comes from the standard solution; a more advanced explanation comes from the derivation of *I*.

Fifth, in order to learn students also need feedback on their work and achievements. Feedback may come from:

- The course materials themselves, with the classic open learning line 'Now that you have answered this question, here is how we addressed it . . .'.
- Other students on the course, if they have (perhaps with your help) formed face-to-face or online self-help groups.
- Tutors, through written feedback on student work (perhaps with marks or grades).

Activity 9

Take one of the activities above and write some feedback for it. This feedback should cover the main types of answer, right and wrong, that you expect students to give, helping them to understand why the right or best answer is right or best.

Our response

'You should have observed that the ruler is much stiffer when bent across its width than across its thickness.'

'The Engineer's Bending Equation tells you that $M/R = E/I$ and the standard solution for the second moment of area, I, for this rectangular beam shows that it depends on the width of the beam but the cube of its thickness . . .' etc.

Sixth, and following reasonably enough from the previous step – you decide what learning resources and what teaching activities are needed to help the students to undertake, with reasonable prospect of success, the learning activities you have previously planned for them; learning activities that will lead them to achieve the specified learning outcomes.

Students will need access to content, in order to undertake the learning activities that will in turn, hopefully, enable them to achieve the intended learning outcomes of the course. Content can take two main forms:

- existing books and other sources including online resources (we shall encourage you below to make maximum use of existing sources); or of course . . .
- . . . specially written content (which is slow and expensive to produce to a suitable standard).

It is not enough to convert lecture notes into 'distance learning' material, even by adding some questions and activities. Lecture notes are designed to support lectures. Open and distance learning materials, by contrast, must work without a lecture. There will probably be a textbook or collection of papers (some of which you may have written) or some websites that contain much of the course content. Use these. Critique them if you need to, but use them. Teaching activities stand or fall by how successfully they engender student learning activities.

Activity 10
Suggest some sources of existing content that you could use.

Our response
There are many books, from the erudite to the enjoyable, on structural mechanics. We have particularly valued *Structures: theory and analysis* by Williams and Todd (2000), and *Structures, or Why Things Don't Fall Down*, by Gordon (1991). With such good texts (Williams and Todd write in an 'interactive' style) there seems little point producing yet another teaching text. But see Activity 12 below and Producing the course materials on p. 86.

Activity 11
Suggest how you could make these available to your students.

Activity 12
In extremis: what (if any), and how much, content will you or someone else absolutely need to write?

Our response
At the minimum we shall have to produce the 'student activity' component that we outlined above. This is needed to link the texts we have chosen to the learning outcomes we have defined. Depending on the learning skills of our students, we may be able to rely on their linking the activity to the text (a resource-based approach). If they are novice independent learners, however, we shall also need to provide a structured commentary to guide them through the texts.

Activity 13
Estimate how much time this is likely to take you.

Our response
We suggest, a few working days.

If you have been developing your ODL course as you work through this chapter, you will already have written some teaching activities when you specified student learning activities earlier.

Finally, you pull all this information into an overall course process, probably best expressed in a course handbook (which is ideally online) and which links to the various learning resources and activities that students and staff will use. Studying by ODL needs a clear structure, framework and schedule, for the students and the teachers. The course handbook must provide this.

Studying by open learning can lack many of the features which give shape to face-to-face study, such as lectures, classes, day-to-day contact with peers, hand-in schedules. You need to put equivalents for these into your open learning if participants are to feel part of a community and are to stay the course. (You may be able to include some face-to-face contact – in the evening, for a day or a weekend or longer. If you can, do. It is usually very highly valued.)

Activity 14
Outline some specific ways you could help your distance learning students to feel that they are part of a course and a community, rather than feeling isolated.

This has sounded like a linear course design process. We add here another dimension – the need to iterate between each stage. We suggested this in discussing outcomes and assessment – will the assessment test students' attainment of the outcomes? A similar feedback loop is needed at each stage. Will the course learning outcomes, if attained, mean that your aims for the course have been attained? And, once the learning outcomes and the assessment processes and tasks are in alignment – are the proposed learning activities likely to be the most effective, attractive (affordable) ways for the students to work towards the learning outcomes and hence assessment tasks? Will the proposed teaching methods and learning resources best support, stimulate, etc. the students to undertake these learning activities? And does the course, as described in the handbook, form a coherent, attractive, optimum, affordable and practical whole? Some of these questions can be answered during course design, based on previous experience. Others must be answered as the course runs, and the course refined in the light of feedback and experience. The advantages of course resources being available online will be clear, where the heavy costs of printing are avoided and the costs of changes are limited to the (nonetheless substantial) costs of academics' and editors' time.

In describing a systematic process of course design we have also been exploring some essential conditions for students to learn, and how you can provide these through open and distance learning. To conclude this section, and taking a step back, two final questions:

Activity 15
From your experience of teaching, what other conditions are essential for students to learn your particular subject?

Activity 16
How will you provide these for your ODL students?

Producing the course materials

If you have followed through the advice given earlier, you can now collect together the materials you have produced, to structure your course under these headings:

- *Study guidance*: aims, learning outcomes, other learning resources, the course schedule and process, contact details.
- *Questions and activities*: a framework of interaction that guides the student through the learning process.
- *Course content*: purpose-designed learning materials or links to suitable learning resources.

If your subject expertise is at the heart of what you are selling with this course, and you therefore must write some of the course content, allow lots of time. Many attempts at open learning founder because the course authors try to write all the content. This is understandable – we are interested in the content we teach! But it can wreck the economics of the course.

Planning the course operation

Student diary

An effective and economical way to plan the operation of the course is to construct a hypothetical diary or log for a tutor, an administrator and a student on the course during one cycle of presentation. This will identify most planning and operational issues and needs.

Activity 17
Do this for your course. Even a couple of pages of rough notes will help you plan the reality of the course.

Administration

The administration of a distance learning course needs to be immaculate. You will need to plan, track and follow every stage of the operation – registration of students, despatch of materials, deadlines for return of work, actual return of work, feedback by tutors . . . everything.

Activity 18
Write down the main administrative functions that your course requires.

Activity 19
Write down how you will make sure that these are met.

Tutoring

Giving feedback to students on their work is a vital part of the teaching on a distance learning course. Cost it into the process – half an hour, more if you can afford it, for the tutor to give detailed individual feedback to each student on each assignment, to ask the student questions, to suggest how they can improve their work for the future. You should add email, and possibly also telephone or even face-to-face contact.

Studying at a distance can be lonely. One-to-one student/tutor contact through any medium overcomes this, and is essential.

Monitoring and evaluation

Pilot early sets of materials and questions on students. Get and use their feedback. This will iron out many possible difficulties. Also pilot the course processes, including tutoring. Find out what students like and don't like, what works and what doesn't. And make the necessary changes.

Activity 20
Write some of the questions that you expect to ask your students when piloting your course.

Similarly, while the course is running, ask for feedback from students, from tutors, and from the course administrator. Evaluate little and often. Act on the results of the evaluation, and show how you have done so – this will increase the response rate for future evaluations. If you don't know what questions to ask, ask the course participants what questions you should be asking them.

Activity 21
Write some questions that you expect to ask your students, tutors and administrators to gain feedback at the end of your course.

Conclusions

The first message of this chapter is that it is possible to produce and run a successful open learning course without huge financial resource, as long as sustained attention is given to the key issues described here:

- a focus on student learning and its support;
- appropriate course content;

- excellent feedback to students, which, along with the course materials and the student activities that they require and support are really your only teaching method(s);
- excellent administration at every stage; and
- commitment to seek and use feedback at every stage of development and operation.

The second message is that some elements of supported open learning can to advantage be included in mainly or partly face-to-face courses in engineering, in a reasonably economical way, again as long as the issues above are given due weight.

References

Biggs, J. (1999) *Teaching for Quality Learning at University*, Buckingham: SRHE and Open University Press.

Gordon, J. E. (1991) *Structures, or Why Things Don't Fall Down*, Harmondsworth: Penguin.

ODLQC (2003) *ODLQC Standards*, London: Open and Distance Learning Quality Council, http://www.odlqc.org.uk/standard.htm (accessed 28 October 2003).

Williams, M. J. and Todd, J. D. (2000) *Structures: theory and analysis*, Basingstoke: Macmillan.

Recommended further reading

EPC (2000) *The EPC Graduate Output Standard*, Interim Report of the EPC Output Standard Project, EPC Occasional Paper No. 10.

Race, P. (1994) *The Open Learning Handbook: promoting quality in designing and developing flexible learning*, London: Kogan Page.

Rowntree, D. (1990) *Teaching Through Self-instruction: how to develop open learning materials*, London: Kogan Page.

6

Widening access – flexible and work-based learning

John Wilcox

Introduction

In both Europe and North America, fewer young people are choosing materials engineering as the career of choice when they leave school. The reasons for this may be many and complex but, in part, it is believed that the subject does not have a high profile in the school curriculum and that the industry is largely ignored by the careers service. Many teachers and careers advisers see the materials industry as declining and lacking in innovation, offering few job opportunities with little excitement.

Industry has responded to this situation by developing its technical staff through other routes. Two particularly successful routes have been the recruitment of more mature individuals moving into the industry as a result of career changes and the development of existing craft employees into professional engineers by planned and structured career development. The new materials engineers, therefore, have a wide variety of qualifications and prior experience, and individual training needs are more varied. Furthermore, competitive pressures are restricting the ability of companies to release staff for training by day- or block-release since there is no longer sufficient cover for absent manpower.

This creates a significant challenge to the educationalist: can the learning programme be customized to meet the individual needs of the companies and the differing backgrounds of the students? Our approach to this has been to devise a learning programme that builds upon the student background and takes maximum advantage of the opportunities that exist in the workplace to deliver the learning. This learning programme is supplemented by more traditional forms of teaching and learning, making use of 'taught class' or distance learning, according to the needs of the student.

Two educational tools are essential to our approach: the accreditation of prior and experiential learning (APEL) and work-based learning (WBL).

Understanding the student's background

The first step in developing an individual learning programme for a student is to assess what the student already knows. Formal procedures for this assessment exist and are termed the Accreditation of Prior Learning (APL) and the Accreditation of Prior Experiential Learning (APEL) in which a person's learning and experience can be formally recognized and taken into account to:

- gain entry to further or higher education courses;
- give exemption from certain parts of a new course of study;
- qualify for an award in an appropriate subject in further or higher education.

APL/APEL is a process that enables people of all ages, backgrounds and attitudes to receive formal recognition for skills and knowledge they already possess, and takes into account:

- organized prior-learning where the learning has been assessed and where certificates are awarded on completion;
- learning gained through unstructured experiences and short courses, arising through leisure pursuits, family experiences and work.

The terms APL and APEL generally describe the same process, but there is a difference in the nature of the evidence provided to support a candidate's claim for recognition of previous qualifications or experience (Nyatanga et al., 1998).

APL generally refers to the situation when the candidate has attended relevant organized prior learning which has been assessed by the learning provider, and for which certificates are awarded on completion.

APEL generally refers to incidental prior learning which is unassessed. Such learning may be gained through unstructured experiences, arising from leisure pursuits, family experiences and work. It also includes unassessed formal training courses. Certificates may or may not be available as evidence that the learning has taken place.

This difference between APL and APEL is significant, and has consequences for both the candidate, and for the accrediting institution. It leads to a number of differences in the approach required, and the timescale and costs of the process. Because APL is based upon prior certificated learning, it is possible to match prior qualifications against specific competences required by an institution in a relatively straightforward fashion, using information on the course content and checking the awarding body's certificate of achievement. This process does require some skill and experience on the part of the institution but the candidate's role is simply to provide this information (course content and certificates) to the institution. In view of this, APL may be a rapid process, taking perhaps six weeks.

In contrast, APEL requires the candidate to find or prepare documents that illustrate the level of skill, expertise, knowledge and understanding (s)he possesses by virtue of on the job training, short courses and life experiences. Because competences developed in this way are not assessed, and are largely uncertificated, witness statements are needed to confirm the authenticity of the claim being made. This makes APEL a more rigorous and time-consuming task than APL. It also requires considerable effort by the candidate and the APEL tutor, who must work together in partnership. The role of the candidate is to review his/her previous experiences, and to seek out and provide evidence of achievement of relevant competences. The role of the tutor is to direct and advise the candidate, and to assess the evidence that is provided.

A likely timeframe for APEL is, therefore, three months. Furthermore, because of the workload required, it is better if APEL can be undertaken when the candidate is free of any commitments to academic study, such as before the course begins or during the long vacation, so that the appropriate amount of effort can be devoted to APEL.

The onus for providing evidence of prior learning lies entirely with the candidate. To complete this step successfully, (s)he will need to work in an organized and timely fashion. However, it is clear from our own experiences that the institution will need to support and advise him/her by:

- Providing self-assessment checklists.
- Supplying written guidelines and videos.
- Appointing an AP(E)L tutor who will organize group workshops and regular one-to-one discussions with AP(E)L candidates throughout this stage. The latter can help in establishing (and achieving) deadlines and milestones, and in bringing planning and discipline to the whole process.
- Matching the skills, expertise, knowledge and understanding achieved by the candidate against the learning outcomes and performance criteria demanded by the institution.

The role of the AP(E)L tutor demands skill and experience. It requires wide knowledge of national and, potentially, international educational systems so that advice can be given and judgements made about the validity and suitability of evidence that the candidate may be able to provide. Subject-specific knowledge is often important in judging the scope and level of learning being submitted for accreditation (Simosko, 1991).

This being so, we observe that many organizations nominate or appoint specific named individuals as AP(E)L tutors and co-ordinators within specific subject areas. Usually, such staff carry out their AP(E)L duties alongside other departmental responsibilities, such as subject leaders or admissions tutors. Their job is to work with candidates and support the AP(E)L process.

In order to ensure consistency of interpretation and implementation of the organization's policy on AP(E)L, an overall APL co-ordinator is usually appointed. His/her role is to co-ordinate the activity of the team of APL tutors dispersed among the departments, schools, faculties, etc., setting out the institution's policy on AP(E)L, monitoring its implementation and ensuring the sharing of best practice among the team of AP(E)L tutors. From our own experiences, we would fully support this team approach. It ensures uniformity of approach, and mitigates against the isolation AP(E)L tutors would otherwise feel in working with candidates in their separate technical areas.

Benefits

APL and APEL improve access to education and training and the awarding of academic, vocational and professional qualifications by recognizing that learning is continuous, taking place at work, home and at leisure, as well as in the classroom. Intending students and those applying for professional qualifications benefit from AP(E)L since it enables them to build upon their experiences so that they do not have to revisit what they already know and can do. It also:

- recognizes the value of their accomplishments;
- shortens the time required to complete formal qualifications;
- saves significant sums of money by giving exemption from course elements or providing credit points and awards towards a qualification;
- assists career development;
- focuses on their individual development and training needs.

However, the benefits of AP(E)L are more wide-ranging and fundamental than the awarding of credit for achievement. There is evidence that those who complete the AP(E)L process become more self-confident, are willing to take greater responsibility for their own development and have a more positive approach to education and training.

Since the outcome of the AP(E)L process is credit towards a professional or academic qualification, institutions also gain from its use. They find they can:

- maximize the effective use of educational and training resources;
- better meet the needs of individual clients, students or employees;

- motivate their clients or employees to participate more willingly in and to complete programmes;
- provide equal opportunities to a greater range of clients;
- diagnose individual strengths and weaknesses.

To be fully effective, AP(E)L needs to be associated with learner-centred training and education. Distance learning and online learning are particularly attractive methods of delivering individual learning programmes provided the learning programmes on offer are sufficiently flexible or focused to meet the needs of the student. Another approach is to utilize the learning opportunities that are available in the workplace.

Work-based learning

Work-based learning (WBL) is learning occurring during paid or unpaid work. It includes learning *for* work (e.g. work placements), learning *at* work (e.g. company in-house training programmes) and learning *through* work, where work-based activities are linked to specific learning objectives.

Learning *for* work has a long history. It includes apprenticeships, as well as periods of work experience or work placements delivered as part of academic programmes. Learning *at* work has traditionally included training courses. These are often not assessed and may not be accredited. However, there have been recent developments where universities have accredited company management development programmes, and accepted them as part qualifications towards a university academic qualification (for example, see Garnett, 2001). Employees then top-up with additional academic modules or credits in order to achieve the full award.

Learning *at* work also includes *workplace* learning where university courses are delivered at the workplace. Here, the course travels to the student rather than the student travelling to the course. A faster rate of delivery is possible (Rose *et al.*, 2001) because the student has developed a grasp of the concepts being taught through workplace experience.

Learning *through* work is a relatively new approach that takes advantage of learning opportunities in the workplace to deliver enhanced skills, knowledge and understanding. It is particularly useful in part-time and distance-learning programmes of study and is also relevant in the continuing development of professionals. It can be distinguished from other approaches to WBL in a number of important ways (Raelin, 2000):

- Learning through work requires the student to review and reflect. This may involve learning from experience, but also includes applying new theories to everyday events and experiences.

- Learning through work involves research, action and problem solving in the working environment, focusing on challenges to the individual employee and to his/her organization.
- Learning through work involves the learning to learn, as well as the learning of new knowledge and the development of improved insight and understanding.

Another of the characteristics of learning through work is that the learning experience of each student is unique, since each learning environment is different. According to Gerber (1998) there are 11 different ways by which workers learn:

1 by making mistakes and learning not to repeat them;
2 through self-education on and off the job;
3 through practising personal values;
4 by applying theory and practising skills;
5 through solving problems;
6 through interacting with others;
7 through open lateral planning;[1]
8 by being an advocate for colleagues, for example through committee work;
9 through offering leadership to others;
10 through formal training;
11 through practising quality assurance.

In our own approaches to WBL, students make use of a number of these and we have researched the impact of some different approaches on student learning.

Example A: Product evaluation – solving problems and applying theory

In this example, students were required to carry out an investigation of a metallic component to ascertain what material was used to manufacture the component and the processes employed in the manufacture. Students were then asked to comment on the materials and manufacturing processes employed. Here, the clear objective was that students should apply theoretical metallurgical knowledge on the structure, properties and processing of metals. The component for investigation was selected by the student from his/her workplace to be worthy of special investigation, for example a competitor product, an innovative new product or a defective product. Many of the students who undertook this assignment were already contributing to product evaluations in the workplace. The assignment provided an opportunity for them to develop their skills further in this area, and to demonstrate those skills to their employer. Student motivation was therefore high, and employer support for the learning was not in doubt.

The investigations that were carried out often threw up challenging metallurgical issues. One student was asked to determine which of two steel castings had been given a normalising heat treatment, and to confirm that both castings met the customer's specification for chemistry and mechanical properties. This raised the question as to why the casting that had not been heat treated managed to meet the specified properties, and a metallurgical reason for this had to be found. In this case an apparently simple investigation became quite thought provoking. Another student discovered that the component he was studying was manufactured from the 'wrong' grade of alloy steel (AISI 4140 instead of AISI 4130). AISI 4140 has a higher carbon content and a higher manganese content than AISI 4130. The component was an oil industry riser running tool that had failed during service on a UK offshore oil platform, but before he could construct a story blaming the use of the wrong steel grade for the failure, he noticed that the microstructure was also 'wrong'. A steel that was supposed to have been quenched and tempered had a microstructure showing all of the possible transformation products from the cooling of austenite: ferrite, pearlite, bainite and martensite. He concluded that the material had not been correctly heat treated. The use of the 'wrong' grade of steel proved to be an interesting diversion. In this way, the application of academic metallurgical theory to commercially manufactured and processed alloys proved to be extremely challenging and encouraged students to read outside the curriculum. For example, some students carried out further independent research in order to learn more about metals processing, metals processing defects and mechanisms of failure. Additional skills, such as gathering background information and report writing, were also gained. However, what proved most interesting was the comment that academic involvement brought a broader perspective to the investigation than would otherwise have been present in the workplace.

Example B: Understanding industry – applying theory

Here, students were required to study (1) the way in which organizations were organized and structured, and (2) the regulatory regime they operate within. Students were then asked to investigate how their own organization applied theories of organization and how they satisfied the regulatory regime. Again, by focusing on the student's own workplace, student motivation and employer support were not in doubt.

In this example, we found that students consulted workmates and company experts as part of their learning process, as well as applying theory provided by the module tutor through self-reflection and analysis. Some students were able to make use of knowledge gained through responsibilities they already held and experience they had gained within the workplace. For them, the assignment provided the opportunity to get credit for prior learning. Others commented that the assignment had resulted in a better knowledge of the structure and operation of their organization and a better understanding of the rationale for certain procedures and structures in the workplace.

Example C: The learner as a teacher – learning through leadership

A third example was provided by a student who demonstrated and developed his knowledge by writing a technical manual for the company. This was designed to be a training aid for process operatives within the manufacturing operation, so there were expected to be company benefits as well as personal educational benefits to the student. Company reference sources were used to support the development of the manual as well as academic text books.

There was an unexpected additional benefit from this work. In carrying out background reading for the manual, the student developed an increased awareness of the benefits of process control to the quality of the product. The student was able to disseminate his improved understanding to the workforce and product quality levels improved as a result.

Interestingly, again the student commented that the academic involvement in the workplace has assisted the process by providing guidance on the content of the manual.

Work-based learning requires a high level of motivation and commitment from the student since the student must be motivated and organized to add another task to his/her daily workload, and be prepared to take that task home for further research, reflection and reporting. It also requires a supportive workplace. There are three aspects to this. First, although the academic establishment provides its own tutorial support, this is necessarily at a distance (apart from specific academic visits to the workplace), so an industrial mentor can usefully provide advice and encouragement through maintaining direct contact with the student. Second, the employer needs to ensure that the student has access to the necessary resources and information and the necessary authority to be able to complete the assignment. Last, our experience indicates that students perform best when there is a culture of learning in the workplace. When this is in place, we find that colleagues are prepared to support the student's learning in several ways:

- Company experts provide specialist advice and information as part of the student's researches to complete the assignment.
- Colleagues debate matters of opinion with the student during conversation.

This support reduces the isolation a student can feel when studying without the peer group interaction that normally occurs within a student cohort attending an academic establishment.

Good work-based learning requires a tripartite partnership between the student, the employer and the academic centre. Ideally, employer, student and academic should agree a work package that will enable the student to meet the learning outcomes required for the qualification yet be aligned to the strategic aims of the employer. This increases the commitment and motivation of the student to complete the task and increases the motivation of the workplace to support the student in his/her learning.

This partnership can be formalized through a written learning agreement (Doncaster, 2000), which is signed by these three parties. This agreement states clearly what assignment the student will undertake, the tasks that will be carried out and the planned deliverables. It also gives a timetable for these actions. Furthermore, it should specify what the learning objectives are and should show how the assignment will meet those learning objectives. The production of this document should cement the partnership between the student, employer and academic. It is also claimed (Laycock and Stephenson, 1993) that these agreements assist students in developing a sense of ownership and responsibility for their studies, while recognizing that others have an important role to play in this. Our own experience is that students find it difficult to develop the learning agreement alone, and that some academic input is required. Unfortunately, this reduces the benefits of the agreement to the student since it reduces his/her ownership of it. However, in our view the learning agreement does have some important benefits:

- it ensures that the assignment will meet the required learning outcomes;
- it establishes a deadline or completion date for the assignment;
- it forces the student to identify the tasks required to complete the assignment and develop a plan for the project.

The University of Queensland, Australia has extended the concept of WBL into full-time programmes of engineering education (see www.uslp.uq.edu.au). It has developed the concepts of traditional vacation work and the sandwich course to ensure greater consistency to the work experience by placing its final year students in industry for a 12-week period in the final year of the degree programme. While in industry, the students continue to study and submit assignments to the university, but also undertake a final year project within the company. Rather like our own model of work-based learning, the students receive tutorial support in the workplace through an industrial mentor and an academic tutor who provides telephone tutorials.

The concept, termed the Undergraduate Site Learning Programme (USLP), is a response to the need for engineers to be better able to apply theoretical knowledge in practice and to acquire the 'soft skills' required in employment

– communication skills, team-working skills, business awareness and basic competence in health and safety. (Such issues underlie the development of the output standards for engineering graduates by the Engineering Professors' Conference.)

Like us, the University of Queensland recognizes the importance of the student/industry/academic partnership to the success of the work-based learning process. If correctly established and maintained, this partnership can result in each of the partners benefiting: the company benefits from the work of the student, the student applies some of the skills required of a professional engineer and the university strengthens its links with those that apply and practise the academic understanding developed and promoted by the University.

Learning through work offers advantages over traditional teaching and learning approaches but also offers some challenges. As academics, we are committed to WBL because it provides opportunities for:

- demonstrating the usefulness and relevance of learning to the working environment, thereby assisting the learning to become embedded in the learner;
- linking theory to practice, so that the student is better able to understand the rationale for current procedures and, indeed, improve or develop current practice;
- applying new skills, knowledge and understanding in the workplace to the benefit of employee and employer;
- developing the 'soft skills' required of the student engineer in the modern workplace;
- demonstrating to the student the continuing and informal nature of the learning experiences in life which underpin continuing professional development.

Research (Costley, 2001) has also shown that WBL students:

- increase their involvement in the workplace, developing a greater understanding of their employer's objectives and their role in delivering them;
- develop increased self-confidence;
- develop project management skills;
- are able to contribute to the breakdown of internal barriers between disciplines in the workplace.

However, we should not underestimate the significant contribution that academic involvement in the workplace can bring to an organization and its staff. It can bring rigour, it can bring fresh thinking, so that new ideas and practices can germinate and take root.

Note

1   This involves having an open, fertile mind to accept new experiences, new information, new methods of learning and, indeed, to actively seek out fresh perspectives.

References

Costley, Carol (2001) 'Organisational and employee interests in programs of work based learning', *The Learning Organisation* 8 (2): 58.

Doncaster, Kathy (2000) 'Learning agreement: their function in work-based programmes at Middlesex University', *Education & Training* 42 (6): 349.

Garnett, Jonathan (2001) 'Work based learning and the intellectual capital of universities and employers', *The Learning Organisation* 8 (2): 78.

Gerber, Rod (1998) 'How do workers learn in their work?', *The Learning Organisation* 5 (4): 168.

Laycock, M. and Stephenson, J. (1993) *Using Learning Contracts in Higher Education*, London: Kogan Page.

Nyatanga, L., Forman, D. and Fox, J. (1998) *Good Practice in the Accreditation of Prior Learning*, London: Cassell.

Raelin, J. A. (2000) *Work-based Learning: the new frontier of management development*, Englewood Cliffs, NJ: Prentice Hall.

Rose, Emma *et al.* (2001) 'Workplace learning: a concept in off-campus teaching', *The Learning Organisation* 8 (2): 70.

Simosko, S. (1991) *APL-Accreditation of Prior Learning – A Practical Guide for Professionals*, London: Kogan Page.

University of Queensland, 'Undergraduate site learning programme' (description), http://www.thiess.uq.edu.au/USLP-description.html.

7

A holistic approach to mathematics support for engineering

Christine Hirst, Sarah Williamson and Pam Bishop

Setting the scene

Engineering is based on both practical and theoretical knowledge in which mathematics plays a central role. Almost all branches rely on mathematics as a language of description and analysis and mathematicians work with a steady flow of engineering problems. The link between the two fields in both academia and industry is well established.

Since the mid-1990s, engineering departments, which are a part of this symbiosis, have had to deal with a growing number of educational issues. Unlike subjects such as computer and business studies, engineering has had problems attracting a sufficiently high proportion of more able entrants. This has resulted in an increasingly diverse range of levels and types of qualifications at entry into engineering courses. There is also growing evidence that many entrants lack basic mathematical skills.

In 1995, the report *Tackling the Mathematics Problem* highlighted many problems concerning the education of mathematics in both England and Wales (London Mathematical Society (LMS), 1995). By 2000, the report *Measuring the Mathematics Problem* presented evidence of a 'serious decline in students' mastery, of basic mathematical skills and level of preparation for mathematics-based degree courses' (Engineering Council, 2000: ii). Since then, this situation has not improved, causing acute problems for those teaching engineering mathematics.

In dealing with this issue the report *Engineering Mathematics Matters* recommended a more systematic programme of study (IMA, 1999). It suggested a closer match between course design and student profiles, the core curriculum being broadened and made more flexible. Another report states that courses should provide a balanced spectrum of learning experiences. 'Fluency and confidence in the knowledge and use of mathematics and science comes with repetition and practice but deeper understanding comes with experience of transferring concepts and principles to new contexts and applications' (The Royal Society, 1998: 6).

Universities have taken a range of steps to address the situation. Academics are providing different methods of assessment, support and broadening courses; they are exploring ways of maintaining the balance between theoretical and practical knowledge and its application to problem-solving processes. Departments have made curriculum changes to include more A-level material in the first year and have introduced new systems such as streaming. Some have established bridging courses or summer schools prior to the start of the academic year. Mathematics Learning Support Centres have been established and provision has been made for extra support modules to be studied alongside the traditional syllabus (Lawson *et al.*, 2001).

Overall, there is a growing thread of innovative teaching methods and support systems, devised to provide students with a more balanced spectrum of mathematical knowledge. This chapter will explore some of these methods and systems.

Teaching mathematics within an engineering context

The changing mathematical background of undergraduate engineers

The report *Mathematics for the European Engineer: a curriculum for the twenty-first century* lists the following mathematical topics as being important to engineers:

- a fluency and confidence with numbers;
- a fluency and confidence with algebra;
- a knowledge of trigonometric functions;
- an understanding of basic calculus and its application to 'real world' situations;
- a proficiency with the collection, management and interpretation of data.

(SEFI Mathematics Working Group, 2002: 3)

A few years ago it was assumed that such topics were thoroughly covered in pre-university education. However, this is no longer the case. There is evidence that some students are struggling to make the transition in science, engineering and mathematics from A-level to degree level study (Lawson, 1997; Engineering Council, 2000).

Sir Gareth Roberts' report *Set for Success: the supply of people with science, technology, engineering and mathematics skills* stated that, for many academics, 'current science and mathematics A-level syllabuses, while covering a wide variety of interesting areas, do not necessarily equip students with the intellectual and conceptual tools required at degree level' (Roberts, 2002: 89).

In addition to the decline in preparedness of entrants, the situation in engineering has been further complicated by the introduction of Curriculum 2000 and the increasing modularization of AS and A2 level courses. Students are entering higher education with a variety of subject knowledge and, perhaps, a mix of scientific and non-scientific AS and A2 level subjects which in some cases can mean the student's choices at degree level are limited. For example, in some universities A-level physics is a prerequisite for electronic engineering but not for computer science. Some students, discovering that they will not be accepted onto an electronic engineering course, apply to study computer science (Roberts, 2002). This, in addition to the attractiveness of the subject, has led to a large increase in demand for computing-based courses while engineering has grown increasingly unpopular. Consequently, the discipline has struggled to find sufficient numbers of students with the desired level of entry qualifications (SEFI Mathematics Working Group, 2002: 4).

Due to these many factors the mathematical knowledge of the engineering student entering university has changed. There has been a gradual shift from a deep foundation to a surface knowledge of facts. Academics are beginning to adapt, first by acknowledging the situation then by making changes within the educational programme. Those who continue to deliver the same course they have always taught are wondering why their students are failing.

Mathematics and engineering practice

Although the content of engineering programmes has changed since the mid-1990s, students still need a broad base of mathematical knowledge that they can apply to engineering processes. This application implies two distinct components – the knowledge and the process. In terms of engineering these can be defined as follows:

- Knowledge is the growing body of facts, experience and skills in science, engineering and technology disciplines; coupled to an understanding of the fields of application.
- Process is the creative process, which applies knowledge and experience to seek one or more technical solutions to meet a requirement, solve a problem, then exercise informed judgement to implement the one that best meets constraints.

(Malpas, 2000: 31)

To help students acquire these concepts, engineering teaching draws on a bank of knowledge comprising of just some of the following:

- *materials* and their physical, chemical or biological properties;
- *science* and key underlying principles of the engineering disciplines;
- *applied mathematics* relating to the discipline;
- *knowledge* required to meet technical objectives such as motion, flow, transfer, control, support, containment and physical or information processing – but often carried out in, or destined for, an environment with technical, financial or time constraints;
- *design, construction, application, maintenance, disposal* of engineering products and systems;
- *information* generation, processing and transmission;
- *modelling and simulation*;
- *innovation and research.*

(Malpas, 2000: 33)

Each forms the basis of factual knowledge imparted in the teaching of engineering. As departments update the content and the nature of their courses to reflect the latest course developments, they are also faced with the diverse mathematical abilities and qualifications of their students. Innovative approaches have been devised to address the different level of mathematical skills and provide effective support mechanisms for the students. These approaches are reviewed in the next section.

Teaching students with diverse backgrounds

For some institutions, streaming is part of the process of addressing the mismatch between prior qualifications and course requirements. The first step is invariably a diagnostic test, which provides the staff and the students with an indication of the different levels of attainment. Students are then allocated to one of the streams, each receiving a tailored programme of study which enables them to master basic techniques and feel confident in applying mathematics to engineering problems. For example, between 1993 and 1996, UMIST identified that a proportion of students entering various disciplines were not coping with the engineering maths courses because of a lack of basic mathematical skills. This was affecting overall curricula and many students were dropping out or failing. A streaming system was put into place with good effect.

Case study: **UMIST**

Students studying Engineering (and other related disciplines) at UMIST receive teaching in mathematics via a streamed hierarchy of courses, P, Q and R: the P-stream being hardest and fastest to motivate the most able students, the Q-stream being an intermediate case and the R-stream being designed to get the best out of the weaker students. Students are allocated to one of the three streams according to a combination of previous mathematics qualifications and a diagnostic test taken at the beginning of the first semester, with opinions from the students themselves also being taken into account.

As well as the end-of-semester exams, assessment comes from coursework assignments taking place during the semester. On the P- and Q-streams, this takes the form of 'take-home' assignments but the R-stream students are asked to sit several short tests during the semester. Each week, students attend two lectures and one tutorial session; the number of students in the tutorial groups varies with smaller groups (and hence a larger share of the tutor) for students on the R-stream. The Director of Service Teaching in the mathematics department is keen to provide further support sometimes following a referral mechanism from the student's personal tutor in his/her own department.

(Steele, 2000)

Many departments face an inhomogeneous student cohort and teaching the whole year effectively has become almost impossible. Streaming provides a means of placing the students in more homogeneous groups to provide more effective teaching and mathematical support (Savage and Roper, 2003).

In establishing a streaming system it is important to have support from the Heads of the Departments involved as well as other members of staff. Usually the streaming system involves both the mathematics and engineering departments and it is, therefore, crucial to establish a good relationship between the two. Teaching mathematics to first-year engineering students is a difficult task. Academics must ensure that the basics are understood and well practised but they also have to motivate each mathematical topic by illustrating how it connects with ideas and topics within the students' engineering courses. The following section looks at ways in which this issue is being addressed.

The need for collaboration between mathematics and engineering departments

Generally, the teaching of mathematics to engineering students is carried out either within the engineering department or through service teaching provided by the mathematics department. What has developed in recent years is the realization that engineering mathematics is not simply a matter of teaching pure mathematical techniques. It requires a direct focus towards engineering (IMA, 1999).

In dealing with these circumstances, certain universities have successfully established a working relationship between the mathematics and engineering departments, based on sharing knowledge and ongoing collaboration. The objective is to establish more effective links between the mathematics being taught and the mathematics used in the engineering course. This is achieved by identifying the mathematics needed for the engineering course and supporting the mathematics lecturer by providing examples which are rooted in the engineering discipline. It enables the lecturer to harmonize notation as much as possible and set the most appropriate examples, given the class profile. This approach has been taken at the University of Edinburgh with positive results.

Case study: University of Edinburgh

A few years ago the mathematics department at Edinburgh looked at the problems of interfacing between mathematics and engineering courses and came up with a system to enable greater student understanding. Based on the *Maths Links Project*, the aim was to establish more effective links between mathematics courses and those given by client departments in which mathematics is used. The results of the project led to the production of material that describes the matrix of connections between mathematics and client courses, and is supported by potential mathematics examples rooted in the various disciplines.

Now all first- and second-year chemical engineering students are taught mathematics by the mathematics department, while the chemical engineering department provides their examples and problems. The engineers supply copies of notes from fluid mechanics lectures including all the tutorials and tutorial solutions. This enables the mathematics lecturers to see the ways in which the mathematics they are teaching is going to be used later on in the course. The mathematics lecturers then select one or two examples, which are presented during their own tutorials and lecture courses. The objective is to teach first- and second-year students in terms of examples that are relevant to engineering to help them see the problems within an engineering context. The comments from the students have been positive. Difficulties still exist but there are fewer complaints based on the fact that the students are seeing the relevancy of what they are doing with the mathematics. This is viewed as the first step towards motivating the students to taking mathematics more seriously.

(Christy, 2003: 18)

The development of contextual teaching methods by both mathematics and engineering departments is resulting in academics introducing a number of different approaches to teaching. One of the most significant is based on the integration of conceptual and practical mathematics through the use of technology. The next section looks at the different types of learning technologies being used by academics.

Using learning technologies for teaching

During the last 30 years, learning technologies have become more widely available. In relation to the engineering mathematics curriculum, this has enabled new approaches to teaching and learning. In addition, sophisticated mathematical software is now commonly available which routinely allows analysis of problems of such size and complexity that only a few years ago would have been regarded as a research activity.

There are definite signs that the involvement of technology in the teaching of undergraduate engineering mathematics is gaining momentum. For example, the graphics calculator has become an integral part of two courses at Napier University. For first- and second-year engineering students, it plays a major role in an integrated technological approach to mathematics.

Case study: **Napier University**

In the lectures, teaching mathematics is based around four stages: explaining the theory to students; worked examples; examples with the aid of the graphics calculator; and illustrating the maths topics in a context relevant to engineering. In the tutorials, the calculator is used in exercises designed to develop competence in mathematical techniques and, in some cases, to develop skills toward mathematical modelling. In both the lectures and the tutorials the calculator provides a visual understanding of graphical solutions and the related arithmetic and plays an integral part in the teaching of mathematics in engineering applications. Generally, it enhances the teaching and learning of mathematics and consolidates the coursework.

(Evans and Jackman, 2003: 20)

Widely available software such as spreadsheets can be a powerful tool for data manipulation. At the University of Bradford, MS-Excel™ has been used to provide simulation facilities for teaching control to engineering students.

Case study: **University of Bradford**

Control is a subject most students find difficult. While the mathematics is not particularly onerous, the understanding required is demanding. Excel has been used to provide simulation facilities in support of teaching control to engineers. This dictates a sampled data approach which fits in naturally with digital implementation of control. The technique also allows students to explore the affects of non-linearities in systems such as control signal saturation. It provides a 'hands-on' dimension which students find valuable. The approach is capable of use with other dynamic systems and is not restricted to teaching control. Indeed, it could be used quite widely.

For example, in chemistry and chemical engineering it is a good way of examining reaction dynamics.

(Henry, 2003: 26)

Specialist software is also playing an important role in teaching mathematics to engineering students. Students studying aeronautical engineering at Queen's University Belfast use MATLAB™. In the first year the software provides the students with programming skills for use in later courses. In the second year, it is used to enhance teaching of linear algebra and to apply mathematical techniques to engineering problems.

Mathcad™ is used in all years of the engineering mathematics course at Oxford Brookes University, to enable students to investigate real engineering problems which have no analytical solution but which illustrate mathematical concepts.

Case study: **Oxford Brookes University**

In order to motivate the students to study engineering mathematics, problems drawn from other subjects studied in the degree are presented which require analytical and numerical solutions. An assignment is given to students early in the course which poses a problem drawn from structural engineering. It comprises a variable coefficient second order boundary value problem relating to beam-columns. The problem requires students to derive a set of finite difference equations for a limited number of internal nodes and solve the linear system of equations produced using Mathcad. Once this simple exercise has been undertaken, the students have to extend their calculations to larger numbers of nodes and compare the results with approximate analytical solutions of constant coefficient differential equations, which bound the true solution. The final part of the assignment which is normally only undertaken by students seeking high grades, consists of then writing a Mathcad program using a 'shooting algorithm' for the same problem.

The exercise has the objective of making students realize that mathematics has a role in engineering, enabling practical problems to be solved. It revises the theory of second order differential equations, which is needed at the end of the course when partial differential equations are encountered. It also extends their knowledge of Mathcad and its applications and consolidates finite difference theory. The requisite mathematical knowledge, such as numerical methods for the analysis of differential equations, is taught by a series of lectures in parallel with the problem being given to the student. Additional Mathcad techniques required for the assignment, such as handling large arrays, are taught in problem classes.

(Beale, 2003: 30)

Additionally, computer programming skills can become a focus for the learning of engineering students. In 1993 at the University of Edinburgh, a module was devised addressing typical chemical engineering problems and requiring the students to write computer programs to solve them.

Case study: University of Edinburgh

The problems were chosen to cover a range of mathematical methods: algebra, ordinary differential equations (linear and non-linear) and some simple linear and non-linear optimization problems. From the engineering standpoint, they also covered the major application areas including separation processes, reactors, material balances and data fitting. The emphasis is very much on practicalities. How do numerical methods work? What can go wrong? How do I write a program for this method? How can I adapt someone else's program? Only what we see as the very minimum necessary amount of theory is developed and issues such as numerical stability are mainly addressed by experiment.

(Ponton, 2003: 34)

Technology-based activities are enriching the teaching environment for students. Sheffield Hallam University is an example where a range of technology is being used to varying degrees across the whole engineering programme, providing a selection of educational tools which are becoming integrated within a number of engineering modules.

Case study: Sheffield Hallam University

Mathematical topics are treated according to 'SONG' – a combination of Symbolic, Oral, Numerical and Graphical approaches – broader than the traditional mainly symbolic approach, and in the same vein as with the 'Calculus Reform' movement in the US. Students are encouraged to engage in doing mathematics and to exploit a range of technology throughout – graphics calculators, spreadsheet, Derive, pencil, etc. The rich interplay of graphic, symbolic and numerical approaches is emphasized.

(Challis, 2002: 32)

For some academics, technology has developed very much into a motivational tool and has become part of the teaching process over recent years. Others focus on creating a more interactive environment in which the student participates. The next section explores an example of a game show format.

Using interactive lectures to enhance student motivation and engagement

Teaching engineering concepts to students who do not have a very strong background in mathematics is always challenging. For some academics, the task has developed from lecturing to providing an environment that combines learning and fun. Here is one such example from the School of Engineering, University of Birmingham.

Case study: **University of Birmingham**

Problem classes are traditionally used in the teaching of mathematics. For a first-year Chemical Engineering course in mathematical modelling, a quiz based on the TV programme 'Who Wants to Be a Millionaire?' has been introduced, in a two-hour problem class supporting lectures. A highly structured approach to modelling is taught in the lectures, with a strong emphasis on the key issue: how does one begin? Students usually struggle to turn a problem expressed in words into mathematical equations, and the problem classes are intended to provide practice at modelling and in solving the resulting equations.

Classes involve 25 to 30 students, and each is repeated, as the whole cohort is 55 to 60 students. The first problem class emphasizes the development of models, beginning with the students criticizing an attempt at modelling from a *Tom and Jerry* cartoon (a short video clip which is used as light relief in an earlier lecture). The second problem class begins with more difficult model building involving second order ODEs and finishes with a quiz.

In order to break up cliques and promote better interpersonal skills (i.e. teamwork), the students are allocated at random to one of four groups as they arrive. Each group works on a set problems for 50 minutes, resulting in the preparation of a few overhead transparencies explaining the group's problem and its solution. The author and a postgraduate demonstrator circulate around the groups giving advice. Strong students are asked to help weaker students, so that all group members understand the group solution (and more interpersonal skills are practised). After a short break, one student volunteer from each group presents to the whole class (4 × 5 min). It is certainly the case that presenting complex mathematical derivations on a few overheads and in a few minutes makes a student have some sympathy with the lecturer!

After the presentations, the Who Wants to be a Modell-er? quiz begins. A second volunteer from each group faces six questions related to his or her group's problem. Four answers are shown on an overhead projector to the student (who comes to the front of the room) and the rest of the class. Typically, one answer will be correct, one will be obviously wrong, and the other two contain typical student errors. The student must choose one. As in the TV show, the student has lifelines. 'Phone a friend' becomes ask a specific group member, 'Ask the audience' means ask the class, and '50:50' works by the author removing two answers (not necessarily at random; a struggling student might be left with the correct answer and an obviously wrong one, while a stronger student might be left to choose between the correct answer and a common trap). The rewards for correct responses are chocolate bars, of the small party pack variety.

The questions are such that it is hard not to get at least five correct. When appropriate, discussion of the incorrect choices and the traps follows a question, using a whiteboard for notes when necessary. The four quizzes take about 40 minutes, completing a 2-hour class.

(Thomas, 2003: 14)

Such levels of interactivity are simple and can be easily produced by anyone. The format could also be applied in other problem classes and many subject areas.

Practices such as streaming, developing links between engineering and mathematics departments, technology and interactive lectures, are each contributing to the learning process. They are becoming part of a growing collection of innovative ideas, which are developing as universities attempt to improve the engineering student's mathematical knowledge.

Supporting student learning

It has been identified that mathematics A-level syllabuses do not always provide sufficient grounding for the undergraduate studying engineering. 'Good grades at A-level, even among bright students, do not necessarily reflect adequate knowledge of or ability to use core mathematical techniques' (Roberts, 2002: 89). Consequently, universities are addressing the situation in two stages:

- an early assessment of the student's mathematical ability through diagnostic testing;
- the development of student support practices.

Diagnostic testing practice

In most cases the tests take place during the induction week or the first few weeks of the academic year. The results assist departments to devise approaches to adjust the mathematics teaching and curriculum to the needs of the group and also to inform subject specialists' expectations of their students' mathematical abilities. Primarily, tests are being used to help devise strategies to support students with different attainment (IMA, 1995).

Two departmental surveys conducted in April 2001 and February 2003 by the LTSN MathsTEAM found there was a rise from 60 per cent to 72 per cent in the number of institutions conducting diagnostic tests. The methodology for the testing ranged from intelligent systems through computer-generated multi-choice questions to paper-based tests. Students' responses on paper-based tests are sometimes read automatically by an Optical Mark Reader (OMR) and marked by the computer, or the whole process may be undertaken manually. The following case studies examine different approaches.

Case study: University of Coventry

Paper-based diagnostic test

The mathematics department at the University of Coventry has carried out a comprehensive diagnostic test since 1991. During the first week of the academic year, 600–700 entrants to a range of science and engineering degrees, and also to courses in the Business School and the School of Art and Design, sit one of the Mathematics Support Centre Diagnostic Tests. There are two tests: one aimed for students on courses with an A-level in mathematics (or equivalent) entry requirement and the other for students on courses with a GCSE mathematics entry requirement. The Maths Support Centre, also established in 1991, manages the procedure but the tests are administered by staff of each of the various participating disciplines. The test is timetabled and takes place in the host department. Engineering students were observed in a large classroom: each was handed an OMR (Optical Mark Reader) answer sheet and a booklet containing 50 questions. A set of instructions was presented on page 1. The student was asked to use an HB pencil to complete the answer sheet; this was necessary for the 'marking machine' to recognize the selected answer. In this instance, a calculator was not allowed. It was also stated that the results of the test would not be used for assessment purposes, they would be analysed and returned to each student indicating either satisfactory performance or areas where extra work was advisable. The results were given back at the end of induction week.

As part of the induction programme, students have a half-hour visit scheduled to the Mathematics Support Centre. During this time, they are informed of the help that is available, shown the various handouts and how to access the Centre website. They are also given back their own diagnosis from the test. The printouts they receive list seven topics and their performance within each. It is hoped that receiving the results in this manner will help the students to appreciate that the diagnostic test is part of a package, which includes ongoing student support. Students can return to the Maths Support Centre for help from staff or use the materials available. Special revision classes are also scheduled.

(Lawson, 2003: 19)

Case study: **University of Newcastle upon Tyne**

Computer-based diagnostic test

DIAGNOSYS was first used by the Department of Engineering Mathematics at the University of Newcastle upon Tyne in October 1993. Developed under the Teaching and Learning Technology Programme (TLTP), the computer package is an intelligent knowledge-based system for testing background skills in basic mathematics or other technical subjects. The testing process includes entrants into the Engineering Foundation Course, Stage 1 of Mechanical and Materials degrees and all first-year students to the Faculty. It is an essential tool in assessing students' mathematical knowledge. It is used to help individual students identify their level of attainment and to provide support for those with special needs.

During the first week of the 2002–2003 academic year first-year students sat the DIAGNOSYS test within a scheduled computer session. Each student entered their name, department and the level of mathematics they had previously attained. Based on this information the package decides the level of questions to ask initially. At the beginning of the test there is an optional tutorial on how to enter different types of answers (number, multiple-choice, algebra) which provides an opportunity for the student to get used to the interface. What follows depends upon the success rate of the students: those achieving a good success rate can quickly pass to more advanced topics; those less successful are taken on a slower route. The test terminates when there are no questions left to be asked or when a time limit is reached.

Each topic area contains several questions at a given level and one is chosen at random for each test. Coupled with the 'expert-system' approach, which gives each student a different path through the test, each student will be asked a completely different set of questions, which helps prevent cheating. The results are stored on the server as individual text files; at the end of the group test they are downloaded by the tutor and transferred to a disk. The information is printed out and given to each of the students.

(Appleby, 2003: 30)

Diagnostic tests in themselves do not assist students. The next section examines the variety of support-based initiatives being implemented within engineering departments throughout the UK.

Support-based practice

In the past, traditional undergraduate engineering programmes consisted of lectures on different mathematical topics that were supported by both tutorials and sets of problems. These were carefully marked and discussed with the students. From the mid-1990s there has been clear evidence that this pattern has changed. There has been a shift to a more diverse selection of teaching and support strategies. The lecture may have been retained, but the tutorials have become more structured or have been replaced by other methods of support for student learning, both independent and staff directed (Anderson *et al.*, 2000).

The different teaching initiatives for supporting engineering students have increased dramatically in recent years. Systems for support have been initiated as a result of diagnostic testing and the identification of the lack of mathematical skills among engineering undergraduates. Each approach attempts to deal with the fact that engineering modules are assuming knowledge and skills which some students do not have, particularly in number and algebra. In addition, they are attempting to address the mathematical diversity of the student intake (Mustoe, 2002).

Support strategies are becoming a part of teaching engineering students for many universities. They aim to provide the undergraduate with an understanding of their mathematical weaknesses and the opportunity to address them. One of the most popular support initiatives is the Mathematics Learning Support Centre.

Mathematics learning support centres

In 2001 a survey of higher education institutions indicated that 46 of the 95 who responded had some kind of Mathematics Learning Support Centre (Lawson *et al.*, 2001). The provisions varied greatly, although there were a significant number of common themes.

In 2003, the LTSN MathsTEAM provided further insight into the developing features of Mathematics Learning Support Centres. Academics from seven institutions provided structured reviews of Mathematics Learning Support Centres, looking at the execution of the learning activities, the support needed, the implementation difficulties, evidence of success and suggestions of how other academics could reproduce the activity. With setting-up dates ranging from 1987 to 1997, each had progressed from the initial stages to a comprehensive strategy of support; one example is based at Loughborough University.

Case study: **Loughborough University**

In 1996 forward-looking members of the Department of Mathematical Sciences at Loughborough secured funding from an internal university learning and teaching initiative to open a Mathematics Learning Support Centre. The main reasons for doing this were to underpin the substantial service teaching commitment of the department to engineers, and to recognize a deteriorating situation regarding preparedness of many of these students for the mathematical demands of their programmes. A full-time manager was appointed with the task of developing the centre, initially for a period of two years. Prior to the appointment of the manager, space was made available within the department sufficient to accommodate the centre itself and an office for the manager. In October 1996 the centre opened, drop-in surgeries were started from the third week of the autumn term, and a vigorous programme of advertising was undertaken to raise awareness among first year engineering students. At the same time, supporting materials were either purchased or developed in-house. These included supporting computer packages such as Transmath, Mathwise, various GCSE and A-level items of software, videos etc.

Almost immediately, the Centre had a positive effect on the student experience. It additionally became apparent that many of the resources available to support engineering students were also highly relevant to students in the physical sciences, mathematics, business and economics. Before the end of the initial two-year period, a decision was made in the university to establish the centre on a more permanent basis and to fund its management by top-slicing all three faculties in the university according to student usage.

In 2002 the centre was relocated and significantly enlarged. It became part of a newly formed Mathematics Education Centre, which is responsible for the development and delivery of mathematics for engineers. A wide range of supporting mechanisms is available. Drop-in surgeries are staffed for 25 hours per week. Leaflets are available covering a very wide range of topics. A variety of pre-sessional materials have also been developed, for example, *An Algebra Refresher* is a booklet which is sent out to all new mathematics students during the summer vacation. Recently, the booklet has also been sent to some groups of engineers and physicists and it has been published by the LTSN Maths, Stats & OR Network along with *A Calculus Refresher.* The Mathematics Learning Support Centre runs regular workshops covering basic topics. A mathematics tutor who can give specialist help to dyslexic students is available for 22 hours per week. For further details see http://mlsc.lboro.ac.uk

In general, Mathematics Learning Support Centres are providing a valuable framework for follow–up support for the student. Still evolving, for many institutions they are becoming an important part of the student's mathematical development.

Peer-assisted learning

Schemes where students help each other to learn are becoming increasingly attractive to university departments throughout the disciplines. This method of support offers a very cost-effective way to implement various pedagogical aims and to train students in useful transferable skills. A good example of this is presented in the following case study.

Case study: **University of Hertfordshire**

Student proctors were introduced in the Faculty of Engineering and Information Sciences in the early 1990s. The aims of this service were to:

- provide students with an additional level of academic support, i.e. beyond that provided by staff;
- allow students to learn from their peers in a one-to-one situation.

Proctors are appointed in the areas of Engineering, Computer Science and Mathematics. The number of proctors appointed each year varies between departments. In the 2001/2002 academic year there were six engineering proctors, ten computer science proctors and one mathematics proctor. These numbers reflect the number of undergraduate students studying in each of these subject areas.

The mechanism for appointing proctors also varies between departments. In Engineering and Mathematics adverts are placed on the student notice boards in the summer term inviting applications from second-year under-graduate students for posts commencing in the following autumn term. Candidates are required to have an appropriate academic background (e.g. a first class or upper second class profile to date), appropriate personal skills, (e.g. be well organized, be able to communicate clearly, be patient with students with difficulties) and to have an interest in helping others. All applicants are interviewed by staff and appointments are made shortly afterwards.

Each proctor is usually available for two or three hours each week. Details of their location and availability are published on the student notice boards. At these times the students requiring help can see the proctors on a drop-in basis, i.e. without an appointment. In Engineering and Mathematics the proc-tors attempt to provide support on any technical problem in their subject area. The proctors are not expected to be able to deal with every problem they are given. In all departments experienced academic staff are available to provide backup to the proctors when required.

The introduction of proctors has been a success and evidence shows that students make good use of the service, especially approaching coursework deadlines and examinations. The support provided by the student proctors is often different from that provided by academic staff, i.e. the proctors have usually been through the same courses as those seeking help and can often bring a different perspective to each problem.

(Davies and Fitzharris, 2003: 24)

Peer–assisted learning can work in a variety of different ways; each has their individual benefits and all of them demand active involvement with the subject and a dialogue with another or others (Donelan and Wallace, 1998). A detailed description of various peer-assisted learning programmes is provided by Goodlad (1995).

Summer schools

Many institutions have introduced a series of short intensive courses which take place before the start of the academic year. They are designed to prepare students for entry to university studies. Many include the subject mathematics, with the aim to address the lack of knowledge among entrants into university programmes such as engineering. Summer Schools in many cases are designed to be intensive and yet fun. An example can be found at the Glasgow Caledonian University.

Case study: **Glasgow Caledonian University**

The Glasgow Caledonian University decided in 1991 to run a pre-entry Summer School to help prepare students entering first year who have a time or a qualifications gap. Entry is by referral from an admissions tutor. There is no cost to the student and if a student matriculates, then he/she can claim travel expenses.

The Summer School is offered flexibly, with students able to attend one evening a week from Easter and then, in addition, during the day from the end of June. The Summer School finishes the week before registration. The three main entry points are as follows: post-Easter for mature students who are making a return to education; late June for students who have the minimum qualifications for entry, but who are perceived by their admission tutors to have a weakness in mathematics; and early August, after the school exam results are published, for students who have failed to make the grade required in a conditional offer.

On the first day the student receives an information booklet giving full details of the operation and assessment, including the marking scheme for the required portfolio and an individualized progress chart giving details of the Computer Assisted Learning (CAL) lessons to be completed and the assessments to be undertaken. The average student is expected to complete the programme in 72 hours. The software (CALMAT) is available on most of the PCs on campus and can be purchased on a CD for home use. Completion data for CAL work done at home is merged with data on the campus server. Many students who purchase the system work at home, only attending supervised sessions when they need help or want to sit a test. In addition to the progress chart containing the list of CAL lessons, each student is given paper-based materials related to the CAL lessons. The required portfolio should contain learning plans, summaries, formulae and enough worked exercises to demonstrate competence in each section of the individualized syllabus. The assessments are computer-delivered, but not multiple-choice.

Mock tests are available and the actual tests are taken under supervised conditions.

(Cook, 2003)

Mathematics support strategies have evolved over recent years. Academics have addressed the nature of the support, the staffing, and student engagement and funding. The result is a collection of developing resources and good practices aimed directly at mathematical issues, which are playing a valuable part in the future development of many engineering students.

Mathematics and engineering – developments

As each university adapts to the educational issues surrounding mathematics and engineering, some practices will be adopted, others will disappear; some will evolve even further. There is no long-term solution, as both academics and students are faced with an ever-changing educational environment. In dealing with the present situation universities can only strive to improve the learning environment and make sure that engineering students who are lacking in mathematical skills are given every opportunity to change their circumstances.

There is a growing need for all universities to be aware of the actual and potential problems facing these students, and to have knowledge of current resources being developed to deal with the situation. There has recently been a great deal of publicity around specific issues relating to student transition to HE in the subject of mathematics. Among these are the Engineering Council report (2000), *Measuring the Mathematics Problem*, which presents evidence of a serious decline in students' mastery of basic mathematical skills and level of preparation for mathematics-based degree courses. Others such as IMA (1995), Sutherland and Pozzi (1995) and Mustoe (2002) have looked at the problem in terms of how it is affecting engineering programmes.

For many institutions this has meant recognizing the issues, identifying the changes required and implementing new procedures. Some universities have made changes at the curriculum level – delivery methods, assessment and content. Some have introduced summer schools or pre-course information to assist the students before entry. For others, the focus has been on providing ongoing pastoral, and other, support through Mathematics Learning Support Centres or drop-in centres. The research carried out by the LTSN MathsTEAM illustrates many examples of such teaching practices. The information gathered provides a broad spectrum of innovative ideas and positive adjustments within the curriculum in establishing methods of support and assessment procedures.

For example, diagnostic tests have been developed because of the need to identify specific weaknesses in students' mathematical knowledge. They also provide valuable information for departments in terms of the future support and development of the students. A recent in-depth study by a small working group surveyed 13 mathematics departments in the UK that use diagnostic testing and produced the following preliminary recommendations:

- academics need to advise students of the diagnostic test and supply revision materials *before* arrival;
- the purpose of the diagnostic test must be clearly defined, i.e. it is not part of the formal assessment;
- there must be follow-up and support for the students.

(Quinney *et al.*, forthcoming)

In order to provide support there is a growing need for the development of educational resources for both the student and academic. As the teaching environment shifts from academics being the 'transmitters of information' to 'designers and facilitators of the educational experience' (Sherwood, 2001) they urgently need resources to support their evolving role. Students also need access to these means to help them 'take control' of the situation. Fortunately, there are some centrally funded projects currently working to produce such material for academics and students.

The **math**centre, the UK Mathematics Learning Support Centre funded by the LTSN Development Fund provides online materials for students and academics at its website www.mathcentre.ac.uk. There is free access – all the materials can be downloaded in PDF format – and clear routing to brief explanations, with more detailed information on essential mathematics topics. There are mechanisms for universities to establish or enhance their own local mathematics support and links to relevant initiatives such as the LTSN MathsTEAM.

mathcentre will also provide a home for the web-based activities of the project 'Mathematics Support at the Transition to University' in the Fund for the Development of Teaching and Learning programme (FDTL). Designed to revise and refresh students' mathematical knowledge and skills, this project is producing e-learning diagnostics, digital video tutorials, associated texts, extension texts and interactive exercises, to be delivered on the DVD-Rom **math**tutor.

Another FDTL project is HELM (Helping Engineers Learn Mathematics). The overall aim is to enhance the mathematical education of engineering undergraduates by the provision of flexible learning materials. As described at www.lboro.ac.uk/helm, the project is developing the following materials:

- forty workbooks of approximately 50 pages, each containing a mathematics topic for engineering simply explained, worked examples and case studies;

- computer-aided assessment for all topics;
- illustrative computer-aided learning segments.

HELM, **math**tutor and **math**centre are each producing valuable resources which will assist engineering departments in supporting their students. Other projects are coming on stream each year via funding opportunities like the National Teaching Fellowships. There is a searchable index of these at www. ltsn.ac.uk/genericcentre/projectfinder. However, they are only a part of an ever-changing educational environment, at both school and university level, which is constantly being reviewed by government.

Reviews such as the *Inquiry into A-Level Standards* sought to resolve the major concerns relating to the grading of A-levels. The report from this inquiry has proposed both medium- and long-term recommendations, which will ultimately affect the school mathematics curriculum and the skill-base of the engineering students of the future (Tomlinson, 2002).

A major project commissioned by the Teaching and Learning Research Programme, *Techno-Mathematical Literacies in the Workplace*, will look at the fusion 'of mathematical, ICT and workplace-specific competencies' and is expected to report in 2006 (TLRP, 2003).

The *Post-14 Mathematics Inquiry* was established in response to a recommendation in the Roberts (2002) report to ensure that the UK has a strong supply of young people with good mathematical knowledge and skills that meet the wide-ranging needs of employers and further and higher education. Recommendations were made on changes to the curriculum, qualifications and pedagogy for those aged 14 and over in schools, colleges and higher educational institutions (Smith, 2004).

Recommendations made in these reports involve major changes that will affect the content, approach and the education of engineers in the UK. Implementation will be a formidable task; the intention is, however, to provide a vision for the future so that each step can progress towards the goal of improving student learning within institutions.

At a structural level, there is now an Advisory Committee for Mathematics Education which is addressing the 'mathematics problem' in a unified way. A National Centre for Excellence in Mathematics Teaching will provide much-needed support for mathematics teachers at all levels, and for students at various transitions, including the move from school to university.

In conclusion, higher education has been aware for some time of a 'mathematics problem' that has arisen due to a rapid decline in students' mathematical skills between 1990 and 2003. Many engineering and mathematics departments have taken individual and collaborative steps to ease the transition from school to higher education. This situation is ongoing, and academic departments will continually need to be aware of developments and adjust their teaching strategies to provide the best possible learning experience for incoming engineering students.

Acknowledgements

The authors of this chapter wish to acknowledge their indebtedness to the many people who contributed to the work of the LTSN MathsTEAM. These include: Paul Chin and Steve Walker, LTSN Physical Sciences; Ellen Packham, The UK Centre for Materials Education; Tony Croft, Loughborough University; Doug Quinney, Keele University; Mike Barry, University of Bristol; Richard Atkinson, University of Birmingham; Bjoern Hassler, Cambridge University.

References

Anderson, J., Austin, K., Barnard, T., Chetwynd, A. and Kahn, P. (2000) 'Supporting student learning', *Teaching Mathematics and its Applications*, 19 (4): 166–172.

Appleby, J. (2003) 'University of Newcastle upon Tyne', *Diagnostic Testing for Mathematics*, LTSN MathsTEAM.

Beale, R. (2003) 'Use of Mathcad to assist in the teaching of second year engineering mathematics', *Maths for Engineering and Science*, LTSN MathsTEAM.

Challis, N. (2003) 'Using technology to teach mathematics to first year engineers', *Maths for Engineering and Science*, LTSN MathsTEAM.

Christy, J. (2003) 'Developing the interface between engineering and mathematics at Edinburgh University', *Maths for Engineering and Science*, LTSN MathsTEAM.

Cook, J. (2003) 'Glasgow Caledonian University mathematics summer school', *Maths Support for Students*, LTSN MathsTEAM.

Davies, A. and Fitzharris, A. (2003) 'Student proctors: a peer support system', *Maths Support for Students*, LTSN MathsTEAM.

Donelan, M. and Wallace, J. (1998) 'Peer-assisted learning – a truly co-operative initiative', *Students Supporting Students. SEDA Paper 105*, Staff and Educational Development Association.

Engineering Council (2000) *Measuring the Mathematics Problem*, London: Engineering Council.

Evans, A. and Jackman, S. (2003) 'Using the graphics calculator to support mathematics for engineering students', *Maths for Engineering and Science*, LTSN MathsTEAM.

Goodlad, S. (ed.) (1995) *Students as Tutors and Mentors*, London: Kogan Page.

Henry, M. (2003) 'Simulation of linear and non-linear dynamic systems using spreadsheets', *Maths for Engineering and Science*, LTSN MathsTEAM.

IMA (1995) *Mathematics Matters in Engineering*, Southend-on-Sea: Institute of Mathematics and its Applications.

IMA (1999) *Engineering Mathematics Matters*, Southend-on-Sea: Institute of Mathematics and its Applications.

Lawson, D. (1997) 'What can we expect of "A" level mathematics students?', *Teaching Mathematics and its Applications* 16 (4): 151–156.

Lawson, D. (2003) 'Coventry University', *Diagnostic Testing for Mathematics*, LTSN MathsTEAM.

Lawson, D., Croft, A. C. and Haplin, M. (2001) *Good Practice in the Provision of Mathematics Support Centres*, LTSN Maths, Stats & OR Network.

LMS (1995) *Tackling the Mathematics Problem*, London: The London Mathematical Society, Institute for Mathematics and its Applications and the Royal Statistical Society.

Malpas, R. S. (2000) *The Universe of Engineering – A UK Perspective*, London: The Royal Academy of Engineering.

Mustoe, L. (2002) 'Paper over the cracks? Mathematics for engineering undergraduates', *Mathematics Today* 38 (3): 67–69.

Ponton, J. (2003) 'Process systems engineering – a course in computing and numerical methods for second year chemical engineers', *Maths for Engineering and Science*, LTSN MathsTEAM.

Quinney, D. *et al.* (forthcoming) *Action Research on Diagnostic Testing and Student Support Project Report*.

Roberts, G. (2002) *Set for Success: the supply of people with science, technology, engineering and mathematics skills*, London: HM Treasury.

Savage, M. D. and Roper, T. (2003) 'Streaming undergraduate physicists for mathematics teaching in year one', *Maths for Engineering and Science*, LTSN MathsTEAM.

SEFI Mathematics Working Group (2002) *Mathematics for the European Engineer: a curriculum for the twenty-first century*, Brussels, Belgium: SEFI HQ.

Sherwood, C. (2001) *Knowledge Management for E-Learning*, International Conference on Engineering Education, Oslo, Norway.

Smith, A. (2004) 'Making mathematics count', the Report of Professor Adrian Smith's Inquiry into Post-14 Mathematics Education, available online at http://www.maths inquiry.org.uk/report/toc.html (accessed 22 May 2004).

Steele, C. (2000) 'A streamed system of mathematics courses II', Paper from the Institute of Mathematics and its Applications (IMA) Conference *Mathematical Education of Engineers III*, Loughborough.

Sutherland, R. and Pozzi, S. (1995) *The Changing Mathematical Background of Undergraduate Engineers*, London: Engineering Council.

Royal Society, The (1998) 'Engineers – the supply side: executive summary', available online at http://www.royalsoc.ac.uk/files/statfiles/document-62.pdf (accessed 29 April 2003).

Thomas, C. (2003) 'A game show format for first year problem classes in mathematical modelling', *Maths for Engineering and Science*, LTSN MathsTEAM.

TLRP (2003) 'Techno-mathematical literacies in the workplace', *Teaching and Learning Research Programme*, available online at http://www.tlrp.org/proj/phase111/hoyles.htm (accessed 14 July 2003).

Tomlinson, M. (2002) *Inquiry into A-Level Standards*, London: Department of Education and Skills.

8

Technology in support of learning

Phil Barker

Introduction

Computers pervade all areas of an engineer's life: controlling machinery and experimental equipment, modelling and simulating real-life processes, data reduction and analysis, communication and information retrieval. Not surprisingly their use in undergraduate engineering courses is commonplace: students need to learn how to use this tool of the trade. However, the role of computers in engineering education is greater than this, computers are used as an aid to teaching and learning. This chapter addresses using technology to learn, rather than learning to use technology. However, it will be seen that there is a link between the two: where a technology-based approach is useful to a practising engineer for solving a problem it is often also found to be useful to a student needing to understand a concept. Thus, we find that students and teachers use computers for their ability to model complex behaviour, to handle large numbers of calculations, for communication and for finding information.

Much has been written about the potential of technology to reform education. Frequently the writer is advocating the widespread uptake of an emerging technology: for example, Thomas Edison is quoted as saying, 'I believe that the motion picture is destined to revolutionize our educational system and that in a few years it will supplant largely, if not entirely, the use of textbooks' (quoted in Cuban, 1986: 9). This chapter is based on reports of technology in use in engineering or similar courses: we hope that by doing so we have avoided talking about what could happen instead of reflecting on what is happening.

Conversational model for teaching and learning

In order to help understand the role of computers in learning and teaching it is useful to have a model for what happens during the learning and teaching process. The model which I will use is Laurillard's conversational framework (Laurillard, 1993), which describes an ideal and idealized teaching and learning scenario in terms of the activities of the teacher and the student, and media used for the interactions between the two. As well as identifying the roles of the teacher and the student, Laurillard distinguishes between the student and teacher operating at the level of descriptions and the student and teacher operating at the level of action within a 'world' which the teacher sets up as a model of the real-world concept being taught.

Acting at the level of descriptions, there is a 'conversation' between the student and the teacher where the teacher provides an explanation of a concept to the student, the student describes their understanding of this concept back to the teacher and, if necessary, the teacher re-describes any part of the concept which they feel the student does not fully grasp. There is also a conversation at the level of actions: the teacher creates a 'world' within which the student can act and sets the student a goal within this world. The student acts to achieve this goal, and the teacher provides feedback on these actions. The student may then modify their actions in the light of the feedback from the teacher. This is illustrated in Figure 8.1.

Operation at the levels of description and action are linked through a process of adaptation and reflection. Thus, the teacher adapts the tasks set for the students in the light of the students' description of the concept, and the teacher reflects on the students' actions in completing this task to modify their explanation of the concept. Similarly, the students adapt their actions in the light of the teacher's description of the concept and reflect on the feedback from the task to modify their own description of the concept.

Readers will immediately recognize real-life teaching is rarely as interactive and adaptive as this model describes, outside of one-to-one tutorials there is little scope for the iterative refinement of descriptions and tasks implied in the model. However, it should not be too difficult to see how real-life teaching includes elements from this model: through lectures and texts teachers explain concepts to their students; through laboratory exercises and problem sheets students are set tasks which involve them in using their understanding of these concepts to achieve a goal, often in a simplified or idealized 'world'. Tutorials and questions during lectures provide some scope for teachers to modify their explanations on the basis of what students tell them of their understanding or how students undertake the tasks which are set for them, however, year-on-year refinement of a course provides much more scope for reflection and adaptation.

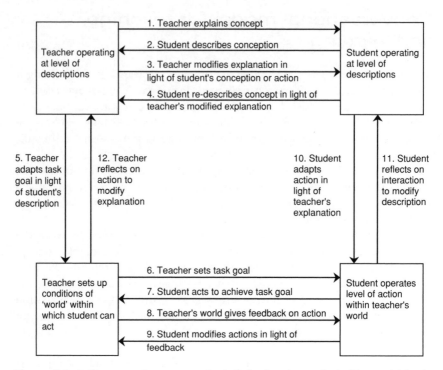

Figure 8.1 A diagrammatic representation of the learning and teaching activities in Laurillard's conversational framework (adapted from Laurillard, 1993)

Other factors in teaching and learning

The conversational model addresses the teaching of skills and knowledge, and the development of understanding. However, during their years at university, students are expected to move from learning what their teacher tells them they need to, using resources supplied by the teacher, to identifying their own learning needs and finding resources which fulfil these. The model does not explicitly address the work that a student might do themselves, individually or in groups, or how a teacher might encourage this.

Also, outside the model of the conversational framework are issues relating to motivation and access. These affect both learner and the teacher: addressing the interests of the student is important if they are to engage in the teaching and learning process, but we must also address the motivation of the teacher, which may be personal or may derive from institutional imperatives. Thus, a lecturer may decide to use a computer-based learning resource because she thinks it will provide her students with a break from sitting and listening to her talk, and she may decide to use a computer-marked assessment in order to reduce the burden of marking when classes are large. Also, it may be necessary to provide students with material which they can access at any time from any place.

EASEIT-Eng: information on the use of technology in UK engineering courses

The following sections describe the features of various types of teaching and learning technologies and their role in engineering education. Where possible these are illustrated with extracts from case studies or literature reports of real-life use of an example of this type of resource in UK higher education. Many of these extracts are taken from case studies produced by the EASEIT-Eng project so it is worth providing some background to this project first.

The EASEIT-Eng project was concerned with providing evaluations of third-party computer-based learning resources with the aim of helping engineering lecturers who wanted to use such resources for their teaching. The project personnel believed that the only way to appraise whether a resource was suitable for use in teaching and learning was to base the evaluation on the real-life use of that resource in a real course. Therefore, they drew up an evaluation methodology which solicited the opinion of teachers and students who had been involved in an implementation of the resource in UK higher education. The information solicited from these evaluations are available as short case studies from the database on the Learning and Teaching Support Network Engineering Subject Centre (LTSN Engineering). For more information on the EASEIT-Eng project and the evaluation methodology used see the EASEIT-Eng website.

We must note here that comments, positive or negative, about a feature of a resource which are made in this report should not be taken as being indicative of whether the overall evaluation of the package was positive or negative. For example, in the section on text and hypertext immediately below, many negative comments come from evaluations material produced by the Electronic Design Education Consortium (EDEC). EDEC materials were, in fact, well received, in fact EASEIT-Eng found them to be among the most widely-used text-heavy computer-based resources for engineering teaching and learning. As a result of them being widely used, negative comments about text are more likely to be sourced from evaluations of EDEC materials than from other, less successful packages.

Technology-based learning materials

Text and hypertext

Leaving face-to-face contact, as in lectures, aside, text remains the primary medium for communication between teacher and students. Lecture notes and text books allow teachers to explain concepts to students in a way that can be accessed by the student at any time, in any place providing they have a copy with them. Hypertext allows text to be structured and accessed in ways which may improve the efficiency of the descriptions, for example the teacher may provide a link to further details which need only be followed by those students who feel they need to be told more. Publishing text and hypertext on the Internet so that it can be accessed on demand can enhance its availability, at least to students with a suitable connection.

Two major classes of student response to text in computer-based resources can be found in EASEIT-Eng case studies. The first is that resources with little text are often perceived by students as lacking depth of coverage: the students often suggest that they should contain links to a glossary or explanations of the more difficult concepts (EASEIT-Eng, 2000–2002, case study 4). On the other hand, where lots of text is presented on the computer students often commented that they would rather have had it on paper (EASEIT-Eng, 2000–2002, case studies 39, 43, 45 and 60). In some cases, individual students listed the 'print button' as one of the most useful features of the resource. This complaint about lack of hard copy of the text reflects on one of the more common observations about students using computers to learn – they tend not to take notes as much as they would in a lecture theatre (EASEIT-Eng, 2000–2002, case studies 28, 32 and 51). This is clearly a problem inasmuch as it deprives the student of familiar revision material, and it may represent a deeper problem in that it seems to indicate that the students adopt a rather passive learning style while reading. Once identified, this problem can be addressed by, for example, having the students fill out a workbook as they go through the material (EASEIT-Eng, 2000–2002, case study 20).

Whatever the shortcomings of expecting students to read text from a computer screen, they are offset by some advantages. One advantage is that text delivered over the Internet in web pages as documents in a virtual learning environment (VLE) is available (in theory) to students off-campus and out of hours. This is dealt with in more depth in a later section of this chapter. A second is that the text can be delivered as hypertext, or with a search facility to direct the students to the relevant section. Students seem to expect the advantages of searchable hypertext when text is computer based: several EASEIT-Eng evaluations elicited comments from students suggesting this, for example that they would like a hyperlinked glossary that a simple page-turning navigation scheme was 'boring' (EASEIT-Eng, 2000–2002, case study 4), and made it difficult to go straight to the relevant section (EASEIT-Eng, 2000–2002, case study 27). However, an over-complex web of pages could leave students feeling lost and unsure whether they had covered all the material (EASEIT-Eng, 2000–2002, case study 21).

Multimedia: images, animation and video

Various multimedia resources are frequently used to enhance the presentation of the concepts being taught, both as a supplement to verbal presentation in a lecture or to textual presentation in a computer-based tutorial. These are frequently well-received by students: in the words of one tutor using such a resource, 'I think the animations do make it click for them' (EASEIT-Eng, 2000–2002, case study 8); and students often remark that they find animations are, if not clearer than textual explanations, at least something which 'keeps you interested as opposed to pages and pages of text' (EASEIT-Eng, 2000–2002, case study 34). However, it should be remembered that the response of an individual student to this type of teaching material will depend on that student's learning style – some students prefer verbal or textual presentations to visual ones. There were two major reasons for using multimedia which can be drawn out from the EASEIT-Eng evaluations: as a substitute for students seeing the real object and to help students visualize complex abstract processes.

Several EASEIT-Eng evaluations were concerned with the output of a project called CALVisual, which has produced a database of images of building sites and construction work for use in teaching and learning civil and construction engineering. Images from this database had been used in lectures and for online learning as a substitute for visits to building sites, which had become impractical due to large class sizes. Given these rather common circumstances, the CALVisual material gave the students an opportunity to see building defects and construction practices to which they would not otherwise have had access (EASEIT-Eng, 2000–2002, case studies 9, 15, 17 and 18). Of course, the direct benefit to the students in this case came from the use of images, not from the technology by which the images were mediated, however, the EASEIT-Eng evaluations noted that: the lecturer found computer-based images embedded in power point presentations to be easier to manage than acetates and slides; and the students preferred being able to access the images online or off a CD-ROM rather than as handouts (EASEIT-Eng, 2000–2002, case study 17).

In other cases, images and animations were used as a supplement rather than a substitute for students seeing the real object. For example, in one case, students prepared for practical lab work by working through a tutorial which contained labelled photographs of the actual lab equipment they were to use (EASEIT-Eng, 2000–2002, case study 19). Both tutor and students agreed that this reduced the amount of valuable lab time which was spent trying to work out which knob to turn and which dial to read in order to perform the experiment.[1] Another example of a similar use of multimedia is a tutorial aimed at familiarizing students with the use of a surveying instrument before field-work. This tutorial was used for self-paced work by the students and for lecture demonstrations. In the words of the tutor: 'you can show this to 80 students on a screen but you can't get 80 students round an instrument to demonstrate it' (EASEIT-Eng, 2000–2002, case study 33).

Animation, in particular, is well received by students where visualization of a physical structure or change can be difficult. For example, rotatable representations of three-dimensional crystal structures in a material science resource were described by a student as 'one of the major pluses . . . [they] explain things so simply'. Or the animation might be of an abstract concept, for example, phase composition changes around a eutectic point, about which a student said, 'you got a picture from the words, but you look at that and you don't need any of the words and you see it just working!' (EASEIT-Eng, 2000–2002, case study 34).

The examples above show multimedia enhancing the teacher's explanation of a concept. In the conversational model outlined above (see Figure 8.1), multimedia can also be used to enhance the student's description of their understanding of a concept in response to the teacher. EASEIT-Eng did not find many examples of multimedia used in this way, partly due to the idealized nature of the conversational framework, and no doubt partly due to the difficulty of producing multimedia for a student report. However, there were examples where students gave the fact that graphics produced while using a computer-based resource could be easily imported into reports written in MS Word or simply printed out and glued into a lab book (EASEIT-Eng, 2000–2002, case studies 58 and 19 respectively).

Modelling and simulation software

Simulations differ from other forms of multimedia in that they use a computational model of a system to mimic the behaviour of that system given different input parameters. It is possible to present students with simulations in such a way that the inputs are pre-defined and cannot be set by the student, however, apart from a certain flexibility for the author, such use of simulations differs little from the use of animation. The present section will only consider simulations which are interactive inasmuch as the student can vary the parameters with which the simulation runs.

The distinction between modelling and simulation software is that with modelling software the student builds the simulation themselves. They may be presented with a toolkit representing component parts and the rules for their behaviour with which the students can build complex simulations of a system under study. The most common modelling software in use in engineering higher education are the various computer-aided design tools for creating simulations of electronic circuits.

Within the conversational framework outlined above (see Figure 8.1), the educational use of simulation and modelling is that it allows the teacher to construct a world within which the student can act to perform tasks.

The important thing is that the student should be actively engaging with the consequences of the ideas which underpin the concept being taught in such a way that brings out any misconceptions that he or she may be harbouring. A typical protocol for achieving this goal is the predict–observe–explain cycle, where the student is asked to predict the behaviour of a system, then to observe what actually happens before explaining any differences. In terms of modelling rather than simulation this corresponds to an iterative design process where observation of the first attempt at mimicking the target system (i.e. the first prediction) is used to inform refinements. It should be stressed that the use of interactive simulations does not, in itself, imply that the student is actively engaged in learning. For example, if the student is required to work through a set of pre-defined tasks using the simulation, changing variables and noting the response, then there is little difference between simulation and demonstration. Thus, it can be useful to distinguish between the potential for interactivity inherent in a simulation and the activity level of the student using it (Friesen *et al.*, 2003).

There is, of course, nothing in the arguments above which gives any reason for using simulation or modelling as opposed to a real hands-on practical task. However, simulation allows students to attempt tasks which simply would not be feasible in any other form. A frequently cited example of this is running a nuclear power station or any equipment where cost, safety and time-scale problems put the real experience beyond the reach of students. Examples from EASEIT-Eng include managing a construction company for two years and designing a Wind Farm (EASEIT-Eng, 2000–2002, case studies 42 and 70 respectively). In other cases the task, in reality, might simply be more error prone (and hence more frustrating, time consuming and potentially misleading for the student), and more expensive. Lecturers and students using circuit simulation software frequently cite such advantages for the simulation over real circuits as the software being quicker, more accurate and cheaper (EASEIT-Eng, 2000–2002, case study 52), allowing rapid trial and error experimentation (EASEIT-Eng, 2000–2002, case studies 31 and 50) and being less prone to faulty connections (EASEIT-Eng, 2000–2002, case study 31).

It is not only the physical systems which can be made more accessible through simulation and modelling: theoretical concepts can also be brought to the student for experimentation. Typically, these concepts would be framed in mathematics which is too complex or too tedious for the student to solve for every what-if scenario worth exploring (EASEIT-Eng, 2000–2002, case studies 52 and 55).

As well as being used as a substitute or supplement to real lab-based activity, simulation and modelling are also used in engineering courses because they are integral parts of real-life engineering design. Thus, teachers say that they give their students tasks using simulation software since in doing so they prepare their students 'for real-life industrial design processes by giving them an opportunity to use commercial, proprietary software and practice' (EASEIT-Eng, 2000–2002, case study 70). Students also appreciate the use of industry standard tools on their course:

> it's like pre-graduating, we can be using these types of programmes [that industry use], it will just make it a lot easier. If we can learn them before we leave, then it'll make the difference between getting a job and not getting a job . . . if we can use these programmes already then it saves [the company] having to give us training.
>
> (EASEIT-Eng, 2000–2002, case study 55)

In one example of how this thinking is embedded into a course (EASEIT-Eng, 2000–2002, case study 50), the tutor accompanied lectures on the subject being studied (electronic circuit design) with a series of practical activities starting with the use of circuit simulation software to design a circuit, then using a computer-aided design tool to plan the printed circuit board, before fabricating the circuit in practical lab sessions.

A cautionary note needs to be made before we move on: simulation in general, and modelling activities in particular, are not always well received by students. There are, perhaps, two main types of adverse reaction caused by the students' lack of familiarity with the software being used and the mode of learning, respectively. Lack of familiarity with the software is most frequently mentioned in EASEIT-Eng evaluations, where students complain that they spend more time struggling with how to use the software with which they are to model an engineering process than they spend thinking about the process itself (EASEIT-Eng, 2000–2002, case studies 21 and 25). Lack of familiarity with the mode of learning is more frequently implicit in EASEIT-Eng evaluations than explicitly commented on, but we can comment that it is more frequently the tutors and lecturers who comment on simulation allowing an experimental 'what-if' approach to learning rather than students commenting on this being the approach which they took.

Communication tools

Communication between tutor and students is a core part of teaching and learning. The role of technology in the initial communication of ideas from the tutor to the students is dealt with in the sections above, and its role in assessment as a form of communication is covered in a later section. That leaves discussion as a means of prompting students to think through and check their understanding of a concept either in the form of communication with the tutor or with other students (possibly with the tutor as moderator). Technologies such as bulletin boards and email have been used to facilitate this communication, as have technologies which facilitate 'polls' which take a snapshot of student understanding.

To take an example reported in an EASEIT-Eng case study (EASEIT-Eng, 2000–2002, case study 38), a tutor set up a discussion forum to which his students were required to submit a minimum of 20 short postings on a topic of their choice. Students could reply to other postings or start a new topic. The tutor felt that participating in the discussions helped his students learn from their peers. Interestingly, some students had reservations about this since they felt they did not know which contributions by their fellow students they could trust as being accurate. The tutor also stated that the technology helped in facilitating an asynchronous discussion, which gave the students time to consider what they would post; students appreciated the asynchronous nature of the discussion since it gave them control over when they made their contributions. In another use of a similar system (EASEIT-Eng, 2000–2002, case study 30) the same tutor went a step further and initiated a web-based peer review system. M.Sc. students posted short articles on topics of their own choice and reviewed the postings of other students. The tutor hoped that this would increase depth at which students studied topics on course and increase their level of engagement with course, and the EASEIT-Eng evaluation results suggest that this was, indeed, achieved.

Perhaps the most difficult aspect of using a communication tool when teaching is persuading the students to use it. This is especially true when students are campus based or have direct access to each other and the tutor (EASEIT-Eng, 2000–2002, case study 18). In the cases discussed above the tutor overcame this problem by making posting to the discussion forum compulsory and assessed.

Computer-aided assessment (CAA)

Assessment represents a form of communication between the student and the tutor with the aim of providing information about the student's level of understanding to either the student or the teacher. If the aim is to provide the student or the teacher with information on their progress towards achieving the required level of understanding then we are talking about formative assessment. In contrast, summative assessment provides information on the level of the student's understanding at the end of the course. Summative assessment would normally contribute to the student's course mark and, ultimately, to his or her degree classification and, as such, it is often described as being 'high stakes', whereas formative assessment is 'low stakes'. Because of this difference, computer-aided assessment is much more frequently used for formative assessment than for summative.

We will start by looking at cases from EASEIT-Eng where computer-aided assessment has been used to support simple quizzes for formative assessment. These are typically short-answer questions: multiple choice, single numerical answers, or the student may be asked to click on the relevant part of an image. A common feature is that the student's answer is marked automatically and the student is provided with immediate feedback. This type of use of CAA is often found in computer-based tutorial packages, which may contain individual questions which the student answers as they work through the material, or may contain tests at the end of the each topic. Sometimes the test is a stand-alone CAA application used to support learning through other resources. There are some advantages relating to the integration of the questions into the resource which the students use for learning. For example, students have remarked that a question in the middle of some text can act to wake them up and set them thinking about what they have just read (EASEIT-Eng, 2000–2002, case study 51). In other examples the answers provided by the student were used by the tutorial software to decide what learning material the student should see next (Badcock *et al.*, 1996; EASEIT-Eng, 2000–2002, case study 61). These points excepted, the feedback from staff and students tends to be similar regardless of whether the formative assessment is supporting learning with computer-based resources or more traditional modes. Three points are worth noting from this feedback: automatic marking is popular with staff; formative assessment is popular with students; students often do the formative assessment before attempting to learn the material and work to the assessment (i.e. they learn what is needed to answer the question). We will look at each of these in turn.

Typical of the lecturer's response to automatically marked formative assessment is that from two case studies which both used commercial computer-aided assessment products to support courses (EASEIT-Eng, 2000–2002, case studies 1 and 39). In both cases the lecturer used the CAA system with dual aims in mind: to provide more rapid feedback to his students without an unreasonable increase in his workload. Both lecturers felt that this had been achieved, although there was an increase in the workload associated with setting the tests: in other words, some up-front work is necessary in using the CAA system before the benefit of automatic marking is accrued. As well as pedagogical benefits for the students, both lecturers found it useful for them to be able to monitor their students' progress: one said:

> all the records are kept online in a database. That's a really good feature, all for minimum effort on my part. It allows me to see what, if anything, is causing a problem to students, so I know if there's something I need to go through more fully and so on.
>
> (EASEIT-Eng, 2000–2002, case study 1)

The other noted that for this to be really useful it was necessary that all students use the system, and so he used the marks from these tests to contribute towards the students' final mark for the course.

Students, on the whole, appreciated being able to check on their progress while working through the course. According to one tutor, students found the self-assessment sections of a computer-based tutorial system 'irresistible'

(EASEIT-Eng, 2000–2002, case study 44). Students especially appreciate immediate feedback whenever they choose to take the test (EASEIT-Eng, 2000–2002, case studies 1 and 39) – in fact, the most common negative comments relate to students wanting more in-depth feedback and students being unable to find computers when they want to take the test. It almost goes without saying that students are interested in formative assessment since they wish to check whether they are doing well enough to pass the end of course exam, and so assessments which are similar to the end of course summative assessment are especially appreciated (EASEIT-Eng, 2000–2002, case study 35). The other issue which emerges from EASEIT-Eng evaluations is related to this, and also shows how students use the formative assessment to inform their learning strategies. Students will sometimes do the assessment for a module before attempting to learn the material in that module (EASEIT-Eng, 2000–2002, case study 36) and will often only do as much work as is necessary to pass the assessment (EASEIT-Eng, 2000–2002, case studies 1 and 52).

At the beginning of this section we drew notice to the distinction between 'high stakes' and 'low stakes' assessment, with the comment that computer-aided assessment was more frequently accepted for use in 'low stakes' assessment. In the succeeding paragraphs we noted that: lecturers can benefit if all students are motivated to take the assessment (i.e. if the mark counts towards the course mark); students will use formative assessment to guide their learning strategy; and, not surprisingly, prefer the formative assessments to reflect the type of assessment that will contribute to their final mark for the course. Thus, it will be clear that successful computer-based formative assessment requires as much care in matching questions to learning objectives as end of course summative assessment.

In focusing on formative assessment so far we have largely ignored two areas of concern regarding computer-aided assessment. First the problem of cheating in exams which count towards the student's degree classification and, second, the extent to which technology can assist assessment of higher order learning objectives. The former problem will not be discussed in depth here since the solutions to it are, by and large, the same as the solutions to plagiarism and cheating in conventionally delivered assessments. We should, however, note that the many CAA systems allow randomization of the parameters in numerical problems, or equivalent problems to be drawn randomly from a larger set. Also, the analysis of marks available in some CAA systems includes a check on whether two students have given similar replies.

Learning objectives can be categorized by the level of learning which they encapsulate. At a low level of learning students may be expected to remember certain facts; at higher levels of learning they would be expected to apply their learning to specific problems or to make judgements as to the validity of different possible approaches to solving a complex problem (Bloom, 1956).

The type of question which can be automatically marked by a computer are objective tests (e.g. multiple choice assessment, answers to numerical problems) which tend to focus on the lower level learning objectives (Heard et al., 1997). In order to assess higher order learning it is necessary to make use of more discursive approaches to assessment such as presentations or report writing. Technology can support this type of assessment inasmuch as it can support discursive activities. In the example of using an online discussion forum discussed above (EASEIT-Eng, 2000–2002, case study 38), the tutor graded each posting, and the average of the top 20 marks for each student counted to his or her course mark. Unlike automatic marking, this use of technology in assessment did not aim to save the tutor time, however the tutor felt that the depth of learning which was made apparent in the discussions justified the extra effort.

Use of technology in delivering learning materials

The use of technology in learning and teaching engineering covers not just the type of learning material which is used, as has been discussed so far, but also the way in which that material is delivered to the student. This section covers two examples of the use of technology to deliver learning materials: tutorial systems which bundle many different types of learning resource into a single integrated package, and the use of the World Wide Web over the Internet or an intranet, including learning management systems and virtual learning.

Tutorial systems

Tutorial systems are software packages which bundle together resources of the types discussed above in an attempt to produce a rounded treatment of a topic. They are typically suitable for students studying alone, although that does not preclude their use by groups of students, and they may be used to replace lectures in a course. Typically they will comprise a textual and graphical explanation of a topic, which may be supplemented with simulation-based activities for the student. Formative assessment is provided in the form of questions interspersed with the main content of the tutorial and there may be some form of summative assessment at the end of each topic. In some cases the path which the student takes through the material may be influenced by diagnostic tests embedded in the tutorial: a simple example of this can be seen in the 'Computer Aided Learning in Fluid Dynamics' course at Clyde Virtual University (Badcock et al., 1996) which is driven by presenting students with a scenario and asking them questions, the correctness of the student's response determines the depth of explanation which follows. Another example of a tutorial system which adapts on the basis of knowledge about the student can be seen in the 'Hypermedia Structures and Systems' course at Eindhoven

University of Technology (De Bra, 2000) where the hypertext links change depending on how far through the course a student is. Thus, for example, every occurrence of a simple term (such as 'hypertext') might be linked to a glossary for a student at the start of the course but once the student has shown that they have grasped that concept the term will no longer be linked. Conversely, a student who has progressed some way through the course who revisits a page from the introduction will find the content has changed to include references to the material which the student has studied since first visiting that page. A simple example of this adaptability is the contents page which only shows links to topics on the course which the student has studied or is likely to understand given the progress they have made through the course.

Learning management systems

A Learning Management System (LMS, also known as a virtual learning environment, VLE) is software which synthesizes computer-mediated communications with online delivery of course materials (usually web based) (Britain and Liber, 1999). This requires that the LMS should allow a course tutor to mount course materials on a web server and create conferencing or bulletin board services for the students. Access to these materials and services should be controlled on a class-level basis, which requires that the system needs to keep a database of users, their status, the courses they are taking, etc. In some systems this database may be linked to an institutional information management system (the ability to link virtual learning environments with institutional management systems gives us what are sometimes known as managed learning environments, or MLEs).

It is worth considering briefly the criteria by which an LMS can be judged or evaluated: hopefully by looking at these criteria we can gain some idea of how an LMS is best used. Britain and Liber (1999) have used two frameworks for describing how an LMS system might best support e-learning: the first is based on Laurillard's conversational framework (Laurillard, 1993); the second is based on a viable systems model (see Britain and Liber (1999) for references). From the conversational framework they conclude that an LMS should: provide tools for discussions which are integrated with the learning material being presented to the students; allow the teacher to adapt the activities which individual students are set in the light of feedback on their progress; allow students to interact with the learning material and how it is presented to them; and help the student and the teacher reflect on the student's actions.

The Viable Systems Model approach to evaluating LMSs focuses on how educators can cope with managing groups of students, and Britain and Liber suggest six functionalities necessary in an LMS: resource negotiation, coordination, monitoring, individualization, self-organization and adaptation.

The requirements that follow from this approach that were not brought out by the conversational framework are the importance of students being able to work together in groups without being led by the teacher, and the importance of students being able to contribute their own materials.

The conclusion of Britain and Liber is that Learning Management Systems have the potential to be of great benefit in supporting modes of learning which are time intensive using traditional methods. Examples are collaborative learning, discussion-led learning, student-centred learning and resource-based learning, which are traditionally supported by tutorials and project work.

Britain and Liber present a picture of what Learning Management Systems are capable of, the EASEIT-Eng evaluations allow us a glimpse at how they are being used.

Many of the case studies of Learning Management Systems show that the main use which is being made of the LMS (whether by design or not) is that of delivering course notes and similar resources. Frequently, these resources might as well be paper-based as computer-based, for example in one evaluation (EASEIT-Eng, 2000–2002, case study 62) a student described their use of an LMS saying 'most of the time we were just printing off notes'. That is not to say such a use doesn't have its value; in the same evaluation students appreciated having an 'archive' which could be used as 'a backup, if you miss a lecture and you miss the notes'. Delivering course notes and other material via an LMS makes them available 'anytime, any-place', something which students do appreciate. However, it is also noticeable that in many evaluations students are accessing material on LMSs using departmental computer labs (since dial-in access may be slow or may not be available) and they may encounter problems if these rooms are frequently booked or otherwise heavily used (EASEIT-Eng, 2000–2002, case studies 18, 38, 39, 43 and 72). The advice which one student said he would give to others taking the same course in the future is worth bearing in mind here. It was that students should have their own computer and printer (EASEIT-Eng, 2000–2002, case study 43).

We have discussed above the benefits and issues around using computer-mediated communications, which stand whether or not the communication tool is part of a suite of tools offered by a Learning Management System. The EASEIT-Eng project did not find any examples of tight integration of communication tools with delivery of learning material in engineering subjects. An example of a system which does this is the Open University's Digital Discourse Environment (see the Digital Discourse Environment, D3E, website for more details) which can be used for what the developers call 'document centred discourse'. The way the system is presented to the end user is quite simple: opening a document (which may be a simple web page or an interactive java simulation) in a web browser also opens a discussion thread on the topic of the document. The document and discussion can be in different frames in the same browser window or can be in two different browser windows. The most readily accessible example of the Digital

Discourse Environment in use is the *Journal of Interactive Media in Education* (*JIME*, and Buckingham Shum and Sumner, 2001).

Final comments

So what technologies can best support learning? From the lecturer and student feedback received during the EASEIT-Eng evaluations it seems that images (especially moving images) and simulations are especially well received, and they are appreciated because they provide ways of understanding a concept which are not otherwise available. Online assessments are also appreciated, they can lighten the assessment burden on lecturers and provide students with instant feedback on their progress. A final thought, students will only do the work they think the teacher expects them to do: if the use of technology seems like an optional extra, then the students won't use it. Technology-based resources must be integrated into the course so that they seem to the student to be as natural a part of the course as lectures, tutorials and lab classes.

Note

1   The implementation of this computer-based tutorial was such that students couldn't do the lab work unless they had worked through the tutorial; with the previously available paper-based preparation material the students tended to wait until the lab session before looking at photographs.

References

Badcock, K., Littlejohn, A. and Baldwin, A. (1996) *Computer Aided Learning in Fluid Dynamics (CALF)*, Clyde Virtual University (online), UK: available from http://cvu.strath.ac.uk/courseware/calf/CALF/index/web_calf.html (accessed September 2003).

Bloom, B. S. (ed.) (1956) *Taxonomy of Educational Objectives, the Classification of Educational Goals – Handbook I: Cognitive Domain*, New York: McKay.

Britain, S. and Liber, O. (1999) *A Framework for Pedagogical Evaluation of Virtual Learning Environments*, Jisc (online), UK: available from http://www.jisc.ac.uk/uploaded_documents/jtap-041.doc (accessed September 2003).

Buckingham Shum, S. and Sumner, T. (2001) 'JIME: an interactive journal for interactive media', *First Monday* 6 (2): February. Available online at http://firstmonday.org/issues/issue6_2/buckingham_shum/ (accessed September 2003), also available as *Technical Report KMI-TR-99*, Knowledge Media Institute, Open University, UK: available online at http://kmi.open.ac.uk/publications/tr.cfm?trnumber=99 (accessed September 2003).

Cuban, L. (1986) *Teachers and Machines: the classroom use of technology since 1920*, New York: Teachers College Press.

De Bra, P. M. E. (2000) *Hypermedia Structures and Systems*, Eindhoven University of Technology, The Netherlands: available online at http://wwwis.win.tue.nl/2L690/ (accessed August 2003).

Digital Document Discourse Environment (D3E) website, UK: available online at http://d3e.open.ac.uk/ (accessed September 2003).

EASEIT-Eng website, UK: available online at http://www.easeit-eng.ac.uk/ (accessed September 2003).

EASEIT-Eng (2000–2002) *Software Reviews and Case Studies*, UK: available online at http://www.ltsneng.ac.uk/resources/res.asp?restype=swcs&keyid=*n* where *n* at the end of the URL is replaced with the number of the case study, for example, case study 60 is available at http://www.ltsneng.ac.uk/resources/res.asp?restype=swcs&keyid=60 (accessed September 2003).

Fluid Dynamics (CALF), Clyde Virtual University, UK: available online at http://cvu.strath.ac.uk/courseware/calf/CALF/index/web_calf.html (accessed September 2003).

Friesen, N., Fisher, S. and Roberts, A. (2003) 'CanCore guidelines for the implementation of learning object metadata version 1.9 section 5.3: Interactivity level', Athabasca University, Canada. Available online at www.cancore.org.

Heard, S., Nicol, J. and Heath, S. (1997) *Setting Effective Objective Tests*, Aberdeen: MERTaL Publications.

Journal of Interactive Media in Education, (*JIME*), ISSN: 1365–893X, UK: available online at http://www-jime.open.ac.uk/ (accessed September 2003).

Laurillard, D. (1993) *Rethinking University Teaching, a Framework for the Effective Use of Educational Technology*, London: Routledge.

9

A critical look at innovative practice from the student perspective

---

Jennifer Case

For the novice teacher looking for advice, or the experienced teacher hoping to do something new, there is certainly no shortage of suggestions on how to improve one's teaching practice, or novel ideas to apply in one's course. There are more conferences, books, societies, magazines and articles on the web than even a team of people could hope to ingest in a lifetime. Indeed, this very book contains an excellent collection of current and useful exemplars of innovative practice. What is, possibly, less written about is the very common experience of finding out that things don't work out quite as one has planned. Although there are often very positive initial student responses to a new and different thing happening in their course, with time it might often become apparent that the dramatic planned for change in student learning is somewhat elusive, at least for part of the class. The present chapter explores student responses to a second-year chemical engineering course where the lecturer had adopted a range of innovative teaching practices with the intention of promoting better learning. In particular, a closer look is taken at instances where student learning outcomes did not match the lecturer's intentions, with the hope that this might provide useful insights for engineering educators who are, themselves, embarking upon change in their classroom practice.

Innovative practice in a chemical engineering course

The course under consideration in this chapter is a second-year chemical engineering course, something of a campus legend due to high student failure rates for as long as anyone could remember. Over the years lecturers had made various attempts to improve this course, including the use of collaborative study groups, more explicit teaching of problem solving and an entire revamp of the second-year curriculum. Latest in this line of innovators was Dr Barnes, who came determined to make a change, especially remembering her own experiences of the second year. In a discussion with me she noted: 'As a student, I struggled to come to grips with the concepts in this course. Now, as a teacher, I hope that I have some insight into the difficulties, and that I can help students to overcome them as well as to develop an enthusiasm for the material.'

In approaching this course she aimed to create a different environment to that which she had experienced as an undergraduate student, and which she had found alienating and unsupportive. She clearly saw her role as supporting and helping students as they went through a process of conceptual, meta-cognitive and personal development. She was convinced that a good teaching and learning environment could assist more students to succeed in this course. She was strongly influenced by a range of current ideas about teaching and learning, having attended a number of teaching workshops and being an active reader of literature on this topic.

Dr Barnes had as chief objective in her teaching of this course the development of students' conceptual understanding and metacognitive abilities, in addition to the existing (and previously almost exclusive) focus on the development of problem-solving skills. She recognized that aiming for deep approaches to learning and associated metacognitive development had implications for curriculum, teaching and assessment. Complementary changes were implemented in each of these domains, and will be described in what follows.

Curriculum

Overloaded curricula are common in engineering courses worldwide and this course was no exception. In order to 'cover' the required material, new concepts had to be presented at an alarming rate. Inspired by the maxim 'Cover Less, Uncover More', Dr Barnes decided that in order to achieve her aim of teaching and assessing for 'deep' understanding, the amount of material in the curriculum would need to be reduced. She already had an idea of which topics she felt were dispensable (either covered in later courses, or not fundamental to chemical engineering knowledge) but decided to enlist the support of her colleagues in this process. A workshop was held with all teaching staff in which the key exercise was deciding on critical outcomes for the various second-year courses. The existing curriculum was then presented and compared with this list, and on this basis the course content was reduced by approximately 25 per cent.

Teaching

The teaching strategies were designed with the aim of getting students to engage actively with concepts, something that is surprisingly uncommon in undergraduate science and engineering lectures. Primarily this involved replacing the traditional one-way transmission from the front of the classroom with methods such as posing questions to students, getting them to try problems on their own, to discuss issues with their classmates, to report back to the class and to ask questions. Following this, whole class discussion was used to tie together discussions, deal with alternative conceptions, and provide questions for further consideration. To try to break the passive note-taking habit, Dr Barnes developed a 'workbook' that had some information provided, gaps for students to fill in information as concepts were dealt with in class, and problems with space for students to try out their approaches. A description of one of Dr Barnes' lectures (from research fieldnotes) illustrates what this teaching approach entailed:

> In this morning's lecture Dr Barnes got the various groups to give feedback on the different types of heat capacity data they had used [in a group exercise started in the previous lecture]. She got the groups to focus in their feedback on the method they had used. Jane and Amina gave great feedback on how to use mean molar heat capacity. Then the class joker, James, reported on the polynomials – and engendered much mirth by scribbling on the board something that was actually incorrect. Dr Barnes then corrected him, at which he made a marginally better attempt. It was interesting that sometime at this stage Geoff (from the same group) gave an explanation from the floor of what needed to be done, which was very good. David reported on the graphical method – although he started writing up long equations which was a bit odd seeing as they hadn't used these. John then gave great feedback on using [mean] molar heat capacities – with a good method to get around the problem. Dr Barnes then asked the class which method they would prefer – and hopefully the case for mean molar heat capacities was made. Dr Barnes then got them to do exercise 1 to practise using heat capacities in energy balances. At the start she gave students time to play around with it – and then got someone to give the energy balance for this problem. Tim asked whether 100 kmol/s didn't imply the need for a $0.5v^2$ term – and she explained why not. She then went into solving the problem on the board. I was surprised that she used the polynomial method after having lauded mean molar heat capacities earlier on – but maybe just for practice I suppose. Students were asked to try exercise 2 for homework, which she will go through in class on Monday.

Dr Barnes also communicated to students a shift in emphasis away from the lecture providing everything that was needed to succeed in the course, towards an expectation that significant learning would take place in the tuto-rials and at home, both individually and with classmates. In a rather radical move in an engineering context, Dr Barnes also introduced a set of weekly journal tasks into the course. Students could choose to hand in the journal tasks, for which they received bonus class marks. Two of these tasks are repro-duced below by way of illustration.

Journal task   WEEK 5

Reflecting on the first class test:

1   Give a general analysis of your performance in the test.

   - You may wish to calculate your % mark for each question.
   - Recall how you felt before and after the test.
   - Are you happy with your performance in this test?
   - Do you think your mark reflects your understanding of the material?

2   Identify your weak and strong points as displayed in this test perform-ance.
3   What are the most important lessons that you have learnt from this test? Is there anything that you need to do differently from now on?

Journal task   WEEK 8

1   Go back through all your notes and problems so far on Energy Balances. Find two concepts (or definitions or equations) that you don't under-stand OR are not too sure of OR would like to find out more about. Write them down.
2   Now go to the recommended texts for this course (Himmelblau, Thompson & Cecklar, Felder & Rousseau, Reklaitis), and look to see if there is anything there to help you with the two problems you have iden-tified above (make use of the contents page, the index, and general browsing to locate a topic). If you haven't found anything to clarify these problems, find a classmate or tutor or lecturer to help you.
3   Make some notes on how you have resolved your confusion. You must clearly state what you have discovered your problem to be, and how you have resolved it. Don't just write out a paragraph from the textbook!!

NOTE: This is not an easy task to do properly. You need to make time to seri-ously think about what you do understand and what you don't understand. If you take the time for this task you should be able to progress significantly in your understanding. Merely copying out notes on a topic will not be considered a satisfactory response to this task – the task requires you to think about your own learning of Energy Balances.

Assessment

Dr Barnes was concerned that the existing assessment question format in the course (traditional numerical problems) did not adequately assess students' conceptual understanding. In previous years there had been an attempt to introduce non-numerical questions, but these tended to require not much more than the recall of 'bookwork'. Therefore, she worked on developing items that were non-numerical and assessed conceptual understanding. Initially she focused on separate 'short questions', but then started adding 'Explain why . . .' and 'What if . . .?' type questions on to standard numerical items. She also altered some multi-step numerical problems so that students had to explain what they would do, rather than performing the actual calculations. These items comprised approximately a fifth of each test and examination. A sample item with conceptual components is provided by way of illustration below.

Question 2   **10 marks**
In a recycle process for the production of ethylene oxide, the ethylene:air ratio in the fresh feed is 1:10, the separator is ideal, the recycle ratio (recycle:waste) is 2 and the overall conversion of the process is 75%.

(a) Draw a flow diagram depicting the process. Label all streams.
                                                                      (4 marks)
(b) Your colleague calculates the concentration of N_2 in the recycle to be approximately 80 mole %. Explain, without calculation, whether or not this answer could be correct and why.   (2 marks)
(c) Your colleague also calculates the conversion per pass to be approximately 90%. Explain, without calculation, whether or not this answer could be correct and why.   (2 marks)
(d) If the fresh feed rate and the reactor conditions remain unchanged and the recycle ratio is increased to 4, which of the following results are true:

   (i)   The conversion per pass increases.
   (ii)   The conversion per pass remains the same.
   (iii) The conversion per pass decreases.   (1 mark)

(e) If the fresh feed rate and the reactor conditions remain unchanged and the recycle ratio is increased to 4, which of the following results are true:

   (i)   The overall conversion increases.
   (ii)   The overall conversion remains the same.
   (iii) The overall conversion decreases.   (1 mark)

In order to de-emphasize memorization, students were allowed to bring in a 'crib sheet' to all tests and examinations. This was one A4 sheet on which they could write anything they wished. Owing to the nature of the questions it was unlikely that students would need to use this very much during the actual assessment, but apart from reducing stress, it was also recognized that the act of preparing such a sheet could be an important learning experience.

The assessment in the course had traditionally been tremendously time pressured. Dr Barnes was concerned that students might ascribe their lack of success in the course to this time pressure, and therefore introduced one test (the third class test) for which students were given practically 'unlimited time' (five or six hours for a two hour test). Time was limited in all the other tests, although she felt that the time allocated was fair.

As can be seen from all of the above, the teaching practice in this course closely resembled the recommendations that one would find in much of the current literature on good practice in higher education. In particular, these actions were carefully designed in an attempt to improve student learning in the course, with a focus on the development of conceptual understanding. This detailed attention to multiple aspects of the course in order to achieve certain student learning objectives has been termed 'constructive alignment' by Biggs (1999), and is argued to be a useful approach to curriculum and teaching development.

Upon discovering what Dr Barnes was planning to do, I decided to follow this course closely for two years, focusing particularly on students' experience of this innovative teaching context. Initially it had seemed that my research would provide a glowing picture of all the wonderful student learning outcomes that such practice would facilitate. And, indeed, there were some very positive happenings, particularly in the first year where the pass rate increased dramatically and many aspects of key learning development among students were noted. In the second year the course was run in a relatively similar fashion, but with dramatically different outcomes. Significantly fewer of the students passed the course, and my research shifted quickly to trying to understand what lay behind student failure in this supposedly exemplary teaching context. Drawing on a number of in-depth interviews with students, some conducted during the course and others two years later, I was able to delve into their perceptions of the course context, and thereby attempt to provide a deeper understanding of student experience. This chapter presents some of the key findings from this research, in order to provide a picture of students' experiences of learning that will hopefully be helpful to other engineering educators as they embark on attempts to improve practice in their courses.

The importance of exploring student perceptions of the course

Although it may seem a fairly obvious thing to consider, it is Paul Ramsden (1992) who has brought to many educators' awareness the importance of

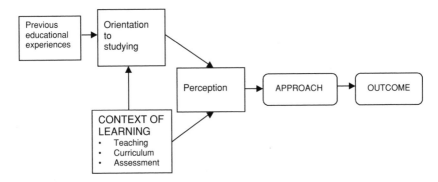

Figure 9.1 A model of student learning in context (Ramsden, 2003: 82)

finding out about how students are perceiving their course. He has pointed out that students respond and react to the situation they perceive, which is frequently quite different to that defined by teachers and researchers. Although a course might formally state certain educational objectives, students could be looking for a simple set of rules for what really has to be done to pass the examination. Instead of focusing on the apparently objective features of a course, Ramsden argues that it is important to look at what students construct out of this as a result of their perceptions. He represents the relationship between students' perceptions, different levels of context, approaches to learning, and learning outcomes in Figure 9.1.

Ramsden describes perception as the 'point of contact' between the context of learning and the student's orientation to studying. He stresses that this diagram should not be taken to suggest a single causal sequence of events but, rather, a 'chain of interactions at different levels of generality' (Ramsden, 2003: 81).

Ramsden's exhortation to explore student perceptions of a course formed the departure point for the research project that is discussed in this chapter. Given the innovative context described above, I was interested to find out exactly how different students perceived this course, and how that related to their learning.

Students' experiences of the course

My research into students' experiences of this course uncovered instances where students were, indeed, meeting the learning outcomes that the lecturer intended by her redesign of the course, and also those where these outcomes were patently not met. Since the assessment so closely matched the curricular intentions, it was not surprising to note that the students meeting the intended learning outcomes during the course also passed in the final assessment, while those not meeting these outcomes also failed. This latter group forms the focus of this chapter. Why, in a context where curriculum, teaching and assessment were all carefully aligned to match the goal of conceptual understanding, did some students fail to meet this goal? In the following section, four students' experiences will be described in order to illustrate the key research findings which address this question.

David   A case of differing interpretation of the course demands

David made the following comments as he reflected on his experience of the course shortly after it had ended:

> I was scared that [the course], you know many people they will tell you that [the course] is difficult, so, I was like making sure that every day I do stuff. But during the course of the year I realized that the course is just fine. Especially the person who was lecturing it is very good, she stopped during the lecture, and she asked questions, she looked around, and she gets you to follow the stuff very well. I was more relaxed than before, than last year. 'Cos, you know, many lecturers they tend to deliver the stuff, and then it's up to you . . . But uh [the lecturer] was like hey, she used to stop during the lecture, and then . . . Actually in fact I would say, I was doing most of my work in the lecture, yeah 'cos that's where I was getting more information, 'cos I used to listen [more] than to write.

As is clear from the extract, David saw the teaching of the subject in positive ways. The extract suggests that he appreciated, and perhaps understood, the ways in which the lecturer of the subject had approached teaching the class. From this extract one might infer that David was a successful student. Quite the contrary – unfortunately he failed the subject outright, and knew this at the time of the interview from which the extract is taken.

The key issue underpinning David's experience of the course appears to be the meanings that he held for the term 'understanding'. David frequently used the word 'understand' when talking about his experience in the course, and felt that understanding was important. His very first statement in the interview, when asked to talk about his experience of the course, was that 'it is a fundamental course in engineering . . . you get to *understand* most of the concepts of the chemical engineering, especially . . . mass and energy balances' (emphasis added). He did not ascribe failing the final examination to a lack of understanding; on the contrary he felt that 'I understand mostly everything'. However, when asked to comment on his examination script, the lecturer's main comment was that his understanding was grossly inadequate, responding to his answers to various questions with: 'He hasn't really got an idea of what he's doing', 'He's just fishing in the dark', 'He's got the wrong end of the stick', etc.

How can we reconcile this apparent contradiction? How could David feel that he understood 'mostly everything' while the lecturer who marked his script feels that he 'didn't really have an idea'? One logical possibility is that while David picked up that understanding is critically important in this course, his meaning for what constitutes understanding was quite different to that intended by the lecturer.

From his examination script it was clear that David had taken quite some effort to memorize key definitions and formulae – quite frequently this is all that he put down in response to a number of questions that required problem solving of a given situation. David's comment that, 'what I wrote in the final exam I got full marks for it', would therefore seem to suggest that he felt that these sorts of answers were adequate, and therefore that he equated 'understanding' with remembering relevant definitions and formulae. Therefore, David had a perception of the required course outcome that was at odds with that defined by the lecturer. This interpretation is backed up by an examination of David's experience of different parts of the course.

Compared to how other students came to the realization that lectures were not the most important part of the course, David found the lectures were so useful that there was not much that had to be done outside class (see quote above). This experience he compared with another course that he was doing in the second semester (at the time of this interview), where the lectures were given in a traditional manner, and where he felt that he had to do more work on his own and to concentrate on the tutorials. We can understand David's perceptions of the role of the lecture by referring to his notion of 'understanding'. When David sat in the lecture, he felt that what happened here was sufficient to build adequate understanding – because, in his terms, having an overall idea of the formulae and definitions constituted understanding. Other students felt that the lecture provided only a starting point and that their real learning happened in the tutorials and when working at home, and this was due to a more inclusive set of meanings that they had for the term understanding.

In terms of judging the standard of the course, David had a pre-subject view of the course as 'difficult' (see initial quote). After the first test, which was widely recognized to be relatively easy, he relaxed, as did many students. However, while other students revised their opinions after the second and third tests, David continued to feel that this was an easy course. He failed both of these two latter tests, and ended up with a 50 per cent course mark (average over the three class tests). David chose to base his expectations for the examination on this course mark, not on the fact that he had failed two out of three tests and said: 'So I got like 50% and was standing the chances to pass'.

Furthermore, he felt that the reason for the poor test marks was due to poor examination technique rather than a lack of understanding. Once again we would interpret this apparent poor judgement in terms of David's meanings for 'understanding' which linked with his expectations of the standard of understanding required to pass in the course.

Geoff   An illustration of the use of a procedural approach

At the start of the year Geoff was feeling positive and confident about the course, commenting that, 'maybe I'm beginning to think like an engineer'. He liked the journal task which had required him to think about his future career, and often talked about this issue. Geoff was a very involved member of the class, often responding to activities in class or asking the lecturer to go over a point, and commented that he 'always felt like [he] was part of the discussion'. He also interacted with a wide range of students, and had fairly close relationships with a number of them.

Geoff recognized that he tended to get adversely affected by stress, both in and out of the test situation, and was feeling at the start of the course that he had this under control. A bit later into the course, however, he started to find the lectures not as relaxed as they had initially been, and he struggled to keep up with the pace. Although he had passed the first test with ease, things started to spiral out of control soon after and he ended up failing the second test. He started to feel tired all the time with the load of assignments, and noted that the vacation week was a 'joke' as he had worked harder than he usually did during the semester. He was not even able to consider doing the short homework tasks that were set in the course as he had so much other work to do. He now became obsessed with time management, and made the striking comment: 'To stop and think . . . at the moment I don't have time for that'. He managed to just pass the third (unlimited time) test but got confused while writing the final examination and noted afterwards that he had some fundamental misconceptions.

Why did Geoff end up not grasping the basic course concepts, even though he was so involved in the course activities and committed to his studies? I followed Geoff's descriptions of what he was doing, and managed to identify his approach to learning. In the literature it is mainly deep and surface approaches that have been identified, yet among these students we had also identified a third approach, termed here a procedural approach, which was used by a number of students including Geoff. Instead of focusing on developing conceptual understanding as required in the course (a deep approach), students using a procedural approach focused on being able to use standard calculation methods to solve problems. From early on in the course Geoff was able to articulate the essential features of his approach to learning, and noted that this approach was largely determined by his experience of stress, saying, 'I don't like doing that, but when I'm stuck, that's my saving grace, I know the equation, just punch it in'.

He also knew that the course was requiring him to use a deep approach, yet this was something that he seldom managed to achieve. Early on in the course he felt that he was building a good understanding of the work, yet as soon as the pressure was on he found himself reverting to a procedural approach, focusing on calculations and methods. After he wrote the June examination, he realized that, despite all his hard work, he still had grave misunderstandings in many important conceptual areas. Following the experience of failing the course he did finally manage to implement his intentions and focus on understanding. During an interview after the conclusion of the course he spoke at length of this new approach, saying for example: 'That's why I'm trying to get this understanding thing in the bag. Because if I can understand it I can do a problem. Rather than if I'm sitting there doing hundreds of problems and getting tired and irritable and whatever.'

He had been advised by senior students to do as many problems as possible during the course, and he now regretted taking this advice. He had worked through countless problems, trying to train himself to remember solution methods and recognize familiar problems, and after the course had ended he realized that this had not helped him in the final assessment. He said that he would now advise students in this course to focus on developing understanding, and described a different way of doing problems where you took one problem and tried to get as much understanding out of it as possible. The reader might at this stage wonder whether Geoff might have similar (problematic) meanings for 'understanding' as did David, reported earlier. A close inspection of how Geoff actually tackled his work, and specifically the problems he now articulated with the procedural approach made it clear that this was not the case. Geoff was now espousing the same goal as the lecturer. He had also shifted from looking for a single method of solving a problem, to wanting to explore as many different ways as possible.

Two years later Geoff again affirmed that failing the course had been a turning point in his approach to learning, noting:

> Like before I came into engineering, I thought let me just pass the course and I get my degree and then I live happily ever after but now I am starting to see that you must understand the stuff. And then failing [the course] and was like the part where I realized that I can't get through like this anymore. I have got to sit down and figure out what is going on. I can't let things pass.

Mike An experience of emotional and personal issues getting in the way

At the time of the course Mike came across as an easygoing student who was not finding the course too difficult and was, possibly, more concerned about his social life. I was aware that his mother had recently passed away, but he assured me that he was coping well with this and that it was not affecting his studies in any way. He frequently missed lectures, but said that this was OK as he always made sure that he never missed two lectures in a row. When he was in lectures he said he often sat back and relaxed while other students tackled the problems that had been set in class.

While waiting to do the first test, for which he had done minimal preparation, Mike panicked when he saw how much work other students had done on their 'crib sheets'. During the test he ended up having what he described as a temporary 'blackout', where he could not remember what to do, but he managed to recover from this in the last half hour. He ended up scoring 72 per cent, and although he was obviously pleased with this excellent result, he felt that he should have worked harder in order to avoid the panic. Despite these good intentions, he did not manage to work any harder in preparation for the second test. He really struggled with this test, felt that he 'couldn't seem to do it', 'couldn't focus', and felt nervous and time pressured. He knew immediately that he had failed, and indeed he had, scoring only 28 per cent. Nonetheless, he still said he was not too worried about the course, as he thought he had a 'feeling' for the subject, and he was concentrating on the assignments in other subjects. Because of this workload he said that he did not have time to do work on the course, although he admitted that 'I suppose to have time you have to make time'. He just glanced through his work for the third test, and scored 56 per cent.

Mike did not work particularly hard for the examination, but felt that what mattered was that he had understood the work. Once again he had the experience of 'blacking out' during the examination, but managed to remember what to do towards the end. He scored a final mark of 52 per cent for the course and said that he was happy to have scraped through. He admitted that he had 'cut it close' in this semester, and planned to work harder in the second semester courses.

In the follow-up interview two years later Mike gave quite a different interpretation of his experience in the course. In the first few minutes of the interview he mentioned his mother's death and how that had had a huge impact on his ability to study. Throughout all the interviews in the second year he had never once mentioned this issue but he now said:

> I really struggled to sit down and concentrate. I would sit down and my mind would be here and there. Not like your mind is always here and there, but actually sort of nothing . . . like I could read through a page and understand nothing and then towards the end of last year again my third year, my second [attempt at] second year, it sort of came together, right at the exams.

He repeatedly returned to this theme during the interview, making comments like 'I kind of lost myself', 'I just lost all drive' and 'That focus it just wasn't there'. He then said that towards the end of the following year his brain 'started sparking again' and he found it amazing that he could actually sit down and study. Nonetheless, he still didn't feel that he had fully regained the abilities that he had demonstrated in his (very successful) first year.

With regard to approach to learning, Mike completely espoused commitment to a deep approach throughout his experience of the course and in subsequent courses. However, his emotional state at the time did not allow him to commit sufficient time and energy to fully implement this approach. Although he actually passed the mass and energy balance course (narrowly), he failed quite a few subsequent courses.

Nomsa   Contradictory feelings about becoming an engineer

From early on in the course Nomsa came across as the 'ideal student', working extremely hard, consulting with peers, asking for advice and generally doing everything that would be advised in a study skills course. She had even revised her first-year notes in the week before the course started. From the start of the year she was concerned that she was not managing her time well enough, and tried to fit even more into the day than she was already doing. She was struggling to understand the problems that were presented in lectures, and had plans to do more problems and to read the textbook. During tutorials she compared herself to her peers and worried that she was not thinking fast enough and questioned whether she was 'fit to become an engineer'. At the end of most interviews when I gave her an opportunity to pose a question she asked me for advice on what was the best way to understand the current course topic.

Nomsa scored 47 per cent in the first test and felt very bad about this, having not understood some of the questions, and having also lost marks through careless mistakes. Long before the journal tasks were due she had worked through the fifth task (see p. 142) in order to analyse what had gone wrong in this test. During the vacation week she had tried to work hard, but found that she was very tired, and although she worked throughout the week she did not achieve as much as planned. After writing the second test she felt that this test had gone better, that she had been confident, and had understood the work. She was disappointed then to discover that she had only scored 40 per cent on this test. This mark she ascribed to silly mistakes and poor time management. She was somewhat happy with the 51 per cent that she scored for the third test as she had passed the course for the first time, although she felt with the time available she should have achieved better. It seemed to her that she did not understand her work as well as she had thought. Once again she started worrying about whether she was fit to be an engineer.

In the final examination she left out most of the long fourth question, and felt that this was due to not practising sufficiently with time pressure. She also recognized that her practice of writing everything in pencil first was very time consuming. She was really upset to hear that she had failed the course, but almost immediately decided to pull herself together and move on to the next challenge.

Two years later Nomsa again gave the impression of a solidly determined student (and had performed reasonably well academically), but she still was really worried as to whether she was going to make it as an engineer. Poignantly she noted: 'Sometimes I doubt I will ever be . . . like in the industry and stuff. . . . I'm really [not sure if I can] stand the pressures and stuff'.

She said that although she was confident with the university education she had received, there were other things required from you as a person in industry and she was not sure she could cope.

What is most concerning is that Nomsa had held a bursary with a large chemical company from her first year and that she had undertaken vacation work at the end of each year since then. Therefore, it was not the case that she was insufficiently acquainted with the workplace, but maybe more that she had so much (negative?) experience here. The issue of students' experiences of vacation work has been further explored in another research project (Case and Jawitz, 2004) conducted recently with final year chemical and civil engineering students. This study showed that black and female students experience particular difficulties as they enter a terrain in which the incoming engineer has historically been white and male. It was also seen how the denial of access to legitimate and meaningful work that is all too often the experience of these students can have negative consequences on the quality of learning that this experience affords them and their emerging identities as engineers. On the converse, situations where they were accepted as legitimate participants in the workplace provided powerful learning experiences for these students and helped develop their identities as black and/or female engineers-to-be.

Lessons for would-be innovative engineering educators

The four snapshots presented above have been selected to illustrate the key issues that emerged in this research project into students' perceptions of the course. These provide a stark illustration of some of the realities of student experiences that can lie behind innovative course environments. In other parts of this research project (Case and Gunstone, 2002) it has been shown how the course environment did serve to promote deep approaches and conceptual understanding for some of the students in the class. The focus on this chapter has been on those students for whom it didn't (of which there were sufficient to be cause for concern). Even though there had been detailed curriculum restructuring, careful and creative use of teaching methods to include active participation, and assessment that demanded conceptual understanding, many students had an experience that fell far short of the desired course outcomes. An exploration of students' perceptions highlighted the following issues, as illustrated in the previous section:

- differing interpretation of course demands (David);
- adoption of a procedural approach (Geoff);
- interference of emotional and personal issues (Mike);
- feelings about becoming an engineer (Nomsa).

We clearly need to move beyond the simple tenets of 'innovative teaching methods' in order to address these issues. Two key suggestions emerging from the research are discussed in what follows.

Watch for the impact of time pressure

In any course, traditional or non-traditional, it is assessment that is most formative of students' perceptions (Ramsden, 1992). The assessment in this course (three class tests and a final examination) had been changed in some aspects in order to reflect the new course emphasis. 'Conceptual questions' which required explanations rather than numerical calculations comprised a significant portion of all assessments, and the term 'conceptual' was consistently used by the lecturer to emphasize this difference. Yet, most assessments were unchanged with respect to their demands on working under time pressure. From the study of student perceptions it would appear that the time pressured tests and exams were the key course feature that so severely limited the learning opportunities for students like David and Geoff. This allowed David an explanation for his poor performance which did not challenge his perception of understanding since he assumed the reason he had failed was due to the time pressure rather than his lack of understanding. The experience of time pressure also led Geoff to think that there was 'no time to think' and that the only viable strategy was to focus on remembering standard solutions (a procedural approach).

This interpretation is further supported by an examination of students' responses to the single untimed test that took place in the course. For a number of students this experience prompted them to seriously query the level of their conceptual understanding and also to rethink their approaches to learning. Unfortunately though, this was an isolated experience, and did not appear to have a long-term effect (especially since the final examination was due to be written under conditions of time pressure). I would suggest that a course environment where a less time-pressured test was the normal experience of assessment might have resulted in more productive perceptions of 'understanding' for a student like David and might have enabled those like Geoff to take more risks in adopting a deep approach.

A compounding effect on time pressure arose from the courses which students were taking in parallel with this course. A key issue here was that while this course had very few assignments to be completed after hours, the other courses had numerous 'hand-ins'. This also led to many students feeling that they did not have sufficient time to spend grappling with the new concepts after class or thinking about the questions which the lecturer had posed that day during the class.

Teach for development of the whole person

From an examination of the experiences of students such as Mike and Nomsa it can be clearly seen that learning is not merely the application of an appropriate approach to a cognitive task, but is a process of identity formation that involves the whole person. Traditionally in higher education, and in engineering courses in particular we have shied away from these issues, often thinking of our students in one dimension (the cognitive domain), assuming that all other issues are best located in the realms of student societies and residences. We need to challenge these perceptions, and work to create environments where students know that there is concern for their whole development. The position is given theoretical support by the learning theory of situated cognition (Lave and Wenger, 1991), which takes learning to be fundamentally about joining a 'community of practice' and taking on a new identity. Lecturers need to realize that what is happening in the 'rest' of students' lives will have an important bearing on their learning, and need to take time to listen to students who are going through difficult personal experiences. In another regard, we have a unique opportunity in our vocationally focused programmes to aim towards the development of students as engineers, and we need to make sure that industry-based experiences are helping students to realize this aim.

These twin challenges urge us to go way beyond 'tinkering' with aspects of our courses but rather to be prepared to make quite radical shifts in our thinking about teaching and learning in order to maximize learning opportunities for all our students.

References

Biggs, J. B. (1999) *Teaching for Quality Learning at University: what the student does*, London: Society for Research into Higher Education and Open University Press.

Case, J. M. and Gunstone, R. F, (2002) 'Metacognitive development as a shift in approach to learning: an in-depth study', *Studies in Higher Education*, 27 (4): 459–470.

Case, J. M. and Jawitz, J. (2004) 'Using situated cognition theory in researching student experience of the workplace', *Journal of Research in Science Teaching*, 41 (5): 415–431.

Lave, J. and Wenger, E. (1991) *Situated Learning: legitimate peripheral participation*, Cambridge: Cambridge University Press.

Ramsden, P. (2003) *Learning to Teach in Higher Education*, 2nd edition. London: Routledge-Falmer.

10

The emergence of studio courses – an example of interactive learning

Linda S. Schadler and
John B. Hudson

Introduction

Innovation in engineering education is not a new phenomenon. There have always been great teachers who have found ways to create a unique classroom environment. In addition, active, collaborative learning has been present in engineering education in the form, for example, of laboratories and senior design projects. There are three relatively recent and significant changes, however, that are stimulating broader innovation in the classroom and paradigm shifts at engineering schools.

In the US, the first stimulus is the National Science Foundation (NSF), which has made it a requirement that research grants have an educational component. This has forced researchers to formally consider changes in their classrooms. The NSF has also developed a set of outstanding young faculty awards that require innovation in education as part of the evaluation criteria (Presidential Young Investigator, National Young Investigator, CAREER awards – in historical order). The Foundation has also increased funding in areas of curriculum and laboratory development and become more rigorous in its requirement for assessing the impact of those grants. In addition, NSF has been funding Engineering Education Coalitions (Coward *et al.*, 2000) and awarding other large grants to schools of engineering rather than to individual investigators to effect broad changes in the curriculum.

The second stimulus, which is not unique to the US, is technology. Laptop computers, the World Wide Web and software innovation are all driving novel educational approaches such as in asynchronous learning, online learning (Lister *et al.*, 1999) multimedia teaching modules (Millard and Burnham, 2002; Iskander *et al.*, 1996; Glinkowski *et al.*, 1997), virtual laboratories (Lyons *et al.*, 1998), lectures (McMahon, 1997), participatory textbooks (Larson, 2001), and design studios (Bucinell *et al.*, 1997; Erden *et al.*, 2000).

The third stimulus is a change in the accreditation process for engineering schools in the US. The new criteria established by the Accreditation Board for Engineering and Technology for the year 2000 (Accreditation Board for Engineering and Technology, 2002) allow engineering schools more flexibility in defining their curricula provided that the graduates develop 11 core competencies. In addition, each discipline has other required criteria. This has led to more flexibility in the engineering curriculum.

As a result, there is a myriad of small projects, innovative tools and teaching methods being developed in the US. It would be difficult, and not particularly instructive, to document them all in this article. Therefore, this chapter will focus on one of the more extensive paradigm shifting changes – namely the studio mode of teaching. Rensselaer Polytechnic Institute (RPI) is one of the leaders in this area (Wilson, 1996) but studio courses are being developed throughout the US (Demetry *et al.*, 2002; Ribando *et al.*, 1999). We will use changes in the RPI teaching approach as an example, while referring to other relevant initiatives throughout.

The studio concept

Despite the great teachers who have found ways to make large lecture/recitation/laboratory courses exciting and informative, there are some serious limitations to this standard delivery method. The first limitation is in the timing of the active laboratory learning. The laboratories are often performed out of sequence with the lecture or several weeks separated from the lecture. Thus, the hands-on learning is isolated from the other learning. While this is often necessary in order to handle the large number of freshmen engineering students taking introductory courses, the laboratories do not help motivate the lecture or vice versa. The second limitation is that attendance is often low in large lecture courses (60 per cent) (Maby *et al.*, 1997). Thus, active learning is difficult in a large lecture classroom setting, and the student interest is low as demonstrated by the attendance. Finally, three different learning environments must be staffed; the lecture, the recitation and the laboratory.

The studio concept attempts to rectify these limitations by combining lecture, active learning (including laboratories, computer exercises, team problem solving) and assessment into one classroom setting (Wilson and Jennings, 2000). The process is facilitated by the faculty, but is focused on interactive learning by the students, and includes hands-on activities. A typical interactive session might include two sets of 10–20-minute lectures on a particular topic with problem solving and experiments after each mini-lecture. This provides quasi-synchronous delivery of material using several different teaching styles to accommodate the diverse learning styles in the classroom. The material is reinforced in a variety of ways. In addition, the switching of activities keeps the students' attention, makes class fun and improves attendance significantly (Maby et al., 1997). Other benefits include the small class size (a maximum of 60 students) and the faculty/student mentoring relationships that develop. Finally, because the student learning is constantly being assessed by monitoring their ability to complete a problem related to the recently delivered lecture, the faculty member has an opportunity to expand on any areas in which the students are having trouble. Analogously, students who are struggling in a course are identified very quickly and intervention can occur.

An appropriate classroom environment is critical to achieving success and requires significant investment. The classroom needs to provide for significant interaction. Students need access to common writing space, technology and the instructor as well as laboratory space. There are special lighting considerations because the portion of the room with computer projection needs to be dark enough that the students can see details on the screen, yet the room needs to be bright enough that students can see to write and work on computers. Two examples of classroom layouts are shown in Figure 10.1. In the classrooms used for Rensselaer's Chemistry of Materials sequence (Hudson et al., 1998), which is described in detail later in this chapter, the students sit in groups of four with Ethernet connections (soon to be wireless) at each table. The instructor has access to computer projection as well as traditional overhead projectors and white boards. Across the hall is a fully equipped laboratory capable of handling 60 students at a time in groups of four. In the circuits/electronics studio, the students sit in two arching rows with the back row elevated somewhat. The students face one direction to hear mini-lectures and complete team problems, and turn in the other direction to 20 learning stations equipped with computers, circuit design space and measurement equipment (Maby et al., 1997). The computer projection equipment is also able to display the data as it is being taken.

There are several instructional components to the studio classroom. The first is a mini-lecture which introduces a topic and provides the basic equations or concepts that will be developed during the rest of the class. The second component is team problem solving. The team problems can be multimedia modules that allow students to practise concepts or simple paper and pen problems. Multimedia modules vary from virtual lectures (McMahon, 1997) to problem solving exercises (Millard and Burnham, 2002) to virtual laboratories (Lyons et al., 1998). There are several advantages to using multimedia problem solving exercises. First, they can be used inside and outside the classroom. Second, if properly configured, the students have the opportunity to complete design exercises. For example, in the circuits and electronics course at Rensselaer, the students can design a circuit on the computer and test the

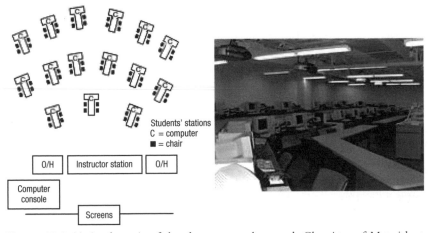

Figure 10.1 (a) A schematic of the classroom used to teach Chemistry of Materials at Rensselaer. The laboratories are across the hall; (b) A photograph of the circuits/electronics studio classroom at Rensselaer

properties of the circuit (Millard and Burnham, 2002). While the students are requested to solve certain problems in class, they have access to the software outside the classroom. These modules are also connected to a computer program called Scribe. This program records the student's interaction with the computer. The instructor can then view the path the student took in solving a problem. By viewing this path, the instructor can determine where students are having difficulty, gain insight into the cognitive process, offer suggestions and better evaluate an open-ended design question. A second strength of this particular multimedia software is a networking technology called WebTeam. Using WebTeam, students from two locations can be assigned a portion of the circuit to design. Because each part of the team can only alter its portion of the circuit, the students at the two separate locations must work together as a team to optimize the design of the whole circuit.

One of the challenges of the team problems and cooperative learning is creating groups or teams that work well together. A unique aspect of RPI is the Archer Center for Student Leadership (ACSL) (McClosky *et al.*, 2003). Personnel from this Center teach two credits of professional leadership in the course of an engineering student's career at Rensselaer. Professional Development I is part of a four-credit sophomore design course. In this course, students are placed in teams and given a project that requires them to design, build and test a product. Engineering faculty and instructors from the Archer Center teach the course together; 75 per cent of the students' grade is determined by the engineering faculty and the other 25 per cent is determined by ACSL. The advantage of this combined approach is that the students learn team building, conflict management and personality types, in the context of being a more effective engineering design team. Thus, they see leadership theories in action. The teams are required to do self-assessment throughout the term and are taught topics such as effective communication and feedback, managing personality differences, conflict management, risk-taking strategies and ethical decision making. Center personnel also teach a one-credit senior level leadership course. We have also used the ACSL to affect team work in Chemistry of Materials studio courses. As an experiment, ACSL personnel came into individual studio classrooms to complete team building exercises. While no formal study on the results was completed, anecdotal evidence from these authors shows that faculty who worked with ACSL found that their student problem solving sessions were far more effective than faculty who did not.

Another component of the active learning is the laboratory component. In some cases, this is indistinguishable from the multimedia modules described above, because these modules provide a virtual laboratory (Lyons *et al.*, 1998) in which data can be collected. In other cases, hands-on laboratories are fun and excellent learning tools. The challenge for the hands-on laboratories is developing experiments that can be completed in 30–50 minutes, but are in-depth enough to provide a meaningful learning experience (Starreett and Morcos, 2001; Hudson *et al.*, 1998b). Examples of these are given in the Chemistry of Materials section that follows. Remote data collection is also a possibility for studio courses. Longlab (Millard and Burnham, 2002), developed at Rensselaer, provides an opportunity for students to make electrical measurements remotely on a laboratory set-up that is real. For example, at a remote location, a beam with a strain gauge attached can be struck and the resulting oscillations measured and compared to the predicted oscillations of the beam in the classroom.

In order to more fully demonstrate a studio course, the details of a Chemistry of Materials course are presented in the following section.

Chemistry of Materials

One of the challenges in engineering education is making the core science courses relevant for engineers. For example, in the 1980s at Rensselaer, engineering students perceived that the General Chemistry sequence was not of great relevance to most of the engineering disciplines. It was too heavily oriented toward preparatory and descriptive chemistry, at the expense of practical topics such as microelectronic materials and corrosion. As a result, Rensselaer developed a two-semester course sequence that combined elements of classical General Chemistry and introductory Materials Science. The sequence that was developed integrated those chemistry concepts that were most pertinent to engineers, such as basic atomic structure, chemical bonding and thermodynamics, with basic materials science concepts such as crystal structure, mechanical behaviour and phase changes. Wherever possible, engineering applications were used to introduce chemical principles. For example, organic chemistry was introduced in the context of polymer synthesis, electrochemistry in the context of corrosion. This idea has been adapted across the country and while this particular combination is not popular (in fact, Rensselaer has changed this into a Chemistry for Engineers and Materials for Engineers sequence), the idea of a Chemistry course that has more applied examples and teaches concepts more relevant for engineers is being developed at other schools (Demetry et al., 2002; Ribando et al., 1999).

This course sequence, named Chemistry of Materials, was initially taught in the classical lecture–recitation–laboratory mode. While this approach was better received by the students than the previous separate General Chemistry plus Materials Science sequence, there were still problems. The large lecture sections, of about 250 students each, were poorly attended, even when efforts were made to recruit the best lecturers among the Chemistry and Materials faculty. The recitation sessions in many cases were just a review of previously assigned homework problems. Laboratory sessions, which were classical three-hour chemistry experiments, were poorly coordinated with the lecture material due to limitations on the number of available laboratory set-ups.

Begun as a pilot programme by one of us (JBH), the course is taken at present by roughly 600 students in the autumn and 400 in the spring. In all cases, the section size is roughly 60 students. The studio format chosen consists of two, two-hour interactive sessions and one, one-hour evaluation session each week. The interactive sessions include presentation of new materials by the instructor, combined with in-class problem solving by the students, working in teams of four. The sections are staffed by the instructor and a graduate teaching assistant, which provides sufficient people-power to interact with the students during problem solving sessions. Initially, the laboratories comprised one whole interactive session, but we have since developed a series of 50-minute laboratories that are integrated into the interactive sessions.

Infrastructure

A central principle of the interactive course has been that the students must be presented with opportunities to participate actively in class sessions. The classroom environment must be compatible with this principle. This was made possible in the present case by renovating two floors of an existing building into interactive chemistry suites, each floor containing an interactive classroom capable of seating up to 60 students, grouped in teams of four, and two laboratory rooms, each with the same facilities. The layout of the interactive classroom is shown in Figure 10.1. There are 15 stations, each accommodating four students. Each of these was originally supplied with a desktop computer, connected to the university network. As all Rensselaer students are required to own a laptop and to use it as appropriate in their course work, these have more recently been replaced by ports that allow connection of a laptop computer by each student. The instructor area at the front of the classroom is equipped with two overhead projectors, whiteboards and a networked desktop computer that is connected to a projector. It is also possible for instructors to connect their own laptops into this projector. The classroom also has an optical microscope that can be used to view fracture surfaces or microstructure and the images are displayed via computer projection.

Format

The interactive teaching format developed uses a modular approach. Each module begins with presentation by the instructor of new material; a concept, an empirical observation or an experimental technique. These presentations are augmented wherever possible by classroom demonstrations or appropriate multimedia modules. Concepts introduced are then reinforced by having the students do a 'team problem' related to the subject under discussion. While the students are working on the problem in their four-person teams, the instructor and teaching assistants circulate around the classroom, providing help and exploring the significance of the problem with those teams that have finished the solution. When the teams have completed the problem, the solution is discussed by the class as a whole. Typically, a module of this sort will occupy about 20 to 30 minutes of class time, with three to four modules being covered in a two-hour interactive session. Laboratory work is embedded within these interactive sessions, with a 50-minute laboratory exercise being carried out on a roughly bi-weekly basis.

As an example of this session format, let us consider the session in which we cover solid state diffusion. The modules of this session lead the students through the phenomenology of diffusion, and then through the concepts of atomic jump frequency, diffusive flux, the vacancy mechanism of diffusion, random walks and the temperature dependence of diffusivity. The session closes with a discussion of practical applications of solid state diffusion to permeation and carburization. The sequence of team problems used is shown in Table 10.1. This session also includes a demonstration of vacancy diffusion by a random walk process in which a random number generator is used to control the motion of a 'vacancy' in an array of two different kinds of 'atoms' (pennies and washers) that can be shown on the overhead projector at the front of the classroom. In recent years, we have coupled this session with a laboratory experiment that measures the permeation rate of hydrogen through a thin palladium diaphragm.

The laboratory component

We have spent considerable time developing laboratory experiences relevant to the course and integrating them into the interactive class sessions (Hudson

Table 10.1 Team problems used to elucidate the principles of solid state diffusion

Concept	Team problem
Atomic jump frequency	For carbon interstitials in BCC iron, the activation energy is 80,000 J/mol, the jump frequency is 6×10^{13} sec^{-1}. At 300 K, how many times does the average interstitial jump from one site to another in an hour?
The diffusion coefficient	Calculate D and D_0 for carbon interstitials in BCC iron at 300 K. In BCC iron, the distance from one interstitial site to another is $a/\sqrt{2}$, $a = 0.28$ nm. Recall that for carbon interstitials in BCC iron, the activation energy is 80,000 J/mol, the jump frequency is 6×10^{13} sec^{-1}.
Random walk distance	A How far, on average, will a carbon atom in BCC iron move in a given direction in one year at 300 K? B What would be the value of D required to get this same average distance in an hour?
The effect of temperature on diffusivity	To what temperature would one have to raise BCC iron in order to get the value of D necessary to move an interstitial carbon atom 660 nm in one hour?

et al., 1998b). This was necessary because the traditional two- or three-hour lab session is not appropriate for the interactive format. Rather, what is needed is experiments that can be incorporated into the two-hour interactive session and can be completed in no more than 50 minutes. The principle illustrated by the experiment must also be tied closely to the material presented in the discussion and problem solving components of the session, and should guide the student to the discovery of a principle or application relevant to the topic under discussion. Another practical requirement is that the cost of setting up and running the experiment must be modest – for this system to work, up to 15 groups of four students must be able to do the experiment at the same time.

Over the course of the past five years we have developed ten new experiments, so that we can include a laboratory, on average, once every three class sessions. These are supplemented by classroom demonstrations that occupy 10 to 20 minutes and are performed by the instructor and teaching assistants. Several of these experiments have been published elsewhere (Hudson *et al.*, 1998a; Hudson, 2000).

Much attention has also been paid to integrating the laboratory material with the related discussion and problem solving material used in the same session. In some cases, the discussion and problem solving lead to a lab session at the end of the interactive session. In others, the lab takes place in the middle of the session. An example of this is the introductory session on mechanical properties of materials. This session begins with definitions of basic

Figure 10.2 A photograph of the desktop equipment used to complete mechanical properties testing in the Chemistry of Materials course at Rensselaer. On the left is the load frame. In the middle is the geometry used for tensile testing including an extensometer, and on the right is the geometry used for three-point bend testing

mechanical behaviour parameters such as stress and strain and the use of the tensile test to illustrate the relations between these parameters. Students then go to the laboratory and carry out tensile tests on a metal and a polymer, using small mechanical testing machines designed specifically for our application (Figure 10.2). These machines are automated, and can be interfaced with the laptop computers that all Rensselaer students are required to own. This permits the students to acquire the tensile test data in the lab and perform the analysis to convert from load v. elongation to stress v. strain. When the data collection is complete, students return to the classroom for a discussion of the various features of the test – elastic deformation, modulus, plastic deformation, fracture, toughness – and how and why these parameters differ between the metal and polymer samples. Related team problems (Table 10.2) cover calculation of the elastic modulus and offset yield strength from the data taken in the lab.

Critique

While it has become clear that classrooms with active learning techniques are more effective than those with passive learning, the studio method has an added component of more complete integration of hands-on learning with other active learning modes. It seems logical, therefore, to assume that the learning will be greater in the studio versions of courses. The results below, however, show that the results are mixed in terms of the gain of technical knowledge, but it is clear that students' communication and teamwork skills improve, that student satisfaction is higher, and that faculty is better able to monitor a student's progress.

Table 10.2 Team problems used to elucidate the principles of mechanical behaviour

Concept	Team problem
Definition of stress and strain	A copper rod 1 cm in diameter and 1.0 m long is loaded in tension to a force of 1000 N. A What is the stress in the sample? B If the sample elongates 0.1 mm under this load, what is the strain on the sample?
Definition of elastic limit and Young's modulus	A Calculate the stress and strain for a point below the elastic limit for one of the samples you tested in the laboratory. (Or use the data given to you by your instructor.) B Calculate Young's modulus for that same sample.
Definition of other tensile parameters	Calculate the 0.2% offset yield strength, the ultimate tensile strength and the ductility for one of the samples you tested in the laboratory. (Or use the data given to you by your instructor.)

Demetry, at Worcester Polytechnic Institute, compared the results of active/cooperative learning in an Introductory Materials Course (Demetry and Groccia, 1997) with results from the traditional approach. The results from three sections taught in the traditional style were compared to two sections taught in the studio-style mode. In this case objective testing of knowledge found that the students learned significantly more in the studio-style course than in the traditional lecture. The students also felt that their teamwork and communication skills had improved. A study by Terenzini et al. (Terenzini et al., 2001) assessed the effect of active teaching on the learning outcomes in design courses. The comparison was made for 17 courses or sections with active learning compared to six courses/sections without active learning across six engineering schools. A statistical analysis of the students' learning showed that the students in active learning classes did significantly better on many of the learning outcomes of a design course particularly in the areas of design skills, communication skills and group skills, but not in problem solving skills. Other studies at Rensselaer show modest improvements in the technical knowledge learned, but an overwhelming endorsement by the students in terms of the style of the course compared to their non-studio courses (Carlson et al., 1998).

Relevant to the comparison of techniques is also the number of students who gain at least the minimum acceptable level of knowledge. One of the advantages of a studio course is that, because of the stronger relationship between faculty member and student, students who are struggling are identified quickly and can receive more attention. One specific example of success in this regard occurred in the circuits and electronics course at Rensselaer mentioned earlier (Millard and Burnham, 2002). Of the 33 students in the pilot studio section, 17 failed the first exam. This is similar to the percentage of students that failed the non-studio version of the course. On the final exam, 98 per cent of the students in the studio version of the course passed. This is significantly higher than the percentage of students that pass the non-studio version. In addition, the students have fun. The course has received significantly higher ratings in the student evaluations carried out at the end of each semester.

Attendance is another clear measure of the success of the studio approach. In the studio courses at Rensselaer, attendance was close to 100 per cent in the pilot studio sections. As the number of faculty teaching studio courses has increased, this attendance has decreased somewhat to about 85 per cent which is still well above the 60 per cent often observed in the large lecture/recitation format. Others teaching the studio mode find similar improvements in attendance (Demetry *et al.*, 2002).

We have also completed qualitative assessments of the 50-minute laboratories developed to accompany the studio course. Formal course evaluations are carried out at the end of each semester at Rensselaer. These include both questions to be answered on a 'one to five' scale, and an opportunity for specific comments on various aspects of the course. In the Chemistry of Materials studio course, the positive response rate on the question 'Did the labs help you learn?' has gone from 55 per cent to 85 per cent as we have moved from disconnected laboratories to integrated laboratories. Only 71 per cent felt they learned from writing laboratory reports. From a careful look at the students' comments, this is probably because we did not discriminate enough between good and poor reports; 77 per cent felt that laboratories were at least somewhat fun (better than lecture was a frequent comment), but that the labs were still too structured.

In addition, we compared the performance of the students on the final exam in 1997, 2000 and 2001. The results are interesting, but not quantitative enough to test the statistical significance. Students were given essentially the same problem on the final exam on mechanical properties in 1997 and 2001, that is, before and after exposure to the laboratory on mechanical testing. (Note that there is no student access to these exams after they are taken.) Under the same instructor, the students in 1997 got an average of 60 per cent on the mechanical properties question, and in 2001 they got an average of 72 per cent.

When a course with 500–600 students is transformed into a studio mode, more faculty must be directly responsible for course presentation, as opposed to being recitation instructors. The change in style takes some adjustment for faculty, but in general, they like the studio format. Observing the students while they are doing their team problems provides immediate feedback to the instructor as to points that have been misunderstood in the presentation of new material. Rapport between faculty and students is also greatly improved which makes teaching more fun.

There are, however, a few limitations associated with the interactive approach. Not all faculty members are comfortable with the studio format. In addition, for some courses, the studio format is more efficient (Wilson, 1996), but for others it is more time intensive. In addition, this approach requires teaching assistants who can work in the classroom, and who can set up and monitor the laboratory equipment or computer software, rather than just working as graders. Finally, the staff support for maintaining computer and laboratory equipment is critical to the success of the course.

Summary

The studio format is an exciting method for teaching introductory engineering courses. It leads to more integrated learning, more interaction between faculty and students, and is fun. To be successful it requires the right teaching space and the development of appropriate hands-on modules (either virtual or real).

References

Accreditation Board for Engineering and Technology Inc. (2002) 'Criteria for accrediting programs in engineering in the United States', Baltimore, MD: Engineering Accreditation Commission. Available online at http://www.abet.org/criteria.html.

Bucinell, R. B., Kenyon, R. A., Erden, A. and Platin, B. E. (1997) 'The International Virtual Design Studio', *Frontiers in Education Conference* 3 (Session F3A).

Carlson, A. B., Jennings, W. C. and Schoch, P. M. (1998) 'Teaching circuit analysis in the studio format: a comparison with conventional instruction', *Frontiers in Education Conference* 4 (Session F4H).

Coward, H. R., Ailes, C. P. and Bardon, R. (2000) 'Progress of the engineering education coalitions', *SRI International Report*, May, available online at http://www.nsf.gov/pubsys/ods/getpub.cfm?nsf00116.

Demetry, C. and Groccia, J. E. (1997) 'A comparative assessment of students' experiences in two instructional formats of an introductory materials science course', *Journal of Engineering Education* 86: 203–210.

Demetry, C., Gurland, S. T. and Kildahl, N. (2002) 'Building bridges to materials properties in general chemistry laboratories: a model for integration across disciplines', *Journal of Engineering Education* 91: 379–386.

Erden, A., Erkmen, A. M., Erkmen, I., Bucinell, R. B., Traver, C. *et al.* (2000) 'The Multidisciplinary International Virtual Design Studio (MIVDS)', *IEEE Transactions* 43 (3): 288–295.

Glinkowski, M. T., Hylan, J. and Lister, B. (1997) 'A new, studio based, multimedia dynamic systems course: does it really work?', *Frontiers in Education Conference* 3: 201–216.

Hudson, J. B. (2000) 'Simple classroom demonstrations in chemistry and materials science', J. A. Jacobs (ed.) *National Educators Workshop: Update 99*, NASA Publication NASA/CP-2000–210325.

Hudson, J. B., Schadler, L. S. and Palmer, M. A. (1998a) 'Integration of laboratory experiences into an interactive chemistry/materials course', J. A. Jacobs (ed.) *National Educators Workshop: Update 97*, NASA/CP-1998–208726, pp. 357–368.

Hudson, J. B., Schadler, L. S., Palmer, M. A. and Moore, J. A. (1998b) 'Integration of laboratory and classroom work in an interactive first-year chemistry/materials course', *Journal of Materials Education* 20: 215–222.

Iskander, M. F., Catten, J. C., Rodriguez-Barcells, A. and Jones, A. K. S. (1996) 'Interactive multimedia CD-ROMS for education', *Proceedings – Frontiers in Education Conference 2, Technology-based Re-Engineering Engineering Education*, pp. 856–858.

Larson, T. R. (2001) 'Developing a participatory textbook for the Internet', *Journal of Engineering Education* 90: 49–53.

Lister, B. C., Danchack, M. M., Scalzo, K. A., Jennings, W. C. and Wilson, J. M. (1999) 'The Rensselaer 80/20 model for interactive distance learning', *Proceedings of EDUCAUSE '99: celebrating new beginnings*, Long Beach, CA, 26–29 October, p. 11.

Lyons, J., Kalidindi, S., Lawley, A., Ruff, G., DiNardo, J. *et al.* (1998) 'The NSF gateway engineering education coalition materials project', *Proceedings of the American Society for Engineering Education Annual Conference and Exposition*, Seattle, WA, 28 June–1 July (Session 1364).

Maby, E. W., Carlson, A. B., Connor, K. A., Jennings, W. C. and Schoch, P. M. (1997) 'A studio format for innovative pedagogy in circuits and electronics', *Frontiers in Education Conference* 3 (Session S3F).

McClosky, L., Allard, C., Reel, J. and Kaminski, D. A. (2003) 'Incorporating leadership training in a sophomore engineering design course', *Proceedings of the American Society of Engineering Education 2003 Annual Conference and Exposition* (Session 2525), Nashville, TN, 22–25 June.

McMahon, C. J. (1997) 'Development of the "virtual lecture"', *Journal of Materials Education* 19 (1–2): 87–90.

Millard, D. and Burnham, G. (2002) 'Interactive educational materials and technologies', *International Conference on Engineering Education*, 18–21 August, Manchester, UK (Paper #445).

Ribando, R., Scott, T. C. and O'Leary, G. W. (1999) 'Teaching heat transfer in a studio mode', *Proceedings of the ASME* 364–4: 397–407.

Sanderson, A., Millard, D., Jennings, W., Krawczyk, T., Slattery, D. *et al.* (Rensselaer Polytechnic Institute) (1997) 'Cybertronics: interactive simulation game for design and manufacturing education', *Proceedings – Frontiers in Education Conference* 3: 1595–1606.

Starreett, S. K. and Morcos, M. M. (2001) 'Hands-on, minds-on electric power education', *Journal of Engineering Education*, 90: 93–99.

Terenzini, P. T., Cabrera, A. F., Colbeck, C. L., Parente, J. M. and Bjorklund, S. A. (2001) 'Collaborative learning vs. lecture/discussion: students reported learning gains', *Journal of Engineering Education* 90: 123–130.

Wilson, J. M. (1996) 'Institution-wide reform of undergraduate education in science, mathematics, engineering, and technology', *Proceedings – Frontiers in Education Conference 2, Technology Based Re-Engineering Engineering Education*, pp. 541–544.

Wilson, J. M. and Jennings, W. C. (2000) 'Studio courses: how information technology is changing the way we teach, on campus and off', *Proceedings of the IEEE* 88 (1): 72–80.

Part 4

How can assessment help student learning?

11

Personal Development Planning and portfolio building: introducing undergraduates to the processes of professional development

---

Alan Maddocks

Introduction

All higher education institutions are asked to have policies on Personal Development Planning (PDP) in place by the academic year 2005–2006. This chapter will examine the introduction of PDP within an engineering context. It will focus on the implementation of the RAPID Progress File, an electronic personal and professional development planning tool, in a range of UK higher education institutions involving over 2,000 students. Therefore, this chapter provides the most comprehensive and in-depth analysis of the implementation of PDP processes with students within engineering.

It is clear that the introduction of PDP is fraught with difficulties. This chapter will draw lessons from this implementation programme, identify effective implementation methods and strategies and offer advice on the critical issues that academics face in engaging students in the processes of PDP.

The RAPID Progress File

The RAPID (Recording Academic, Professional & Individual Development) Progress File (http://rapid.lboro.ac.uk/) is a web-based personal and professional development planning tool. It enables registered users to input and maintain information on a password-protected database. It has been developed by Loughborough University as part of the DfEE (Department for Education and Employment) funded project 'Recording Achievement in Construction' (1998–2000), and has been widely implemented through the HEFCE (Higher Education Funding Council for England) funded project, 'RAPID 2000' (2000–2003). The RAPID Progress File has been designed to enable students (within Construction and Civil Engineering disciplines) to maintain a record of achievement and to audit and develop skills compatible with the competence requirements of relevant professional institutions. There are currently eight contextualized versions of the RAPID Progress File. However, this chapter will focus in the main on the implementation of the Civil Engineering version of the RAPID Progress File within Civil Engineering undergraduate degree programmes.

The RAPID Progress File has two main components: PACE and SPEED. The PACE component of RAPID acts as the 'record of achievement'. Here, students maintain their personal details, a record of their achievements (including qualifications), a summary of relevant work experiences and a 'personal statement' that they are encouraged to keep up to date. The information in PACE is downloadable to enable a Curriculum Vitae (CV) to be produced from the data stored. The SPEED component of RAPID contains up to 60 separate skills compatible with the professional competence requirements of the respective professional institution. Each skill is presented in the same format. This template offers the student four statements, ranging from a fairly low level to a high level of competence in the skill. Students are expected to self-audit their competence in a broad range of the skills offered and to record evidence to support the claim of competence that is made. Moreover, students are encouraged to engage in the SPEED skill development process that involves action planning to develop their skills, reviewing and reflecting upon the development activities undertaken, and documenting evidence of competence gained. This process mirrors that required for the completion of most competence-based professional development programmes.

The RAPID implementation programme

The RAPID Progress File has been implemented with well over 2,000 students in a range of UK higher education institutions. These institutions included both research-led institutions and institutions more traditionally focused on learning and teaching. Programmes included M.Eng., M.Sc., B.Eng., B.Sc., HND and HNC courses. The RAPID Progress File was imple-

mented in a variety of contexts including integration within existing programmes, supporting project-based activity, assessing work-based learning, as
an introduction to professional development, and to enhance dialogue
between students and personal tutors. The comprehensive and varied range of
this implementation across a range of institutions and programmes offers a
wealth of experience regarding PDP in engineering, probably unmatched by
any other source.

PDP – what is it?

The current drive towards offering students opportunities for PDP was initiated as a result of the publication of the report of the National Committee of
Inquiry into Higher Education (1997), commonly referred to as the 'Dearing
Report'. The recommendations of this report included the statement that
students should have a 'Progress File', consisting of two elements:

- a 'transcript' in which students' achievements would be recorded
  following a common format devised by institutions collectively through
  their representative bodies; and
- a means by which students could monitor, build and reflect upon their
  personal development.

Progress File for higher education

Following consultations throughout the HE sector, a policy for the Progress File
was developed by the sector, and approved by Universities UK and the Standing
Conference of Principals (SCOP). The policy is being promoted through a collaborative process involving Universities UK, SCOP, the Quality Assurance
Agency (QAA) and the Learning and Teaching Support Network (LTSN).
When implemented, the Progress File will provide each student with a transcript
– a record of their learning and achievement – and a means by which the
student can record evidence of, and reflect upon, their personal development.
The term Personal Development Planning (PDP) is used to denote this latter
process and higher education institutions are expected to have their own
policies in place for the delivery of PDP by the academic year 2005–2006.

The transcript

The transcript provides a comprehensive record of the learning and achievement of an individual learner. It is a formative statement, produced by the
student's institution, which should help students to monitor and reflect on
their progress, and to plan their further academic development. Higher education institutions were encouraged to introduce a system for the production of
individual student transcripts by the academic year 2002–2003.

Personal Development Planning (PDP)

PDP is a structured and supported process undertaken by an individual to reflect upon their own learning, performance and/or achievement and to plan for their personal, educational and career development. The QAA Guidelines for the introduction of PDP state that all students must be offered the opportunity to engage in the processes of PDP at each and every stage of their degree programme. These guidelines also state that the opportunities for PDP should be made explicit, and that students should be supported in terms of the processes of PDP. The policy guidelines for the introduction of Progress Files in higher education state that each higher education institution can determine the way that PDP is used and the contexts for its use. In this manner, institutions can design opportunities and strategies for implementing PDP within their programmes, and provide support and guidance mechanisms that are meaningful to them. In doing so many institutions will be looking to adopt and adapt strategies that have already proved successful within a higher education context, and in incorporating systems, electronic or otherwise, that support such strategies.

The professional context

PDP may be new to higher education but is not an unfamiliar concept within other sectors of education. At secondary level, the National Record of Achievement (NRA), now known as 'Progress File', has been widely used. Although lacking acceptance by many university admissions tutors and employers, such initiatives have offered students the opportunity to engage in recording achievement and managing their own learning, processes that are fundamental components of PDP.

However, of greater interest to both tutors and students may be the increasing emphasis by professional institutions and employers upon Initial Professional Development (IPD) and Continuing Professional Development (CPD). This emphasis, reinforced by moves towards competence-based assessment and performance appraisal, is changing the face of human resource development within employment (Harvey et al., 1997). As such, PDP in higher education will prepare students more effectively for the realities that face them upon graduation when they enter the workplace. This will apply even more where the PDP activities that students engage in mirror those that are prevalent in the occupational sector into which they graduate. This is of considerable significance to students in degree programmes within the engineering disciplines where there is already, through the accreditation system, a strong link with professional institutions.

Lifelong learning

Thus, the introduction of PDP promises to go a long way towards bridging the gap that currently exists in the students' experience of higher education and the world of work, which awaits them on graduation. As such, PDP offers the higher education community the opportunity to more fully engage with the concept of lifelong learning and, in so doing, provide a more seamless progression into and from higher education. Moreover, PDP encourages students to take a more active role in managing their own learning, to adopt a more holistic approach to their development, and to reflect upon their higher education experience. By developing such attributes, students are being better equipped to capitalize on opportunities for CPD and lifelong learning.

PDP – why?

The introduction of PDP into higher education should have profound implications for both higher education institutions and their students. There will, over time, be substantial changes to professional practice and procedures, as well as to the way tutors think about teaching and learning.

Benefits to students

The primary objective for PDP is to improve the capacity of individuals to: understand what they have learned; how that learning was acquired; and take responsibility for their own future learning through the processes of planning and reflection. In so doing, students may be expected to become more effective, independent and confident self-directed learners. Students may be expected to more fully understand how they are learning and relate their learning to a wider context. Students should be able to improve their general skills for study and career management, to articulate personal goals, and to evaluate progress towards their achievement. Moreover, students would be adopting a 'deep', as opposed to a more shallow 'surface', approach to learning (Marton and Saljo, 1976; Marton et al., 1997). In so doing, one might expect students to adopt a more positive attitude to learning.

The benefits described are, in the main, assumed as there has been little opportunity for research into exactly what are the effects on student learning and progression through engagement in the processes of PDP, although such research is under way. As such, the assumed benefits are based on intuitive assumptions rather than concrete experience. Nevertheless, the expectation must be that, in providing students with the opportunity to take a more pro-active role in their learning, they will more readily develop self-management skills in terms of their own learning and will become more self-directed in terms of how they engage with their learning. In short, one might expect that students, by engaging more fully in the processes of PDP would become more aware of their strengths and weaknesses, have greater self-knowledge and become more reflective. In turn, this should make students more self-confident, more motivated and, in turn more employable.

Implications for higher education institutions

The introduction of PDP in higher education could have profound implications upon the way that institutions deliver their educational 'product'. On the one hand, institutions must devise strategies and practices that offer students the opportunities to engage in the processes of PDP, while supporting them in that engagement. On the other hand, students may begin to respond to their educational experience in different ways, becoming less passive and adopting a more critical and evaluative approach. Students' expectations may well rise, and the response required from the institution may need to more readily address individual need than the collective provision of resources. Thus, while the introduction of PDP offers institutions the prospect of more enthusiastic, well-motivated, self-sufficient learners, it also implies that the learning experience offered needs to meet and address the needs of students in a more holistic manner. There is clearly a challenge here for the higher education community to adapt its culture to accommodate changing realities.

PDP – the experience

Pockets of PDP-type activity have been undertaken by academic tutors across the higher education spectrum for a number of years. It is probably fair to say that this activity has been, in the main, isolated and gone unreported. Some case studies have been produced, mostly focusing on the implementation of PDP at institutional level. Some case studies detail implementation within discipline areas but there are precious few in the engineering disciplines. To view case studies of the implementation of PDP in higher education visit the Centre for Recording Achievement (http://www.recordingachievement. org/) and the LTSN Generic Centre (http://ltsn.ac.uk/genericcentre/index. asp) websites.

Thus, the results arising from the implementation of the RAPID Progress File offer the engineering academic community the most comprehensive and in-depth analysis of the implementation of PDP processes with students within engineering. This chapter details four specific examples or case studies. As much of the implementation has been developmental and represents pilot programmes, the identity of each institution is not specified.

Case study 1: **Institution A**

Institution A has used the RAPID Progress File on Civil and Structural Engineering programmes in the academic years 2001–2002 and 2002–2003. In that time over 200 students have been inducted in the use of the RAPID Progress File. It has been used mainly as a support mechanism for project-based activity.

The RAPID Progress File was introduced in conjunction with a paper-based portfolio. The portfolio provides basic notes on skills recording and on how to use the web-based RAPID Progress File. The main strategy adopted has been to introduce paper-based exercises, which relate to skills awareness and recording, that students undertake in timetabled slots, usually as part of some project work (either as individuals or in groups). Students are encouraged to maintain notes in their portfolio and to update their RAPID record. In addition, students are expected to bring a summary printout to their tutor review session. The use of the RAPID Progress File has been voluntary with no assessment involved.

The main success of this approach has been to encourage students to recognize the team-working and problem-solving skills involved in project-based activity. Within this context, the timetabled paper-based exercises have worked well, though some students failed to make the link between this and the web-based RAPID Progress File, thus not seeing the activity as part of a coordinated whole. The voluntary basis of the engagement predictably saw a significant minority of students not perceiving the benefits of using the RAPID Progress File and thus choosing not to use it in any meaningful capacity.

Case study 2: **Institution B**

Institution B has used the RAPID Progress File on all programmes (including Civil Engineering) within its School of the Built Environment. The RAPID Progress File has been used in academic years 2001–2002 and 2002–2003. In that time over 600 students have been inducted in the use of the RAPID Progress File. The use of the RAPID Progress File has been integrated fully into programme specifications with active student engagement becoming a pre-requisite for progression.

Within Institution B the use of the RAPID Progress File is linked to assessment in one module in each level of every programme. The modules were identified by the programme leaders and the use of the RAPID Progress File is incorporated into the module specifications. Students are inducted in the use of the RAPID Progress File in the first semester and produce a 500-word report that asks them to identify where they are now, how they have got to where they are, and how they plan to develop in the future. These reports are assessed and contribute towards module marks.

The main success of this approach was that all the students used the RAPID Progress File. In addition, the responsibility for implementation was spread across all teaching staff within the School. Students appreciated the opportunity that they had been given and understood the rationale for engagement in PDP-type activity, supported by the RAPID Progress File. In particular, part-time students – many of whom were mature students – appreciated the benefits of this approach. The main reported difficulty surrounded students leaving the report to the last minute, causing a high demand for networked stations, and consequently there being little evidence of much reflective thinking going into what they produced.

Case study 3: **Institution C**

Institution C has used the RAPID Progress File on a number of Year 1 construction-related programmes including Civil Engineering. The RAPID Progress File has been used in the academic year 2002–2003 with approximately 50 students, including 20 Civil Engineering students. The RAPID Progress File was integrated into pre-existing modules.

Within Civil Engineering the use of the RAPID Progress File was embedded within a single module. This module has always included a significant component of self-assessment set in the context of challenges faced during a period of fieldwork. The RAPID Progress File was used to record and develop this. The work produced through using the RAPID Progress File was assessed, providing 25 per cent of the module mark.

This approach was deemed to be a success by both students and teaching staff. The opportunity to record activity and skill development that might otherwise have gone unrecorded was appreciated. The primary difficulty encountered centred upon the tendency for many students to overstate their levels of ability in some skills. In addition, the use of the RAPID Progress File encouraged most students to reflect more thoroughly upon the work they were engaged in within that module. Moreover, some students commented as to why this approach was not being more widely applied in other modules.

Case study 4: **Institution D**

Institution D has used the RAPID Progress File within a work-based module with both full- and part-time surveying students in the academic years 2001–2002 and 2002–2003, involving approximately 30 students. The RAPID Progress File was used to assess student performance within this module.

Tutors at Institution D developed an assessment framework based on achievement of different levels of competence within a range of skills. The RAPID Progress File provides such competence levels for each skill included

within it. Students used the RAPID Progress File to self-assess their competence against a range of skills at the start and end of the module, and to build
a portfolio of supporting evidence over a 12-month period. The students'
RAPID portfolios were then used to assess their progress.

The main successes of this approach included acceptance by students that
key skills development is a necessary part of their educational development.
Tutors reported a noticeable improvement in the performance of students
returning from the work-based year following this module. Difficulties
included convincing academic staff to support the initiative, and the time-
consuming process of portfolio assessment.

PDP – the lessons

The above case studies reflect the breadth of the implementation strategies
adopted by higher education institutions involved in implementing the
RAPID Progress File. Other institutions adopted similar approaches but in
each case the implementation reflected the nature of the programmes offered,
and often sought to enhance a particular feature of academic practice that the
academics delivering these programmes identified as open to improvement.
This comprehensive implementation was fully evaluated by an integrated evaluation programme. The data arising from this programme offers significant
lessons in relation to the practice of PDP.

The evaluation programme

The evaluation strategy employed sought to make evaluation a fundamental
feature of the implementation process. Data gathered through evaluation
activity was used to shape both the development and implementation of
the RAPID Progress File, with the growing body of evidence shared
with those engaged in its implementation. Evaluation workshops, involving
academic practitioners, students, representatives from professional institutions
and expert contributors were held. An external evaluator was employed to
provide expert guidance and advice when required, and an outside perspective on the work of the project. The evaluation programme of the final year's
implementation included student surveys, student focus groups, staff interviews, as well as progress and summary reports from each institution. This
produced a wealth of quantitative and qualitative data. This data has been fully
analysed so as to draw tentative conclusions on the effective practice of PDP
within an engineering context.

Primary lessons: common threads

The analysis of the data gathered demonstrates a number of common threads.
These signal the existence of both barriers and motivators with respect to the

effective implementation of PDP in higher education. These barriers and motivators are, to a large extent, intertwined.

Discussions with students helped to identify some common *barriers* to effective practice. Most students felt that the case for participating in the activities supported through the RAPID Progress File had not been made sufficiently explicit to them. Most felt that a stronger case needed to be made in justification of the activity as an activity in its own right, as opposed to just another element of a particular module or an assessed item of coursework. In addition, students felt that there was a lack of clarity in respect of why they were being asked to engage in these PDP processes, what learning outcomes were intended and what benefits they could derive from participation. This was even more apparent where their tutors, themselves, appeared unenthusiastic or lacking commitment about the activities. Students saw their engagement as being for short-term rather than long-term benefit. Many students cited insufficient, superficial or rushed induction as a reason for low engagement with the PDP processes.

Teaching staff commented upon apathy or low motivation from many students, possibly triggered by poor previous experiences in a similar type of activity. Closer inspection revealed that this might, indeed, result from students having weak skills in terms of self-assessment, action planning and reflection.

Motivators that were identified included the electronic mode of delivery, contextualization, links to professional institution practice, and integration with academic practice and processes. Students favoured being able to record their achievements, assess skills, plan development activity and build their PDP portfolios through the web-based medium. The accessibility and portability of such a system was strongly commended. Both teaching staff and students commented that the contextualization provided by a tool that had been developed with their specific discipline in mind was a very positive factor. Indeed, many claimed that they would favour a tool designed for their specific programme. Many students commented that the links to the professional institutions made them take the RAPID Progress File and the activities it was supporting much more seriously. An overriding consideration for students was that engaging in PDP processes was deemed acceptable if it was embedded within the degree programme and fully integrated into academic practice and procedures. A key plank of this was that PDP practices would be valued if they were included within the overall assessment framework.

Thus, primary lessons include: the need for staff to promote PDP enthusiastically, to provide a comprehensive induction programme, to help students develop relevant skills such as self-assessment, and to contextualize and integrate the PDP processes fully within the curriculum. Additionally, the use of an IT system to support these processes, and links with professional practice as determined by professional institutions were also important.

Secondary lessons: individual threads

Conclusions that arise from the individual case studies presented earlier also provide important lessons.

- Case study 1 demonstrates that it is wise to select activities, such as project-based work, for which PDP processes clearly add value. This case study also reveals that asking students to participate on a voluntary basis sends the wrong signals to students about the value being attached to the activity.

- Case study 2 demonstrates that there is much merit in making participation in PDP processes a requirement of the programme. Such a policy ensures student engagement. On the other hand, this case study also reveals the need to develop student enthusiasm, and to develop their skills in terms of processes such as reflective thinking.

- Case study 3 demonstrates that using PDP systems to enhance existing practice can gain a positive response from students. Students can recognize the benefits they gain from such a PDP system but quickly ask why it is not used more comprehensively in their programme. This case study also demonstrates the need to develop the students' skills in self-assessment.

- Case study 4 demonstrates the potential of PDP processes, especially when supported by an appropriate tool, to enhance certain academic practices such as work-based learning. In this particular case the use of the RAPID Progress File enabled this activity to be assessed and provide academic credit. This case study also highlighted issues of time management and staff resources in relation to support of students and the assessment of their portfolio work.

These case studies, and the evidence arising from the comprehensive evaluation of the implementation of the RAPID Progress File across a range of higher education institutions, provide valuable lessons. The main lessons confirm the anecdotal comments of those higher education practitioners who have been involved in the practice of PDP. Moreover, they reflect the early findings arising from the fledgling research activity in this field. As such, they provide clear pointers for those intending to introduce their students to PDP. Nevertheless, despite these lessons, there remain some outstanding issues.

PDP – outstanding issues

Any process of change is likely to encounter a certain level of resistance. Introducing PDP will be no different. It will require much groundwork to overcome such resistance. The goal must be to create a favourable climate for such change (Trowler et al., 2003).

Student motivation is likely to be low at the outset, particularly if their previous experience of such activities has been negative. Students often have a very instrumental approach to their studies. Generating a more self-directed, holistic culture with emphasis on the long term as opposed to the short term among students will take considerable time, effort and support. The effective marketing of PDP by academics within their departments will be critical in developing such a culture.

Staff engagement is another critical issue. The implementation of the RAPID Progress File across the institutions involved, depended to a large extent upon the enthusiastic championing of it, and the PDP processes it supports, by a small number of academic practitioners. An extensive application of PDP will inevitably involve academic colleagues who are less committed or supportive of such an approach. Indeed, there may even be some open hostility to engaging students in PDP-type activity. This is, in many ways, the biggest challenge facing the implementation of PDP. The best possible approach may be to examine in what ways PDP offers solutions to the primary problems faced by academics in terms of delivering their teaching programmes.

This brings us neatly on to the need for integration. The experience of the RAPID Progress File implementation programme clearly demonstrates that students will more readily engage in PDP where that engagement appears a seamless part of the overall academic practice and procedures on their programme of study. Thus PDP, to be effective, needs to be more fully assimilated into programme and module specifications, and stated learning outcomes. Indeed, academic review and subject benchmarking processes increasingly emphasize the need for transparency of the development and monitoring of skills within the programmes of study offered within higher education. Academic practitioners and managers are expected to demonstrate that not only do students have the opportunity to develop such skills, but also that they are made aware of the skills content and process of their learning programmes. It is also increasingly expected that academic practitioners identify, monitor and assess the impact of such activity upon their students. A well thought out and integrated PDP system would, indeed, offer academic practitioners a means of meeting these challenges.

PDP – the engineering perspective

Thus, PDP offers the academic community a major challenge but also a golden opportunity. For the engineering academic there is the added incentive that PDP prepares their students to more effectively meet their future professional challenges. By adopting PDP processes in higher education we merely reflect the processes of professional development used by many of the engineering professional institutions.

In engineering, knowledge is of little value in itself unless it can be applied to provide solutions for real world problems. As such, our engineering graduates need to be not only knowledgeable but skilled and competent in applying such knowledge. They need to be systematic in their approach, able to think critically, apply creative but practical solutions, and to reflect upon their practice. By engaging in PDP, students are encouraged to develop these attributes and adopt the style of thinking required of the practising engineer.

Thus, from the engineering perspective PDP should be welcomed not shunned.

References

Harvey, L., Moon, S. and Geall, V. (1997) *Graduates Work: organisational change and students' attributes*, Birmingham: Centre for Research into Quality, University of Central England.

Marton, F. and Säljö, R. (1976) 'On qualitative differences in learning – 1. Outcome and process', *British Journal of Educational Psychology*, 46: 4–11.

Marton, F., Hounsell, D. and Entwistle, N. (1997) *The Experience of Learning: implications for teaching and studying in higher education*, Edinburgh: Scottish Academic Press.

Trowler, P., Knight, P. and Saunders, M. (2003) 'Change thinking change practices', Learning and Teaching Support Network (LTSN) Generic Centre publications.

Part 5

Leading the change

12

Integrated Learning:
one university's approach
to change

James McCowan

Introduction

Among the points made clear by earlier sections of this book is the rapid pace of curriculum change in the past decade or so. This change has been driven by the reports of numerous professional, academic, governmental and employer bodies which have studied engineering and engineering education (e.g. ACEC, 1994; ASEE, 1994; CAE, 1997, 1999; Felder, 1993; Heitmann et al., 1995; Meyers and Ernst, 1995; NAS, 1995; Simmons, 1995, 1996). Despite the fact that these reports reflect the situation in different countries, and despite the fact that they were undertaken by widely differing groups, their conclusions have remarkably common themes, particularly regarding the need for engineers to acquire a broad range of professional skills.

In the US, the Accreditation Board for Engineering and Technology, or ABET, has provided both direction and incentive for the improvement of professional skills through the adoption of the outcome-oriented criteria known as ABET 2000. These criteria apply to all accredited engineering programmes in the US. Among the 11 attributes which engineering graduates are now expected to possess, one finds eight which fall within the professional skills area: an ability to function on multi-disciplinary teams; an ability to identify, formulate and solve engineering problems; an understanding of professional and ethical responsibility; an ability to communicate effectively; the broad education necessary to understand the impact of engineering solutions in a global/societal context; a recognition of the need for, and an ability to engage in, life-long learning; a knowledge of contemporary issues;

and an ability to use the techniques, skills and modern engineering tools necessary for engineering practice.

Note the extent of the ABET concern with skills and attitudes rather than content. The criteria are not framed simply in terms of knowledge but, rather, emphasize the ability to utilize that knowledge (e.g. 'to identify, formulate and solve', 'an ability to use', 'an ability to function'). The ABET criteria recognize that an education concerned only with knowledge and comprehension, valuable though it is, falls short of what can be achieved through activities at the higher levels of application, analysis, synthesis and judgement. In other words, these criteria address the learning process as well as the learned content. Any effort to address these issues must deal not only with matters of content but also with matters of delivery and learning.

In the US, there have been some outstanding responses associated primarily with single institutions. These certainly include the Integrated Teaching and Learning Laboratory at the University of Colorado (Carlson and Sullivan, 1999) at Boulder and the development of studio approaches at Rensselaer Polytechnic Institute (Thompson, 2002). However, the greatest part of the development of the techniques needed to develop these attributes has taken place within the *coalitions* funded by the National Science Foundation. These coalitions, which began with the Synthesis Coalition in 1990, include most of the best-known engineering schools in the US, as well as some that are less well known. Although each coalition originally had a relatively specific mandate, there has been a tendency for the mandate to widen. The websites of the major coalitions (Coalitions, 2003) contain much of interest.

In Europe, there has been much attention given to engineering education, but much of the energy at the international level has been related to European unification and to changes which create more uniformity in engineering education throughout Europe. The goal has been to create more mobility in the engineering profession in Europe, possibly through a European system of programme accreditation. Continuing education has been given much attention too. On a Europe-wide basis, there has been less effort devoted to issues of professional skills, or to the development of deeper learning, than one sees in the US and elsewhere. There has been no exact counterpart to the coalitions, or to the funding that goes with them. Nor is there, yet, any European counterpart to ABET, with its ability to shape curriculum design throughout its home area.

There have, however, been forces working to increase professional skills and to improve the quality of learning at the national level. In the UK, for example, the efforts to develop European-wide standards have led both the Engineering Professors' Council and the Engineering Council to develop standards somewhat akin to the accreditation criteria in Canada and the US. The most recent version from the Engineering Council (EC, 2003) gives prominence to technical, commercial and managerial leadership, to effective communication and professional skills, to professional conduct, and to a recognition of obligations to society, the profession and the environment.

On the learning side, the UK government's creation of the Learning and Teaching Support Network (LTSN, 2003) has generated much activity related to improved learning across many disciplines. Among the centres is one devoted to Engineering and another to Materials Science and Engineering. These have contributed to 'collating and disseminating good practice and innovation in learning and teaching in engineering education' and to 'providing co-ordination and support for learning and teaching in engineering'. Such activities parallel those of the US coalitions in some ways, but are more centrally directed by national policy.

There have also been some very significant innovations among individual European universities. One of the earliest of these continues to be one of the most comprehensive and effective. Aalborg University uses team-based, project-based learning in all years of all programmes, including programmes in the humanities and the social sciences (Kjersdam and Enemark, 1994). Established in 1974, Aalborg University provides every student team with a permanent office. It has a two-tier lecture structure, in which some lectures deliver fundamentals while others present specialized material required for projects. Project results, and the contribution each student makes to the team, are the major bases of assessment. Projects in the last year and a half of the five-year programme are largely drawn from industry. Aalborg has developed a very substantial industrial linkage, with both research and undergraduate components. Faculty training is exemplary.

Elsewhere in the world, Australian universities have been very innovative, and continue to be so. With engineering education having been given critical analysis early by Williams and later by Simmons (Simmons, 1995, 1996), examples of innovation have been widespread, and found equally in the country's oldest and newest institutions. In Canada, innovations have been fewer, and more modest. An exception, certainly, is the Mechanical Engineering programme at the Université de Sherbrooke, which has pioneered several notable innovations (Proulx et al., 1998). Sherbrooke continues to break new ground, with the Electrical Engineering programme recently embarking on an ambitious approach. Don Woods at McMaster University has been a pioneer in, and advocate for, problem-based learning.

The Canadian Engineering Accreditation Board is steadily increasing its requirements in the professional skills areas, and universities will be required to respond. In addition to humanity and social science content, the CEAB requires 'studies . . . on the impact of technology on society'. They also require developing 'each student's capability to communicate adequately, both orally and in writing'. The Board further expects 'appropriate exposure to ethics, equity, public and worker safety and health, concepts of sustainable development and environmental stewardship'. Finally, they expect the curriculum to 'prepare students to learn independently'.

While many engineering schools accept the value of the changes urged on them by so many people, most are uncertain about how to achieve them. There is no shortage of models, as we have seen. But few engineering schools have access to the funding which has fuelled the coalitions in the US. Fewer still have the greenfield site and radical mandate which Aalborg had. While all of us can learn much from the advances made in Aalborg and in the coalitions, few of us can emulate them, lacking either the funds, or the freedom, or both.

For most of us, the challenge is to find ways to increase the development of professional skills within the context of a university with conventional buildings, established procedures, inflexible interfaculty linkages, highly independent academic units, and staff who are schooled in an expository teaching style. We must do so at an affordable cost and without extending the time taken to obtain a degree. It is no small challenge. But while we may never be completely satisfied with the results, there are ways to make improvements despite the constraints, ways that involve using every learning opportunity to its maximum.

Integrated Learning

Integrated Learning is the response of Queen's University to the challenge above. It seeks to develop professional skills and to achieve deeper learning through an increased emphasis on how technical material relates to other ideas and subjects. It links material in one course to materials in other courses, links material in one engineering discipline to approaches and material in other engineering disciplines, and links engineering to business, environmental and social contexts. It emphasizes how to elevate theory to practice. And it tries to utilize everything from the structure of the building to the operation of its facilities to achieve these aims.

Implementation of Integrated Learning includes the following:

- provision of facilities for students from different engineering disciplines to work together and to learn something about the technology, objectives and skills of other disciplines;
- provision of incentives to those teaching the same theory in different programmes to collaborate in projects or some other practical activity, again so that students gain insight into other disciplines;
- commitment of resources to the development of facilities in which these provisions can be realized, and in which high standards can be reached in environmentally responsible design and operation, in safety, in air quality, and other aspects of engineering practice;

- organization of opportunities for engineering students to work with students from business, science, medicine, rehabilitation therapy, law, art, education and so forth;
- promotion of *integration* – of material in each course with material in other courses, of theory with practice, and of the application of theory to the environmental, social and economic context;
- promotion of activities outside of the classroom which enhance activities inside the classroom, e.g. support for students entering international and national design competitions such as the solar car, aero design, concrete canoe and robotics competitions;
- appointment of some staff who are not academics in the traditional sense but who have successful records of professional practice;
- provision for members of staff with a knowledge of innovative learning methods who can champion change and provide guidance and support for staff wishing to try something new;
- development of multiple links between academia and practising engineers.

The Integrated Learning Centre

The Integrated Learning Centre contains several types of space which are currently scarce or lacking elsewhere on campus. At its heart are meeting rooms for students. Large plazas support practical work from different programmes. There are also single examples of several novel facilities. With these the expectation is that experience in their use will guide the university in the design of facilities in future buildings.

The design of the ILC was created over a long period of time, by a committee working on general issues for approximately two years followed by a building committee functioning for a further two years. Visits were made to several institutions in North America and Europe. There was widespread input from academic staff, technical staff, alumni and others, and, most especially, from students.

The facilities include the following:

- Forty-two group rooms accommodate student team meetings. One-third take up to 12 students and two-thirds take up to 6. These rooms may be booked by a team for planning or discussing projects, preparing presentations and other team activities.
- Plazas contain benches equipped with standard test equipment suitable for supporting a significant fraction of second and third year labs. A specialized chemical plaza provides fume hood capability and a power plaza supports work with very high power requirements. The large general plazas bring students from different years and different programmes together on the same floor. Data are stored centrally and are recoverable through the net.

- A teaching studio consisting of two concentric rings of seating in which students are in lecture mode facing inward and in application mode facing outward. Such a room creates an active learning situation in which the link between theory and application is strong and immediate.
- A design studio and associated prototyping centre allows students from one discipline or from several to work in teams on design projects and then, where appropriate, manufacture a prototype.
- Two first-year studios support team-based, project-based learning in year one by providing tools, benches, chairs and tables, storage lockers and computers to support a wide range of simple projects.
- An 'active learning centre' contains tables and chairs which can be easily rearranged into any configuration. Students can move from, say, concentric, inward-facing circles for central discussion or lecturing to groups of four for team projects and back again. Storage and projection add to the versatility of the centre.
- A multimedia facility allows students to develop their presentation skills.
- A large area subdivided into lockable rooms provides a base for the competitive teams. A large adjacent central assembly area and a separate paint shop serve all teams. Although these activities are outside the curriculum, they are excellent examples of team-based, project-based learning.
- A site investigation facility allowing analysis of field data by people with a wide range of field-related interests, particularly in environmental, geological, civil and mining engineering.

The Integrated Learning Centre meets high standards in environmental design, achieving four-leaf status on a BREEAM Green Leaf evaluation (BREEAM, 2003). It is too common for universities to recommend high environmental standards in lectures but to fall far short of those standards in new buildings, typically concluding that funds are too limited for environmental standards to be addressed. Students learn from experience. And if their experience teaches them that engineering promotes one standard but lives by another, that is the lesson which they will carry into practice. It is not an attitude which any of us should want to perpetuate. Engineering schools, surely, have a duty to attempt to inculcate their students with the highest standards, not in any cursory way, but in effective ways that lead to those students choosing to accept high standards of practice when they enter the profession.

Although we worked under rigid budget limitations, there was no compromise on matters of health or safety, and the interior air quality should be exemplary. We met our budget by postponing the construction of some facilities, to be incorporated in future construction, and by eschewing any form of luxury. Luxury should not be equated to comfort or aesthetics, however, and a great deal of thought and consultation went into creating a warm, attractive and exciting atmosphere within the financial constraints imposed.

The structure and operations of the building are utilized in the educational programme through a *live building* concept in which the performances of many aspects of the building, such as water consumption, electricity use, temperatures and beam loading, are monitored and the data put online. These illustrate the theory learned through formal instruction in particular topics and can be used as the basis for projects. Live building data, in combination with daily experience in the building, also have the potential to increase student understanding of the building as a complex system interacting with its occupants and with the environment.

The availability of such data also offers opportunities for outreach, not only to primary and secondary schools but also to the public generally. The ILC hopes to be in a position to employ at least one, and preferably two, people in outreach roles. Increasing student and public awareness of, and comfort with, alternative energy sources and other aspects of 'green' technology has a high priority. We believe that engineers, in their practice, will be much more willing to adopt green technology if they have become familiar with it, and comfortable with it, over a period of years. This is but one of many attempts to use experiential learning in the ILC to enrich the education of engineering graduates.

Integrated Learning employs structured experiential learning in a very extensive way, particularly through team-based, project-based learning. In this, it is not unusual. It is unusual, however, in the extent to which it provides unstructured experiential learning opportunities such as in the green technology example above. This building, with high environmental standards and exemplary practices in health and safety, in minimizing waste and in professional behaviour, teaches the lessons we want our students to learn.

Staffing

We believe that it is essential to introduce into the programme a corps of 'master practitioners', whose experience complements the research experience and theoretical knowledge of the regular academic staff. In the Integrated Learning Centre, the Director is drawn from industrial practice, not from academia or even from industrial research. So is the Operations Manager. And practising engineers from industry and government will be involved to the maximum extent possible in the supervision of projects and other roles. In addition, a Chair in Design Engineering has been created and has been filled by a colleague who has had a career in industrial design, spanning large mineral processing equipment, medical equipment and consumer products. The Design Chair will develop interdisciplinary design experience in all of our undergraduate programmes. The skills and knowledge of these experienced practitioners complement the research expertise and theoretical knowledge of the regular academic staff.

A Chair in Engineering Education Research and Development has also been created, the DuPont Canada Chair. We wished to be as knowledgeable and as quantitative as possible in evaluating the success of all of our educational techniques, and the creation of a Chair and of a graduate programme in this area gives us that capability. It provides an expert base for faculty training and development. And it provides expertise in assessment and other areas important to success. Most of all, it provides a research base to facilitate the continuing evolution and improvement of Integrated Learning.

Both the Chairs, in Design Engineering and in Engineering Education, have been hired as *faculty appointees* (responding to the engineering Dean and serving all engineering students equally) rather than, as has been universal until now, *departmental appointees* (responding to the Head of that department and primarily serving the students and programme in that department). And provision has been made for adding more faculty positions if the situation warrants it. The availability of such positions provides an effective way of hiring and supporting someone whose interests span several departments. Such people can be invaluable, especially where interdisciplinary approaches are valued and promoted, but it is often difficult to fit them into a single department. The new rules provide much more flexibility.

In addition, it is intended that at least one position will be created for assisting staff in developing new projects and laboratory activities. Staff members, and especially young staff members, may have excellent ideas but insufficient time to develop them. In a research-intensive university, we believe that the provision of technical assistance to faculty for developing new undergraduate activities is essential.

Finally, we are developing roles for senior students helping junior students. As every teacher knows, teaching a subject is an excellent way to master it, and so the use of senior students to teach younger students serves to strengthen the learning process for both. Indeed, it has numerous advantages. We have had success already using final year students as mentors to first-year student teams, and plan to increase these opportunities when the new facility is open.

Changing the curriculum: managing the transition from conventional delivery to Integrated Learning

Mention was made earlier of the opportunities available to a new institution which are, in practice, unavailable to an established institution. In an established institution, one inevitably finds academic colleagues who are reluctant to change. Many will be deeply involved in successful research programmes from which they do not wish to take time to develop new teaching approaches. Many will have found lectures an effective way for *them* to learn when they were undergraduates, and will be sceptical about the need for new methods. Some will have had careers of almost unbroken research, and will have little or no experience of, or understanding of, engineering practice. Some will find it difficult to forsake the role of authority figure for the role of mentor. Some will see university education as being concerned entirely with content, not with techniques and skills, and will feel that any diminution in content weakens the education. Such people often combine a conviction that projects will result in reduction of technical material with a desire to pack *more* technical material into a programme. And for all, continuation of the status quo will mean less work, less effort and less risk.

It is a formidable list of obstacles, and can be daunting to any group interested in promoting change. Draconian methods imposed from above are possible, and have even been known to work, but a system that accommodates and encourages gradual change is less disruptive, more collegial and more likely to make converts.

At Queen's, Integrated Learning is being introduced gradually. Some key courses, including most of those in the first year, are being altered, and some pilots of those changes have been under way for a few years. Some of the staff members who have been heavily involved in the development of Integrated Learning are keen to utilize its capabilities and will alter the delivery of their courses accordingly. The new Chairs in Engineering Education and in Design Engineering will utilize active-learning techniques and will encourage others to do so. But much will stay unchanged for a while. Integrated Learning is designed to accommodate slow change, dissident viewpoints and gradual adoption. Those who prefer a lecture format in their courses can continue to use lectures, but the fraction of the education delivered in this way can be expected to decrease with time. Faculty members who cannot relinquish control, or cope with open-ended learning sessions, or afford the time to develop new delivery methods, will still find a place for their approach. Administrative units responsible for other disciplines – for Science, Arts, Medicine, Law, whatever – will not be affected if they wish to be unaffected. Old style lecture rooms and laboratories will continue to find use, certainly by these other faculties but also within engineering. But with time, change can be achieved. Future facilities will be designed to support active-learning methods. And in time, as the fraction of the programme delivered in conventional formats decreases, some older facilities can be renovated to new uses.

The approach to Integrated Learning outlined here is an appropriate one for engineering schools with established academic staff used to a different approach to teaching, and with a large investment in conventional academic buildings full of lecture halls and laboratories. Integrated Learning is an approach that most institutions could adopt.

This accommodating approach is doubly useful, because Integrated Learning anticipates constant change, experimentation and improvement in the future. An approach which accommodates change due to changing attitudes also accommodates change due to growth, innovation and experimentation. Provision for change has been built in wherever possible. In the Integrated Learning Centre, for example, services are placed in outer walls, not in partitioning walls, to accommodate future rearrangement of the space.

Administrative and support staffs present their own list of obstacles. Few will want to give students authority to make decisions about building operations. The separation of capital, energy and maintenance budgets will interfere with adoption of procedures that represent a net benefit to the university, but represent a net cost to one particular budget. Many support staff will be accustomed to standard technology, established suppliers and standard procedures, and will be unwilling to make the effort necessary to learn about newer ways. Building codes can be slow to adapt to new technologies. And any positive data regarding technology used elsewhere but not in one's own university may be viewed with scepticism.

There are administrative areas where the approach described above, the policy of gradual change, will not work. Few academic colleagues will consider a change which adds to their load with no benefit, and hardly any will consider a change which actually affects them adversely in terms of finances. For a new system to work, the budget and administrative system must be rethought so that, wherever possible, it rewards people who contribute successfully to the new initiatives. And in no case can it punish them.

Integration and analysis

A central aspect of the curriculum changes involved in the adoption of Integrated Learning is to add synthesis and integration to analysis in one's approach to a subject. In teaching engineering, we regularly rely on *analysis*, on separating complex systems and situations into simpler elements. By isolating each element, we focus attention on a smaller and simpler subject, and avoid the complications that arise from its interactions with other subjects. Thus, we obtain a clearer view of the subject than could be obtained otherwise. The student is struggling with new concepts. Understanding can be achieved more easily, more quickly, and with less danger of misunderstanding, if the complexities of interactions are cut away.

Without doubt, analysis is a fundamental approach to teaching which all of us will continue to use. But the fact is that in real practice, such isolation is rare. The practising engineer must merge the technical ideas of any subject with the technical ideas of other subjects, and with the economic, political, environmental, ethical and social issues that pertain. While isolation is an excellent way to introduce a subject, the engineering student must also learn about the interactions with other technical subjects and, ultimately, with the economic and other considerations. Indeed, these interactions will be at the heart of most professional practice.

What creates many of the concerns about engineering education is that we educators too-often stop at analysis. If, as often as possible, we follow the analytical presentation of theory with an application of that theory in some context, we are, in fact, introducing the student to the situation that he or she will actually face in professional practice. Understanding the theory is essential. But to become an engineer who is much in demand, one must also be able to link it to other technical material, and to the economic, social and environmental factors which are relevant. The synthesis of material with material from different fields is rarely trivial. Developing the necessary skills requires repeated practice, each practice accompanied by constructive feedback.

Such experience is not only directly relevant to engineering practice, it has other benefits as well. The application phase typically involves active rather than passive learning. Such learning deepens, consolidates and extends the student's understanding of the theory and leads to much longer retention.

And while the understanding of theory can be strengthened by active learning techniques such as team projects, such active methods are virtually the *only* way to develop professional skills. Therefore, deploying active-learning methods reinforces one aspect of the education while providing experiential learning of the other, developing self-learning, communication and team skills applicable both inside and outside of engineering practice. And the active experience adds to the range of learning modes available to the student.

Summing up

Integrated Learning attempts to transform an existing, conventional engineering curriculum into one that places more emphasis on active learning, gives increased attention to the development of professional skills, and attempts wherever possible to link theory to the complexities of practice.

The Integrated Learning Centre and its Integrated Learning programme can be seen quite differently from different perspectives (McCowan, 2002). Students see it as a professional workplace for professional activities, complementing the classroom experience by providing the offices, meeting rooms, design space, project space, prototyping facilities and multimedia facilities in which the student integrates material from different sources, practises the skills needed to elevate theory to practice, and learns to deal productively with fellow professionals in other fields. Academic staff see the ILC as a place to try other ways of teaching and learning, a place where versatile learning spaces can be reconfigured to suit the needs of the class, where professional help is available to assist in developing innovative learning and in monitoring and evaluating its results, and in which constraints imposed by timetabling are as few as is possible. The administrators of the engineering faculty see the

Integrated Learning Centre as a way to integrate the faculty's teaching in those areas where it is beneficial to do so, while still retaining a departmental approach to most research and much of the teaching. Members of all departments in the faculty (and some outside of it) collaborate in offering courses of relevance to several programmes, and in providing students with a broader understanding of engineering principles and practice than any one department can provide. For society, the ILC offers an opportunity for outreach to schoolchildren, and for demonstrating new technology. Combining live building features on the ILC website with visits to the Centre, it offers opportunities to everyone to learn something of green technologies, of building technologies, and of the role of engineers in society. All of these aspects of Integrated Learning interact in a constructive way, each in some way helped by the others and each contributing, in turn, to the success of the others.

Acknowledgement

The author thanks Prof. R. D. Heyding for his thoughtful and helpful comments on this chapter.

References

ACEC (1994) *From Potential to Prosperity: human resources in the Canadian consulting engineering industry*, Section 3.6; Association of Consulting Engineers of Canada.

ASEE (1994) *Engineering Education for a Changing World*, American Society for Engineering Education.

BREEAM (2003) Websites are http://www.breeam.com/ and http://216.58.80.108/products/BREEAM%20GL/breeam_gl.html (as of September, 2003).

CAE (1997) *Engineering Education in Canadian Universities*, Ottawa: Canadian Academy of Engineering.

CAE (1999) *Evolution of Engineering Education in Canada*, Ottawa: Canadian Academy of Engineering.

Carlson, L. E. and Sullivan, J. F. (1999) 'Hands-on engineering: learning by doing in the integrated teaching and learning program', *International Journal of Engineering Education* 15: 20–31.

Coalitions (2003) Selected coalition websites are http://www.gatewaycoalition.org/, http://synthesis.stanford.edu/, http://echo.ecsel.psu.edu/index.html, http://www.succeed.ufl.edu/default.asp and http://www.foundationcoalition.org/ (as of September, 2003).

EC (2003) *United Kingdom Standards for Professional Engineering Competence*, London: Engineering Council (UK).

Felder, R. M. (1993) 'Engineering education: current issues and future directions', *International Journal of Engineering Education* 4: 286–289.

Heitmann, G., John, V., van Oort, H. and Waszcyszyn, Z. (1995) *Educating the Whole Engineer*, Annual Meeting of the European Society for Engineering Education (SEFI).

Kjersdam, F. and Enemark, S. (1994) *The Aalborg Experiment*, Aalborg University Press.

LTSN (2003) website is http://www.ltsn.ac.uk/ (as of September, 2003).

McCowan, J. D. (2002) 'An integrated and comprehensive approach to engineering curricula: Part Three – Facilities and staffing', *International Journal of Engineering Education*, 18: 644–651.

Meyers, C. and Ernst, E. W. (1995) *Restructuring Engineering Education: a focus on change*, report on a Workshop of the National Science Foundation, Washington.

NAS (1995) *Engineering Education: designing an adaptive system*, Washington: National Academy of Sciences.

Proulx, D., Broullette, M., Charron, F. and Nicolas, J. (1998) 'A new competency-based program for mechanical engineers', Canadian Society for Mechanical Engineers Annual Forum, Toronto.

Simmons, J. M. (1995) 'The new environment for engineering education', *Australasian Journal of Engineering Education* 6.

Simmons, J. M. (1996) *Changing the Culture: engineering education into the future*, Report to the Institution of Engineers of Australia.

Thompson, B. E. (2002) 'Studio pedagogy for engineering design', *International Journal of Engineering Education* 18: 39–49.

Part 6

Reflecting on reflecting

13

Beyond reflection: where next for curricula which concentrate on abilities?

John Cowan

Once you have learnt how to ask questions – relevant and appropriate and substantial questions – you have learnt how to learn and no one can keep you from learning whatever you want or need to know.

(Postman and Weingartner, 1971)

Introduction

Twenty years ago, when Alan Harding and I were delivering staff development workshop programmes in the Middle East, we prepared and followed a support booklet which we titled 'Beyond Instruction'. Our purpose in doing this was to make clear our firm belief that there should only be a limited role for instruction in engineering, technological or scientific education. We argued that engineering educationists should especially value higher level abilities. We emphasized the importance of such abilities as true analysis, diagnosis, judgement, developing production techniques, identifying requirements and, especially, the creative ability which features strongly in design. For such learning outcomes, we pointed out, a teaching approach based upon instruction was unlikely to prove effective. Hence, we maintained that teachers should set rather less emphasis on instruction as an appropriate mode of teaching, other than in respect of the assimilation and regurgitation of content, and the mastery and use of routine algorithms.

Time has moved on; much of higher education has moved beyond instruction, at least to learner-directed and generally constructivist learning. The educational scene has changed, with much that used to be the work of graduates competently handled by the new technologies. For ten years or so, people who like to portray themselves as being at the forefront, educationally and in terms of Continuing Professional Development (CPD), have been quoting Schön (1987, 1991). His writings, which are perhaps more frequently referenced than read, have led to a plethora of encouragements to be reflective practitioners, and to help students and professionals to be reflective practitioners – for example, Moon (1999), Brockbank and McGill (1998) and Boud and Feletti (1991). Yet, it is questionable if many teachers are really clear about what is intended in being reflective, about how that can be achieved – and to what avail the effort might be undertaken (Warner Weil and McGill, 1989).

It seems to me that, in 2004, the concept of reflection as a single entity is as educationally passé as was instruction, 20 years ago. I rate reflection as a somewhat out-of-date and unhelpfully vague concept, because we are now able to differentiate to good effect, and for educational reasons, between different forms and purposes of reflection. These varieties all merit separate titles, as well as distinct modes of facilitative teaching. In engineering education, for example, much has been achieved by concentrating on that type of reflection which analyses *how* tasks are undertaken, and so is helpfully described as *process analysis*. The move to learner-directed learning, and lifelong learning, is being well served by reflection that stems from considering *how well* tasks are being performed; this is usefully thought of as *self-evaluation*. Learners who venture into the domain of interpersonal relations, in group work of various types, encounter experiences which surprise, puzzle or worry them; in reflecting objectively on these experiences, they question themselves about what they can learn from these experiences, and so they often practise *critical incident analysis* to good effect.

Therefore I suggest that it behoves teachers of engineering to expand, deepen and refine for better use, this vague and general concept of 'reflection', which encompasses so many potentially useful, but distinct, options.

Outline

In this chapter, I hope to develop the above argument, by considering innovatory practice in engineering education in this decade. I cover (with examples in which the characters, teachers and students, are drawn in what I hope is a balanced and helpful manner between both genders):

1   a brief definition of reflection, promptly subdivided into the several different types and purposes I have already mentioned;

2   the use of each type to good effect within an engineering curriculum, followed by the rationale for that type of approach;
3   some thoughts about facilitating reflection, of whatever type;
4   suggestions about how teachers of engineering can best employ these types of reflection in tomorrow's curricula.

Defining reflection

For Dewey (1933), reflection was 'the kind of thinking that consists in turning a subject over in the mind and giving it serious thought'. Moon (1999) takes us to the sharper statement, that in common usage 'reflection' involves: 'a form of mental processing with a purpose and/or an anticipated outcome that is applied to relatively complicated or uncomplicated ideas for which there is not an obvious solution', this being a process which is initiated 'in a state of doubt, uncertainty or difficulty'.

Example

A teacher of engineering is reflecting when she wonders why her feedback comments, which she intends to be helpful, seem to have little subsequent effect on her students' work; and so she wonders what she could do to communicate more effectively.

Example

An engineering student is reflecting when he notices that his searches on the Web usually generate a great deal of material which he does not use; and so he wonders how he can make more efficient use of his searching time.

Process analysis

In process analysis, we ask ourselves 'How do I . . .?' or the more general question 'What is happening when I . . .?' (Taras, 2002). Typically we can do this to advantage when we work out how we do tasks which bear a family resemblance to each other, and then try to generalize from that, in a way which can enhance our practice when we are next called upon to tackle another task of that type. A student would be engaging in process analysis if he identified the key features of his method of searching for information on the Web, and then tried to pinpoint aspects of that process which might be leading to inefficiencies in his searching process.

Example

Even nowadays, students of engineering are often called upon to answer computational questions which call on them to follow a similar algorithm, question after question. They can be prompted to good effect to engage in process analysis. I get them to take time after *one* such successful experience to identify 'How did I . . . solve that last problem?'; and hence to write advice to themselves about how to tackle the next problem of this type. Next time round, they are prompted to check that advice to see if it was effective, or needs further refinement.

Example

Some tasks in engineering education can be complex, and extend over a long period as, for example, in group projects. In these circumstances, I have facilitated activities in which students are regularly required to take a short 'time out'. During this period, I push them to identify, in general terms, 'How do I . . . tackle the complex task we are encountering?' (Cowan, 1998). Usually they are at first unable even to identify and describe in general terms the elements in their approach. It takes some effort and time before they can cope with the demand to describe in detail what these component activities have entailed, and how they have been making the decisions within them. When they eventually arrive at *generalizable* summaries, their *particular* performances tend to improve markedly. For they have seen scope for enhancement more clearly in their generalized algorithm than amid the detail of a particular (and past) solution. Consequently, next time round, they usually don't need to be persuaded to take time out to think about what they are doing and how they are doing it. They will have discovered the usefulness of doing that.

I have found that this type of engagement in analysing can have even more impact on students' development if they are told that I will expect them to keep notes of how well they followed their own advice; when they deviated from it, and why; and with what effect. I warn them that they will be expected to compile revised advice, after the next problem task, based upon the success or otherwise of this current advice. This is iterative process analysis, focused on key activities, and incorporating what Kolb (1984) called 'Active Experimentation', of which more later in this chapter.

I hope it goes almost without saying that these two teaching examples illustrate the use of an ability (that of process analysis) which I value. Consequently, in accordance with the principle which Biggs (1999) has called alignment, I recognize and attempt to discharge the obligation to teach for the development of that ability, and to assess (and reward) its achievement. How that is done, is perhaps, another story.

Rationale

My justification for embodying process analysis in engineering curricula is that I have found (Cowan, 1987; Boyd and Cowan, 1986) that those who are encouraged to think about how they do 'it', whatever 'it' is, will on the whole become more effective and efficient thereafter (Kolmos and Kofoed, 2002). This seems to be so, because – having derived a refined generalization in their own words – they apply their generalization methodically to future examples within the same category, without 'going back to the beginning again'. Process analysis thus leads through specification to development of generic abilities.

The consequent improvements can be dramatic. Rust *et al.* (2003) have reported how the experience of merely one 2-hour session to assist students to identify and then think about what is required of them in their assignments, led them to consider how they could match up to that expectation, and hence to statistically significant improvement. Similarly, Open University teachers on their HELD project (George, 2001), who spent time finding out how to match their style of feedback comment to their students' preferred modes of tuition, found that enhanced effectiveness of learning ensued.

The potential of process analysis for enhancement is only *fully* realized when each generalization is followed by a thoughtful planning of what Kolb (1984) called 'active experimentation'. This is the stage in which we deliberately plan to test out the generalizations we have formulated, in the new but similar situations we have yet to encounter. For example, first-year students of civil engineering were provided (as described later in Critical incident analysis, Example, on p. 210) with analytical methods and concepts to enable them to analyse behaviour in working groups of which they were members. Time was arranged for them to plan to test the effectiveness of the generalized 'advice for next time' which emerged from their analyses. They reported, with persuasive examples, widespread improvements in group working, even outwith their course activities (Cowan, 1987).

Self-evaluation

In self-evaluation, we ask ourselves 'How well do I . . .?' or 'How well could I . . .?'. So, when self-evaluation takes place, we formulate judgements about our present performance, usually with intent to bring about improvement, or to satisfy ourselves that improvement is not needed meantime. The teacher is engaging in self-evaluation when she scrutinizes the impact of her feedback on the working of student groups, and judges it less effective than she would have wished. Similarly, a student engages in self-evaluation when he deems the efficiency of his web-searching capable of improvement. Notice that while the judgement of effectiveness may often be associated with analysis of process, the two entail different approaches. Nevertheless, self-evaluation is usually accompanied or preceded by process analysis.

Example: Process analysis and self-evaluation combined

In a class of 400 first-year students who had been engaged in project-oriented learning, a pilot group of 25 student volunteers were recruited. They were asked to take part in a two and a half day activity in which they were facilitated to identify and analyse the demands which they had encountered in this first project learning experience. They next evaluated their performance. Then, looking forward to a next project yet to be specified, they wrote advice to themselves on the basis of their self-evaluation, about how they might do better next time. The emphasis here was on 'How well could I do this kind of task next time, without brain surgery or working much harder?'

At the end of that second semester, their forceful feedback to the facilitative tutors was that this experience must never happen again. The tutors asked the reason for that frank feedback, and were told: 'We have had such an advantage over the other 375 students. You must never run an activity like this again, unless *everyone* in the class can take part and benefit as we have.'

Example

Recently, I ran a brief workshop activity, along these lines:

- Students brought along, in draft, an open-ended assignment on which they were working. For the meantime, they set it to one side.
- I asked them to prepare to make a choice in an imaginary situation, wherein they had won a holiday in a competition. They should choose the headings under which they would judge the half-dozen possibilities to be offered to them, and outline the method they would use to make their choice. This was to be done in such a way that someone else could follow their 'instructions' in their absence, and reach the same decision!
- Only then did I display my six options, and ask them, and their partners, to follow one set of instructions, and make choices (which should have been the same) accordingly.
- We talked briefly about how to make headings and instructions more usable, and realistic.
- We repeated the activity, but with the prize of a car in mind.
- Now we followed something of the same procedure yet again, in first choosing relevant criteria and comparing performance with criteria. The students were asked to formulate a judgement of their own draft assignment, in effect determining 'How well did I . . . prepare this draft assignment?'

- They were then left to decide how to respond to that formative re-evaluation.
- Subsequently, they were expected to follow a similarly systematic procedure before submitting a self-evaluation with the final version of their assignment.

The results of this activity were that a quarter of the students contacted me by email to request that they might substantially revise their (as yet unsubmitted!) draft – to which the response was 'Of course!' – for I welcome self-determined improvement. Consequently, after the preparatory workshop I have described, the overall standard of all submitted work was markedly superior to that of similar assignments submitted without self-evaluation.

Example

A student engaged in self-evaluation of submitted work questioned the criteria she was using. In effect, she was asking herself the convoluted question: 'Have I settled on effective *and* appropriate criteria to use when I judge how well I am judging the work I am to submit?'. She had noted that, in carrying out her tasks, she was working in what she described to be a typically female manner – multi-tasking. Rather than the linear approach followed by the males in her group, and by her (male) tutor, she felt it suited her way of thinking to be juggling several associated but different demands, at the same time. She was freely accorded permission to cover this heading in her self-evaluation, and to make use of it there. She set about deciding how to describe and judge the effectiveness of her multi-tasking – and, in particular, to identify if she was tackling too many, or too few, tasks at the one time. The outcome was that she determined the optimum balance of tasks, and showed, to her own and the assessors' satisfaction, that by so doing she had improved both the efficiency and the effectiveness of her performance.

Rationale

The justification for building self-evaluation into our curricula derives from the effect on the learning process when a student is charged with self-evaluation (Boyd and Cowan, 1986). In these circumstances, the criteria or headings under which the judgement will be assembled must be known and understood by the student, *and* accepted; otherwise the judgement cannot be made. Consequently, self-assessing students are aware from the outset of precisely what outcomes are intended, or of the changes which they themselves have subsequently made to their chosen outcomes (when they have such freedom) – *and they then direct their learning accordingly*. This is similar to working consciously to the hidden curriculum of assessment (Snyder, 1971) – which as we know prompts learners to concentrate only on that which the system will examine and assess. Thus, the self-evaluating learner is consistently self-directing.

Further, when the students understand that they are to be self-evaluating, they do not delay their judgements until a task has been completed. Evaluation – tentatively – happens as events proceed. Even as the learning progresses, the learner will note likely deviation from desired outcome, and modify learning behaviour and activity accordingly. Thus, the self-evaluating learner is powerfully self-managing, as well as self-directing.

Critical incident analysis

Critical incident analysis begins when we note an incident which puzzles, perturbs or opens up a new prospect for us – and when we then ask ourselves an open question about what we can learn from that experience. We ask: 'What should I take from considering this incident?'. A teacher could have been engaging in simple critical incident analysis if she had noted that several of her students had asked similar questions following her general feedback to them, and wondered what these questions suggested about scope for improvement in her explanations. A student would be engaging in critical incident analysis if he set out to examine why he had been subject to an ill-tempered confrontation with a member of his project group.

Example

First-year students of engineering participated in a programme in which there were a range of group activities – regular laboratory work, workshops of an afternoon's duration, three-week assignments, term-long projects (Cowan, 1987). These experiences were of mixed quality, and brought out some noteworthy, and predictable, problems. In a preparatory input to a forthcoming workshop and group activity, tutors outlined common behaviours in groups, using examples they took from behaviours they had observed during that day's workshop itself. They then offered simple means of transactional analysis.

The programme now provided that, for a period of some six weeks, the students would meet once a week in base groups. Base groups were constituted so that no member was associated with someone with whom they had recently worked within another group. . Members of the base group reported what they had classed as critical incidents in their main group work in the week that had passed. Their peers helped them to analyse what had happened, and formulated advice about how it *might* have been handled, or might be returned to during the next week. Members learnt a great deal, they opined, from the discussions of the incidents reported by others – more so than from the discussion of their own incidents. They also learnt from subsequent reporting of the active experimentation with the conclusions reached. This is an outcome which has much in common with what is reported as happening for participants in action learning sets (McGill and Beaty, 2001). At the end of the term, students enthusiastically volunteered the opinion, substantiated by examples, that the working of the main class groups had improved in consequence of analysing critical incidents.

Example

An engineering professional agreed to take part in a pilot scheme for CPD. He was asked to identify each week a critical incident that, in some way, raised questions in his mind. He might be questioning because he did not understand, or because he was uncertain about what to do or about what he had already done; or when he had felt strongly challenged. It was suggested that he could find it helpful to summarize his thoughts at that time, and to take these forward, if he found that possible.

After a time gap of about a week, he was asked to return to this personal record, and to note any impact on his subsequent work which he could recall as having been occasioned by his reflection. At that later stage, he was surprised to discover just how much effect the analysis of critical incidents had had, in terms either of changed or developed approaches to tasks, or helpful recall of the reflection upon the incident when another similar situation occurred.

Rationale

Critical incident analysis can lead learners to move on from possibly intense consideration of a particular event at a particular time – into a more generalized and transferable appreciation of issues and possibilities arising from an open question, identified by the reflective learner.

Critical incidents which puzzle, perturb or open up a new prospect for us, should generate in our minds the type of searching question of which Postman and Weingartner (1971) wrote – a question which is almost always relevant and appropriate and substantial. Thus, any activity which encourages learners to ask themselves what they should do to pursue some aspect of an incident to good purpose will concentrate their learning on key aspects of the subject area, and on the application of that learning in practice.

Further, course contexts in which students are expected to be on the alert to identify potentially critical incidents will lead more naturally to such questioning, thinking and learning. Placements, for example, often feature several incidents which are important to the learner concerned, and whose analysis and review can lead to important learning for, at least, that learner. When there is a structure in place for such incidents to be noted and recorded briefly at the time, and then reported and analysed while they are still fresh, the opportunity for learning is less likely to be lost.

Open-ended reflection

In process analysis, we set out to analyse a process that occurs commonly in our experience. We know that the outcome we seek is an analysis. In self-evaluation, we set out with the clear purpose of reaching a judgement of some aspect of our activity. We know that we seek a judgement. In critical incident analysis, we ask ourselves a less specific question, but we still know clearly that we hope to identify what, if anything, we are to take from an incident which seemed critical at the time.

In contrast there is a form of reflection which is open-ended. The range of possible outcomes is wide and difficult to anticipate. The reflection is open-ended in that we do not know, when we begin, where it will or should take us. It is also open-ended in that the question we ask of ourselves may take one of several distinct forms. For example, we may set out to consider how to act in a given situation, but without knowing if we will be able to identify options for action, let alone choose between them. We may set out seeking meaning or understanding, without knowing if we can find it. Our search is essentially open-ended, as far as we are concerned.

Open-ended searching

Purposeful open-ended searching begins from a carefully considered question which is important to the learner, who at the outset has no preconception or idea of what form the answer may take. It continues into a search for an answer, or part answer, which could be of assistance to the person reflecting. Our engineering teacher would be searching around an open-ended issue if she took time to think or write about possible answers to the question: 'Is it worth my while devoting effort to thinking about ways of providing feedback to my students?'. Our engineering student would be searching open-endedly if he asked himself: 'What can I do to persuade the others in my group that I have a better idea for our design than the one we seem to be settling on?'.

In my experience, both as a teacher and as a reflecting person, some of the most fruitful and constructive reflections I have encountered have occurred in reflective journals with an open remit, as far as the choice of question is concerned. The journaller identifies a question, of whatever focus, for which they presently have no answer, and where an answer, or part answer even, would be of value. After briefly summarizing the salient facts of the situation, to ensure that describing does not seduce the journaller from the demands of reflection, the writer searches for a solution, while writing. They write as they are thinking their way into the answer, rather like thinking aloud, except that the thoughts accompany writing rather than talking.

Example

Journals were kept in the manner described above, by first-year students of civil engineering at Heriot-Watt, almost 20 years ago (Cowan, 1987) and more recently by computer science and social science students in UHI Millennium Institute (Cowan *et al.*, 1999), over the first four years of degrees in that institution. In many cases, these journalled reflections have led to dramatic insights and developments in ability, which the writers can evidence Weedon and Cowan, 2001). Questions could range from 'Why am I troubled about the ethical implications of the enquiry we propose into the effect of the human–computer interface on disclosure?' or 'How can I overcome my fear of interviewing?' to 'What *is* more important to me, then – to score as high marks as I can, or to prepare myself to be successful in professional practice?'. A similar activity, this time involving experienced teachers in Napier University, has led to significant self-directed changes in their practice following relatively brief engagement in this type of journalling with comments (Cowan and Westwood, 2003).

Example

Facilitation of such journals, in the form of Rogerian commenting from a tutor, is labour intensive. However, there may be a way round this difficulty. Recently, an engineering colleague of mine from Colombia, who was teaching a large class in Pamplona in Spain while studying there for a Ph.D., needed a labour-effective way of enabling constructive commenting on his students' reflective writings. He and I (Gonzalez, 1999) devised a method of engaging the members of his class of 180 students in peer commenting on each other's reflections, anonymously and formatively. It was successful. So at least we know now that that *is* possible. I now seek an electronic version of the same approach.

The expectation that facilitation of journals will be labour intensive is certainly accurate. When this factor is is coupled with the problem of establishing outcomes to the satisfaction of external and even internal examiners who come from traditional backgrounds, there is little viable possibility, in today's educational climate and funding, of acceptance of what, in my own experience, has been perhaps the most powerful form of reflection there can be.

Rationale

Focusing on particular and open-ended questions of immediate importance to the writer can lead to dramatic changes in ability, attitude and values. I have seen several final summary journals in which students claimed and demonstrated convincingly to be completely different people from the person of six months previously, and for this to have been noted and commended by family, employers, friends – and even accepted by a distinctly questioning external examiner.

Serendipity

We should never overlook the reflection which begins when something prompts us to wonder, leading into that wonderful occurrence, serendipity – which is literally full of wondering.

Serendipitous reflection begins when, for no reason that we can identify at the time, we suddenly perceive, question, spot another option, or have an insight. Serendipity may come to the aid of the engineering teacher if she suddenly notices, as I once did, that students respond much better to being asked for 'the headings' under which they will judge their design – rather than 'the criteria' – and so she wonders what that observation says to her about her future practice. Serendipity may prompt a student's thinking, when he is told that mathematicians value elegance in proofs – and so begins to wonder what it is that *engineers* value, and why.

By definition, serendipitous reflection is not something we can purposefully set out to generate. Nevertheless, we will welcome it when it occurs, and will hope that habits of questioning and reflecting developed in the other forms of facilitated reflection will carry over to good effect.

Facilitating reflections

I define teaching as the purposeful creation of situations from which motivated learners should not be able to escape, without learning or developing (Cowan, 1998). Accordingly, I am not content to leave learners on their own to undertake and profit from the various reflective activities I have exemplified here. I do, indeed, leave it to them to find and construct their own understanding and personal development, from the experiences which I create and, often, in meaningful social contact with peers; but I feel that this development can be more effective if I give careful and constructive thought to both the structuring of these activities, and to my facilitative prompting of learners as they engage in them. Thus, they may be nudged to reach out into what Vygotsky, an educational psychologist, has called their 'Zone of Proximal Development' (Wertsch, 1985).

Some of us find this a useful concept rather than obtrusive jargon. It prompts our reconsideration of the role of the teacher in helping the learner to dig out understanding which they may not be able to identify if left to their own devices. The teacher may then provide, not instruction, but 'scaffolding', with whose support the learner reaches further forward into that Zone of Proximal Development than they could otherwise have managed.

With such enhancement in mind, the search to identify and harness the features of effective and non-directive facilitation seems to me to be something to which engineering teachers like me should give careful attention. I have long found many useful suggestions in the writings of Rogers (1967, 1983), subsequently helpfully illustrated by McGill and Beaty (2001). He drew close parallels between effective counselling, and the effective facilitation of learning and development of abilities.

Rogers maintained that there are three conditions – empathy, congruence and unconditional positive regard – which contribute to supporting the construction of understanding and development of abilities from experiences. I recognize that these words are probably not in common usage for most engineering academics. In addition, these conditions call for attitudes and actions that are far removed from those which characterize the lecturing style that is still appropriate for certain aspects of our curricula. Therefore, I suggest that the teachers who aspire to facilitate learner-centred development in parts of their curricula can usefully attempt to appreciate, and to incorporate in their practice, Rogers' three conditions.

Empathy

Empathy is 'intellectual or emotional identification with another' (Anon, 1958). We display empathy when we understand (or show that we are wishing to understand) the position, values, circumstances and emotional state of others – in this case, our students – and act accordingly. A staff development officer displays empathy when she recognizes the consequences which dread of computers and ICT have for an experienced engineering lecturer faced with the demand to put his material on the Web. She shows this learning colleague that she appreciates his fears and his desire to evade the task at any cost. She does so by echoing what she has been told by him, in terms which seem to him an adequate description of how he feels.

Rogers, in an extensive set of statements about empathy (Rogers, 1975), included such phrases as: 'entering the private perceptual world of the other and becoming thoroughly at home in it', 'being sensitive, moment to moment, to the changing felt meanings which flow in the other person' and 'frequently checking with him/her as to the accuracy of your sensings, and being guided by the responses you receive'.

Congruence

Congruence entails matching ourselves up with the other person. Rogers talks of congruence in these terms: 'There is a close matching, or congruence, between what is being experienced at the gut level, what is present in awareness, and what is expressed' (1942: 35).

Example

A group of students become frustrated when it becomes clear to them that they have made a significant mistake in their project plan. Their tutor displays congruence when her response to her students' frustration matches in all ways what she is truly feeling. Within this facilitative (rather than directive) relationship, she is genuine and authentic in what she says and volunteers to these learners, remembering, though not necessarily mentioning, her own similar experience on her M.Sc. Thus, this tutor displays congruence when her facilitative comments are expressed in terms and with intent which consequently come naturally to her.

Unconditional positive regard

Unconditional positive regard entails wholehearted acceptance that a learner's questions, however difficult to locate relative to the immediate learning task, are genuinely of importance to that learner. According to McGill and Beaty (2001), it is 'a non-possessive caring for the learner, an attitude which believes fundamentally that the other person is trustworthy and worth caring for. It accepts the feelings of the other person as relevant to their learning'.

Displaying unconditional positive regard is the most difficult aspect of facilitation for many of us. A lecturer displays unconditional positive regard in showing acceptance, or perhaps in merely seeking to find a basis for it, when acceptance itself proves difficult.   Cranston (2002) has cautioned me that perhaps we should add a caveat to that definition – making it 'an attitude which believes fundamentally, *until given good reason to the contrary*, that the other person is trustworthy'. This quality is sometimes called prizing, warmth or most commonly respect; it meets the need which any learner has to experience for themselves, as making a positive difference in the experience of another.

Combined example

Some years ago, in a personal development planning module wherein we asked engineering students to set their own worthwhile educational objectives, criteria, assessment and study plan, three newly arrived students of Chinese extraction from Singapore approached me. They brought the news that, coming from the directive educational culture they had experienced, they wanted to learn to be self-directed learners. I enthused. 'How will you do that?' I asked. Their spokesman replied, 'We would like you to teach us to be self-directed'.

I found little difficulty empathizing with their aim, and their reasons for giving it high priority, as students in a department with a distinctly learner-directed ethos. I hope I identified with unconditional positive regard with their thoughts about how to reach that from the starting point of their prior experience in Singapore, as they described it and as they now perceived it. I tried very hard to be the true me, in a congruent manner, while tackling a remit which I would certainly not have chosen for myself. We negotiated an arrangement in which I would 'teach', as they called it, for half of the time; this on the condition that they would take charge, as best they could, for the other half.

Some 12 weeks later their spokesman approached me to report, in a delightfully courteous manner, 'We do not think we need your assistance any longer, Professor Cowan. We feel we are now ready to take charge of our own further development as self-directed learners'.

The implications for our curricula – and teaching – in the future

How should we approach the development of abilities in our forthcoming engineering curricula, and in our teaching? What has emerged, would I claim, from this chapter, which now points towards answers to these questions?

I suggest that:

- Abilities will matter more and more in engineering education, as ICT takes over more of the routine tasks, and as content has a lesser and lesser half-life.
- If we value abilities, we should specify and declare them as learning outcomes, assess them, and provide effective learning and teaching activities in which they should be purposefully developed.
- We should expect to depend upon purposeful and appropriately structured reflection in developing students' abilities.
- In developing abilities, we should appreciate that various types of reflection will make different contributions, and should be facilitated in different ways – by suggesting different questions on which learners can usefully focus.
- Reflection, in its various forms, is a complex and unfamiliar demand for students of engineering, and even for their teachers. We must find out how to explain what is entailed, and to assist especially the initial responses to such unfamiliar demands.
- This facilitation can be expedited if we, and our learners, think specifically in terms of, and differentiate between, process analysis, self-evaluation, critical incident analysis and open-ended questioning.
- These reflective abilities, being important for learning and lifelong learning, should themselves be taught for, and assessed.

Teaching being a process which itself depends on (teaching) capabilities, it follows that all that we ask of learners, and facilitate for them, should be paralleled by similar reflective activity by us as teachers. That presents a fresh challenge, as we must surely, ourselves, seek ways of facilitating reflection on our own part. For we are no better able to do all of this on our own than are our students. We, too, will benefit from ideas, pointers, facilitation – aye, and encouragement. How will you plan that for yourself, then? For me (Cowan, forthcoming), that entails asking nothing of my students which I do not ask of myself, in respect of my own development.

References

Anon. (1958) *Webster's New World Dictionary of the English Language*, New York: World Publishing Co.

Biggs, J. (1999) *Teaching for Quality Learning at University*, Buckingham: Open University Press and SRHE.

Boud, D. and Feletti, G. I. (eds) (1991) *The Challenge of Problem-based Learning*, London: Kogan Page.

Boyd, H. R. and Cowan, J. (1986) 'The case for self-assessment based on recent studies of student learning', *Assessment and Evaluation in Higher Education* 10 (3): 225–235.

Brockbank, A. and McGill, I. (1998) *Facilitating Reflective Learning in Higher Education*, Buckingham: Open University Press and SRHE.

Cowan, J. (1987) *Education for Capability in Engineering Education*, D.Eng. thesis, Heriot-Watt University, Edinburgh.

Cowan, J. (1998) *On Becoming an Innovative University Teacher*, Buckingham: Open University Press and SRHE.

Cowan, J. and Westwood, J. (2003) *Continued Reflection on Professional Practice*, outline supporting workshop on this topic, for SEDA Conference on Values and Change in Higher Education, Birmingham, November 2003.

Cowan, J., Joyce, J., McPherson, D. and Weedon, E. M. (1999) 'Self-assessment of reflective journalling – and its effect on the learning outcomes', paper delivered to 4th Northumbria Assessment Conference, University of Northumbria, September 1999.

Cranston, W. B. (2002) Personal communication, helpfully commenting on an early draft of this chapter.

Dewey, J. (1933) *How We Think*, Boston, MA: D. C. Heath and Co.

George, J. W. (2001) *Higher Education Learning Development: final report*, Open University internal paper, Edinburgh.

Gonzalez, G. (1999) Letter following a long and constructive discussion while walking on the Pentland Hills.

Kolb, D. A. (1984) *Experiential Learning: experience as a source of learning and development*, New Jersey: Prentice Hall.

Kolmos, A. and Kofoed, L. (2002) 'Developing process competencies in co-operation, learning and project management', *Proceedings of International Consortium for Educational Development (ICED) Conference*, Perth, Australia.

McGill, I. and Beaty, L. (2001) *Action Learning*, 2nd edition, London: Kogan Page.

Moon, J. (1999) *Reflection in Learning and Professional Development*, London: Kogan Page.

Postman, N. and Weingartner, C. (1971) *Teaching as a Subversive Activity*, Harmondsworth: Penguin Educational Specials.

Rogers, C. R. (1967) *On Becoming a Person*, London: Constable.

Rogers, C. R. (1975) 'Empathic: unappreciated way of being' *The Counseling Psychologist* 5 (2): 2–10.

Rogers, C. R. (1979) *Carl Rogers on Personal Power*, London: Constable.

Rogers, C. R. (1983) *Freedom to Learn for the 80's*, Columbus, OH: Merrill.

Rogers, C. R. (1989) [1942] *The Carl Rogers Reader*, H. Kirshenbaum and V. L. Henderson (eds), London: Constable, pp. 118–25.

Rust, C. (2002) Workshop at ISL Conference, Brussels.

Rust, C., Price, M. and O'Donovan, B. (2003) 'Improving students' learning by developing their understanding of assessment criteria and processes', *Assessment and Evaluation in Higher Education*, 28 (2): 147–64.

Schön, D. A. (1987) *Educating the Reflective Practitioner*, San Francisco: Jossey-Bass.

Schön, D. A. (ed.) (1991) *The Reflective Turn*, New York: Teachers College Press, Columbia University.

Snyder B. R. (1971) *The Hidden Curriculum*, Cambridge, MA: MIT Press.

Taras, M. (2002) Personal communication following Cowan's *Reply to Hinett*, in ILT members only website.

Warner Weil, S. and McGill, I. (eds) (1989) *Making Sense of Experiential Learning*, Buckingham: Open University Press and SRHE.

Weedon, E. M. and Cowan, J. (2001) 'Commenting electronically on students' reflective journals: how can we explain its effectiveness?', in C. Rust (ed.) *Improving Student Learning Using Learning Technology*, Oxford: Oxford Centre for Staff and Learning Development.

Wertsch, J. V. (1985) *Vygotsky and the Social Formation of Mind*, Cambridge, MA: Harvard University Press.

Index

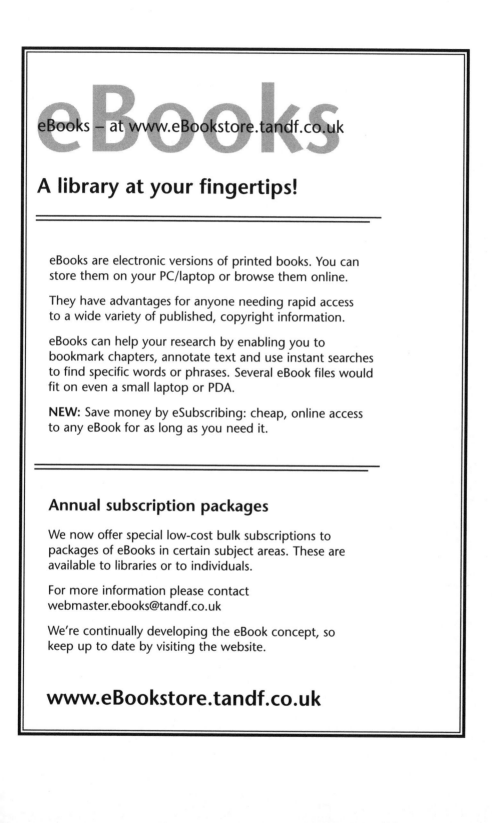